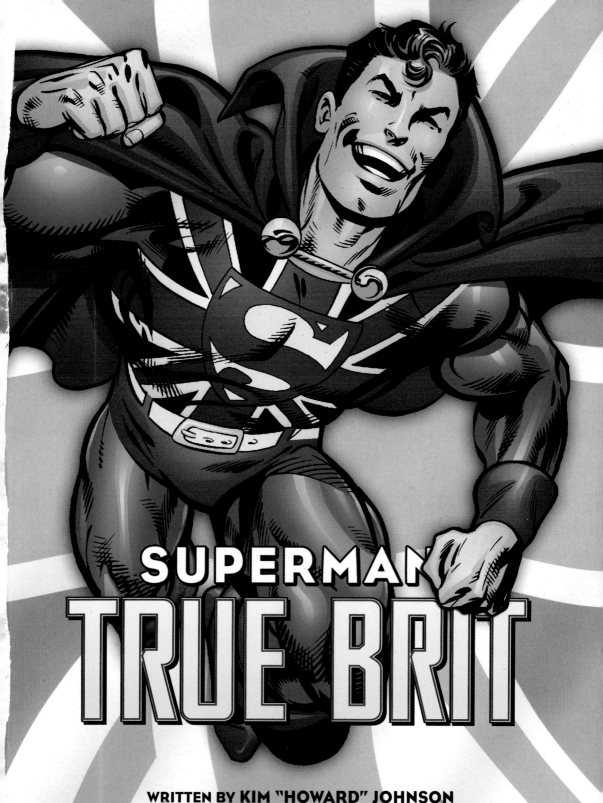

SUPERMAN
TRUE BRIT

WRITTEN BY KIM "HOWARD" JOHNSON
WITH SOME HELP BY JOHN CLEESE

ART BY JOHN BYRNE & MARK FARMER

LETTERED BY BILL OAKLEY & JACK MORELLI
COLORED BY ALEX BLEYAERT

SUPERMAN CREATED BY JERRY SIEGEL AND JOE SHUSTER

SPECIAL THANKS TO JOHN HODGKINS

SUPERMAN: TRUE BRIT.
Published by DC Comics,
1700 Broadway, New York, NY 10019.
Copyright © 2004 DC Comics.
All Rights Reserved.
All characters featured in this issue,
the distinctive likenesses thereof
and related elements are trademarks of
DC Comics. The stories, characters and
incidents mentioned in this
magazine are entirely fictional.
DC Comics does not read
or accept unsolicited
submissions of ideas, stories or artwork.

HC ISBN: 1-4012-0022-2
SC ISBN: 1-4012-0023-0

Printed in Canada.
DC Comics, a Warner Bros. Entertainment Company
Cover design concept by John Byrne.

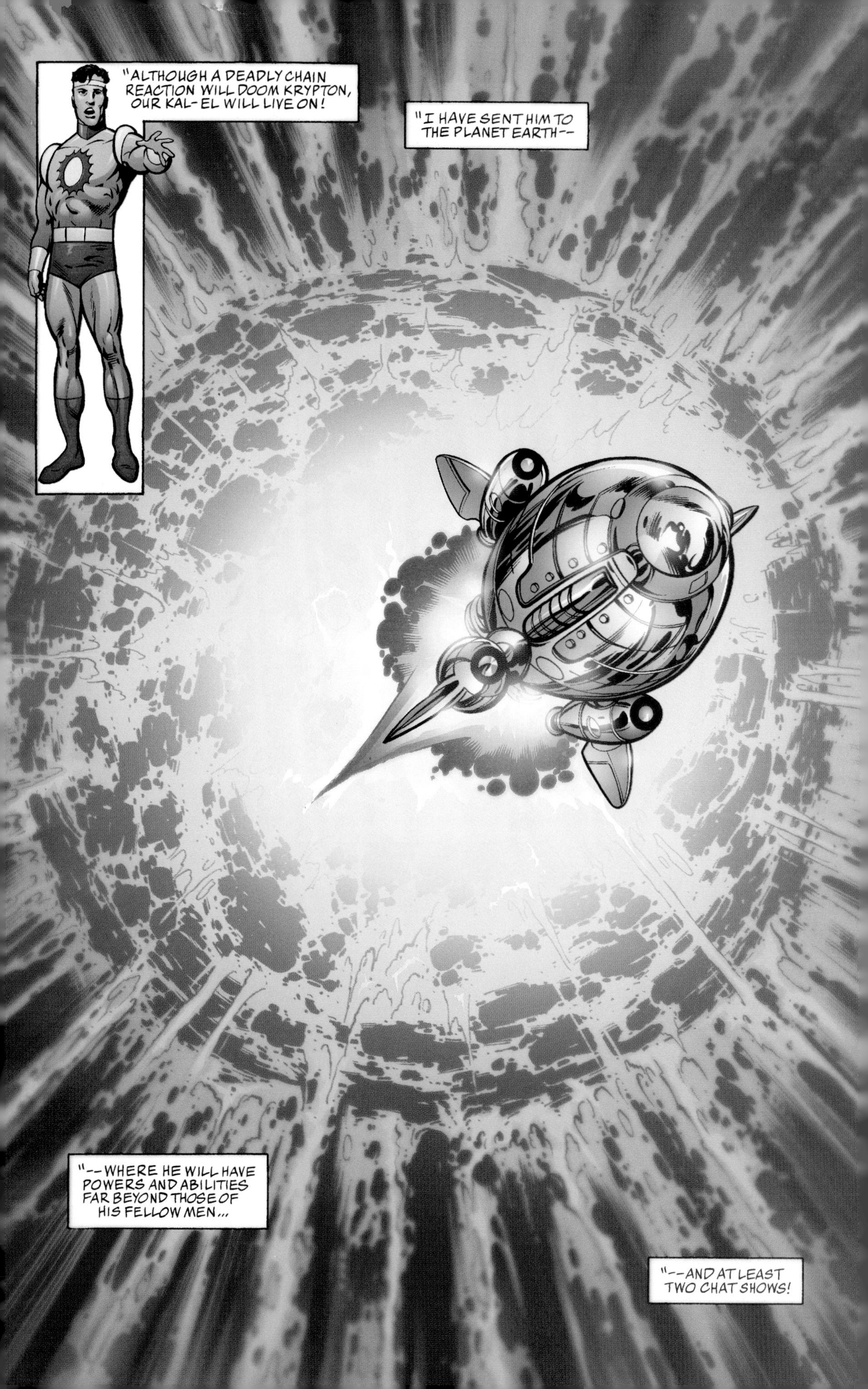
"ALTHOUGH A DEADLY CHAIN REACTION WILL DOOM KRYPTON, OUR KAL-EL WILL LIVE ON!
"I HAVE SENT HIM TO THE PLANET EARTH--
"--WHERE HE WILL HAVE POWERS AND ABILITIES FAR BEYOND THOSE OF HIS FELLOW MEN...
"--AND AT LEAST TWO CHAT SHOWS!

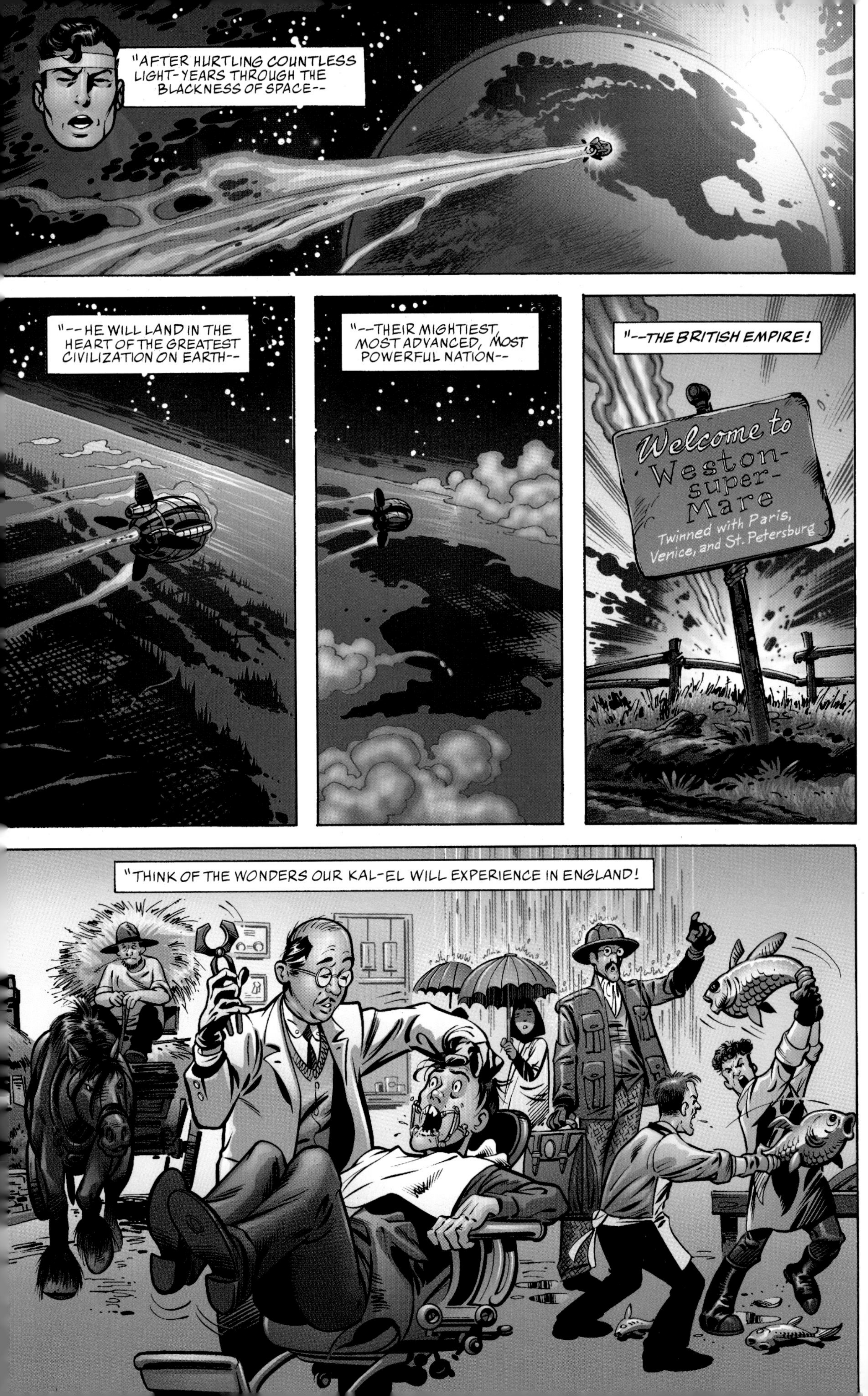
"AFTER HURTLING COUNTLESS LIGHT-YEARS THROUGH THE BLACKNESS OF SPACE--
"--HE WILL LAND IN THE HEART OF THE GREATEST CIVILIZATION ON EARTH--
"--THEIR MIGHTIEST, MOST ADVANCED, MOST POWERFUL NATION--
"--THE BRITISH EMPIRE!
Welcome to Weston-super-Mare
Twinned with Paris, Venice, and St. Petersburg
"THINK OF THE WONDERS OUR KAL-EL WILL EXPERIENCE IN ENGLAND!

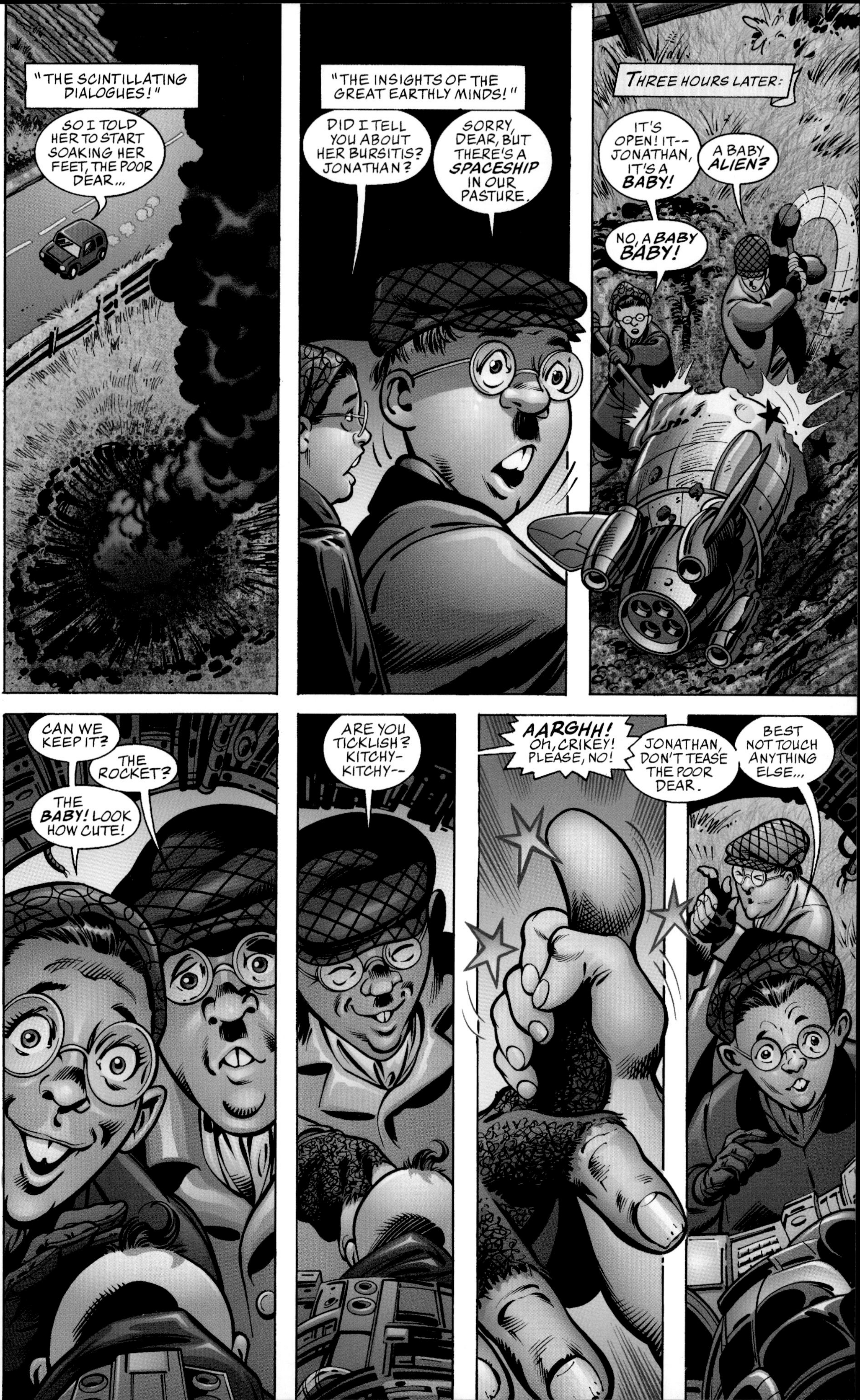
"THE SCINTILLATING DIALOGUES!"
SO I TOLD HER TO START SOAKING HER FEET, THE POOR DEAR...
"THE INSIGHTS OF THE GREAT EARTHLY MINDS!"
DID I TELL YOU ABOUT HER BURSITIS? JONATHAN?
SORRY, DEAR, BUT THERE'S A SPACESHIP IN OUR PASTURE.
THREE HOURS LATER:
IT'S OPEN! IT-- JONATHAN, IT'S A BABY!
A BABY ALIEN?
NO, A BABY BABY!
CAN WE KEEP IT?
THE ROCKET?
THE BABY! LOOK HOW CUTE!
ARE YOU TICKLISH? KITCHY-KITCHY--
AARGHH! OH, CRIKEY! PLEASE, NO!
JONATHAN, DON'T TEASE THE POOR DEAR.
BEST NOT TOUCH ANYTHING ELSE...

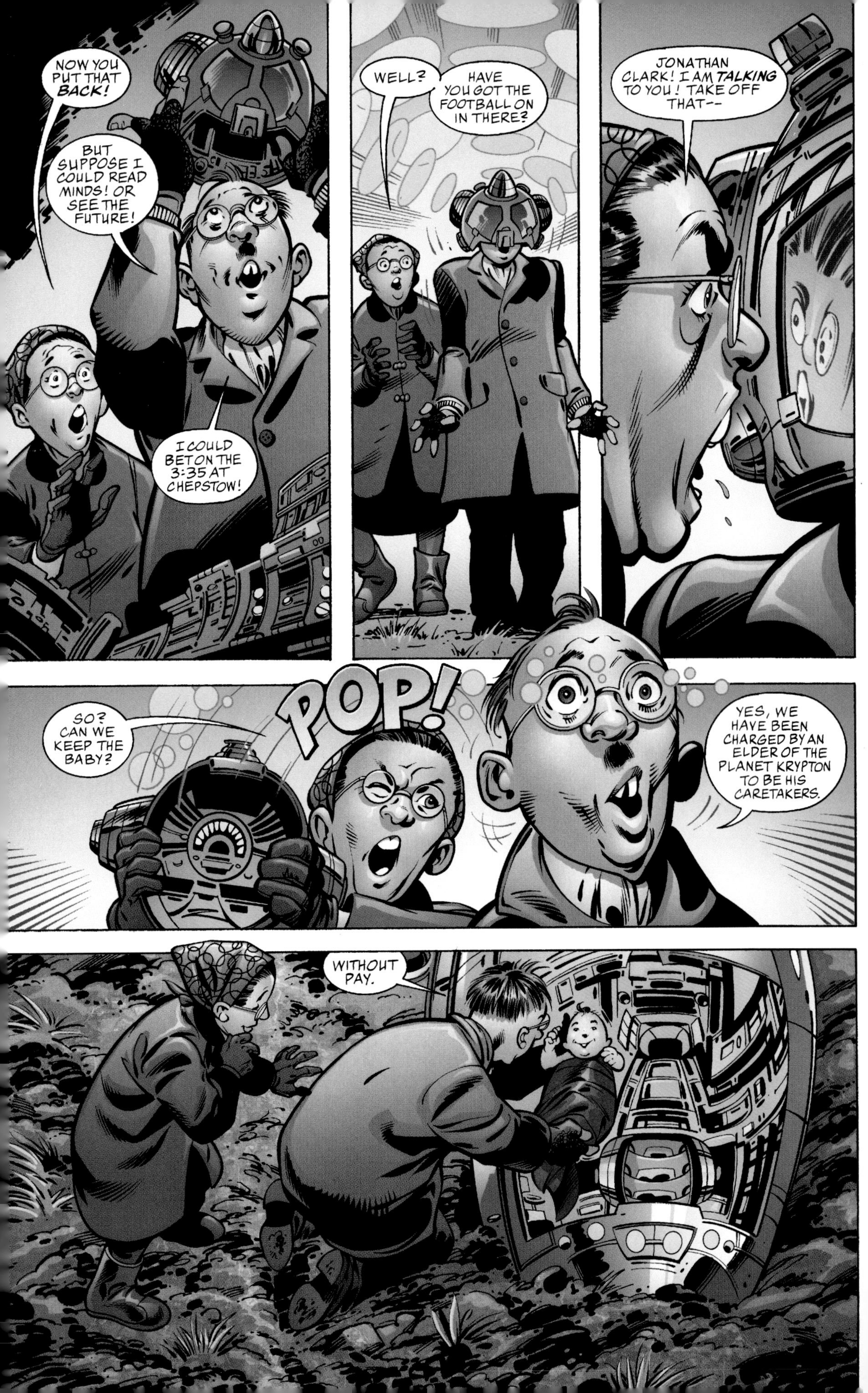
NOW YOU PUT THAT BACK!
BUT SUPPOSE I COULD READ MINDS! OR SEE THE FUTURE!
I COULD BET ON THE 3:35 AT CHEPSTOW!
WELL?
HAVE YOU GOT THE FOOTBALL ON IN THERE?
JONATHAN CLARK! I AM TALKING TO YOU! TAKE OFF THAT--
POP!
SO? CAN WE KEEP THE BABY?
YES, WE HAVE BEEN CHARGED BY AN ELDER OF THE PLANET KRYPTON TO BE HIS CARETAKERS.
WITHOUT PAY.

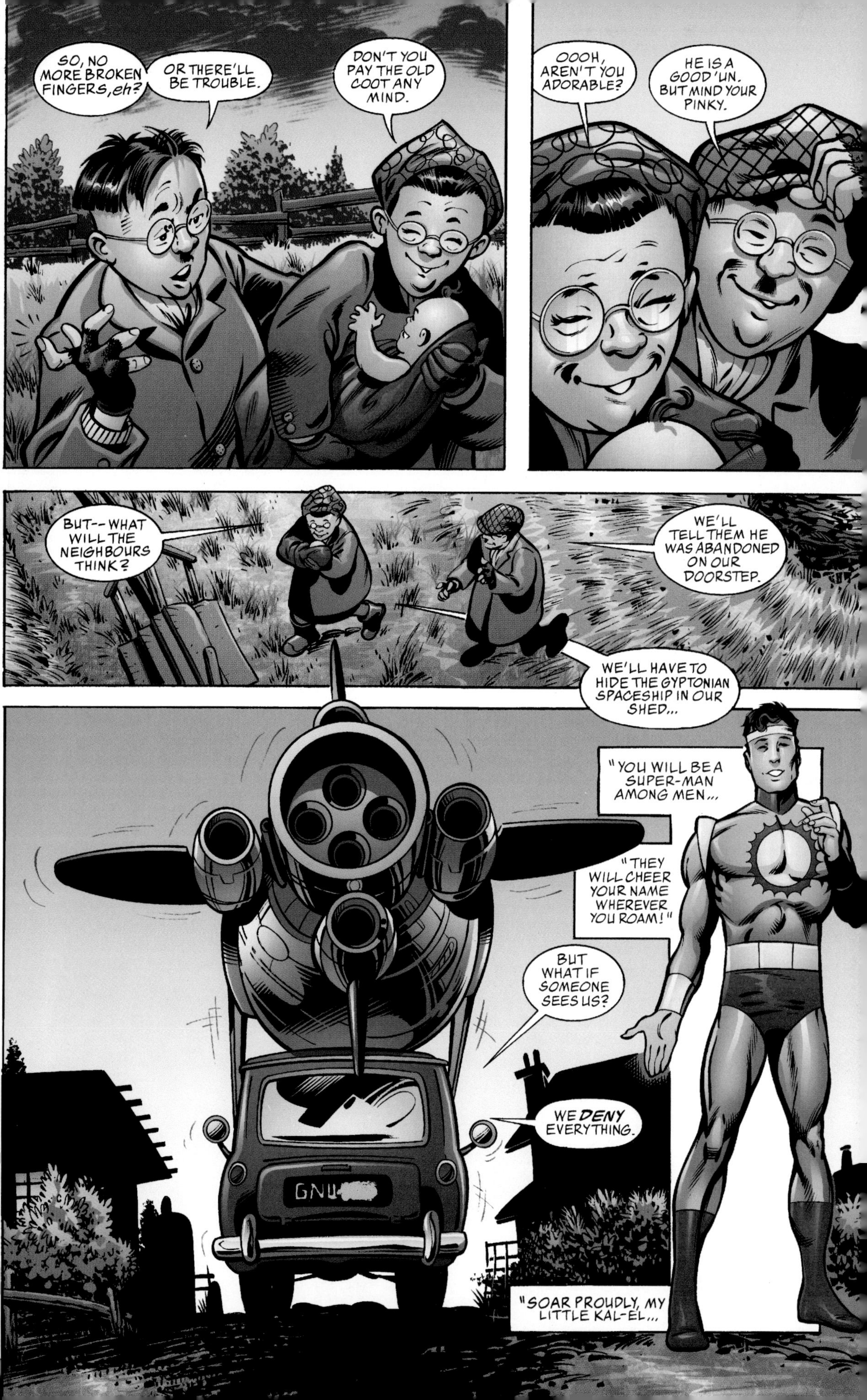
SO, NO MORE BROKEN FINGERS, eh?
OR THERE'LL BE TROUBLE.
DON'T YOU PAY THE OLD COOT ANY MIND.
OOOH, AREN'T YOU ADORABLE?
HE IS A GOOD 'UN. BUT MIND YOUR PINKY.
BUT-- WHAT WILL THE NEIGHBOURS THINK?
WE'LL TELL THEM HE WAS ABANDONED ON OUR DOORSTEP.
WE'LL HAVE TO HIDE THE GYPTONIAN SPACESHIP IN OUR SHED...
"YOU WILL BE A SUPER-MAN AMONG MEN...
"THEY WILL CHEER YOUR NAME WHEREVER YOU ROAM!"
BUT WHAT IF SOMEONE SEES US?
WE DENY EVERYTHING.
"SOAR PROUDLY, MY LITTLE KAL-EL...

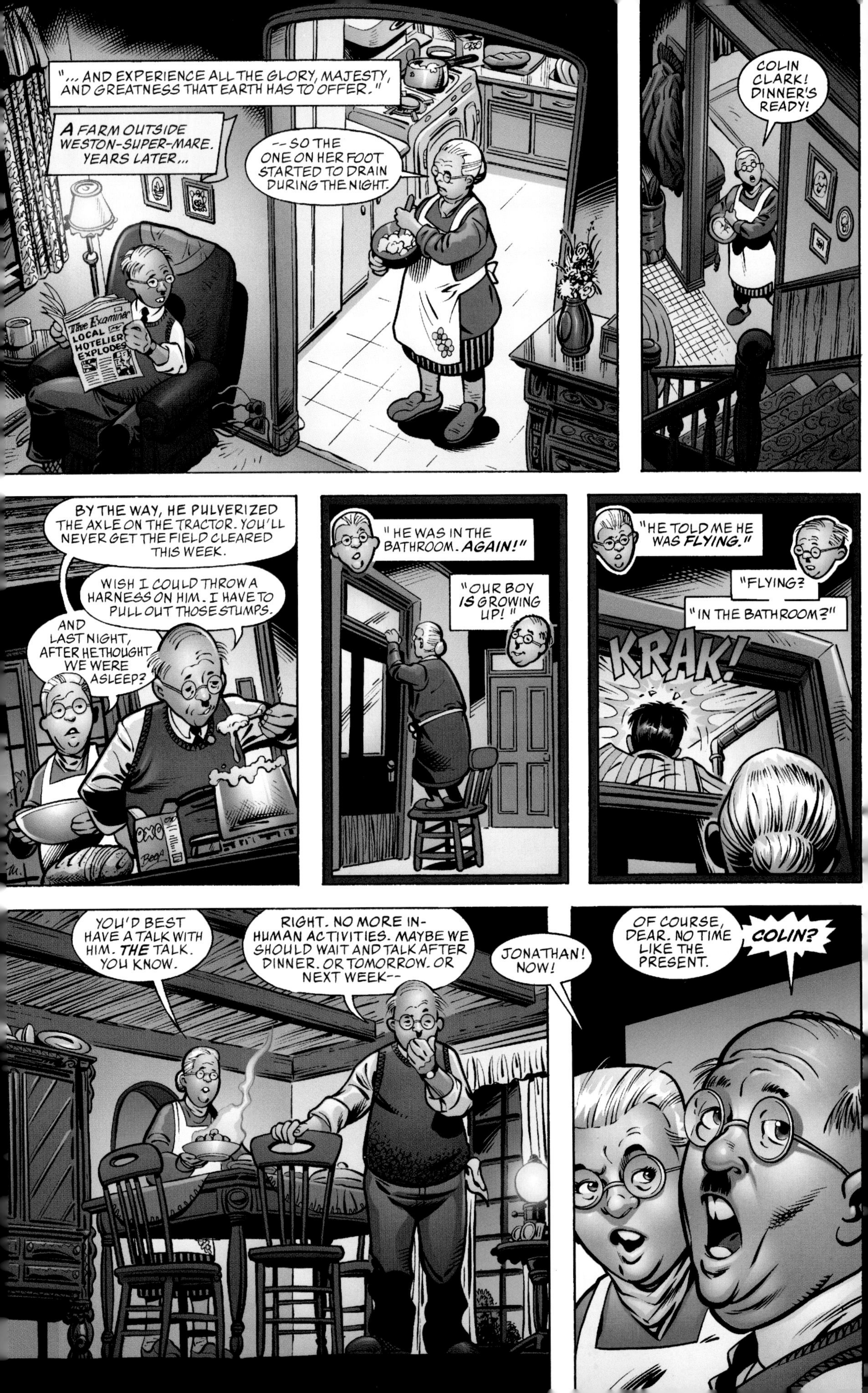
"... AND EXPERIENCE ALL THE GLORY, MAJESTY, AND GREATNESS THAT EARTH HAS TO OFFER."
A FARM OUTSIDE WESTON-SUPER-MARE. YEARS LATER...
--SO THE ONE ON HER FOOT STARTED TO DRAIN DURING THE NIGHT.
The Examiner
LOCAL HOTELIER EXPLODES
COLIN CLARK! DINNER'S READY!
BY THE WAY, HE PULVERIZED THE AXLE ON THE TRACTOR. YOU'LL NEVER GET THE FIELD CLEARED THIS WEEK.
WISH I COULD THROW A HARNESS ON HIM. I HAVE TO PULL OUT THOSE STUMPS.
AND LAST NIGHT, AFTER HE THOUGHT WE WERE ASLEEP?
OXO
"HE WAS IN THE BATHROOM. AGAIN!"
"OUR BOY IS GROWING UP!"
"HE TOLD ME HE WAS FLYING."
"FLYING?
"IN THE BATHROOM?"
KRAK!
YOU'D BEST HAVE A TALK WITH HIM. THE TALK. YOU KNOW.
RIGHT. NO MORE IN-HUMAN ACTIVITIES. MAYBE WE SHOULD WAIT AND TALK AFTER DINNER. OR TOMORROW. OR NEXT WEEK--
JONATHAN! NOW!
OF COURSE, DEAR. NO TIME LIKE THE PRESENT.
COLIN?

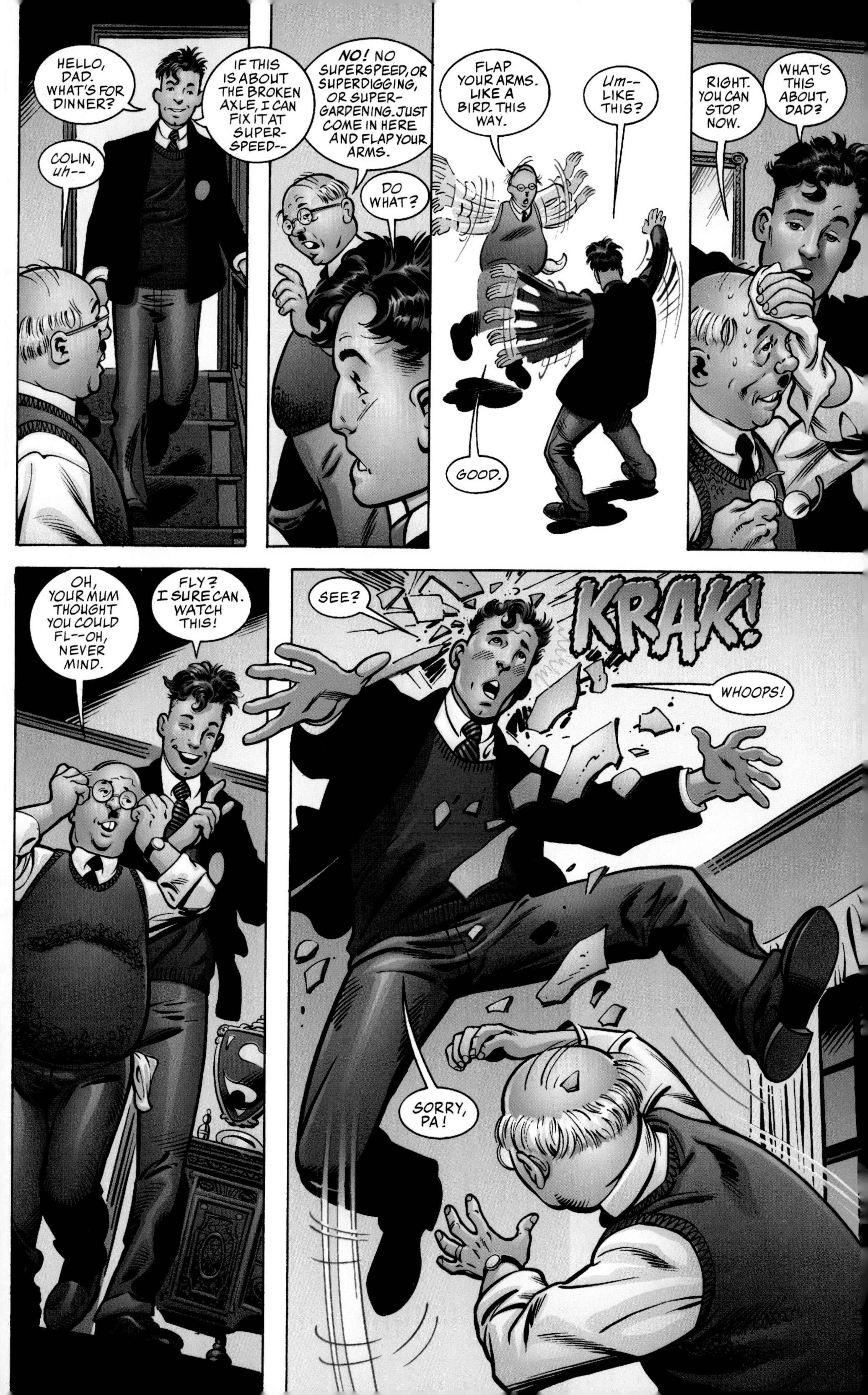
HELLO, DAD. WHAT'S FOR DINNER?
COLIN, UH--
IF THIS IS ABOUT THE BROKEN AXLE, I CAN FIX IT AT SUPER-SPEED--
NO! NO SUPERSPEED, OR SUPERDIGGING, OR SUPER-GARDENING. JUST COME IN HERE AND FLAP YOUR ARMS.
DO WHAT?
FLAP YOUR ARMS. LIKE A BIRD. THIS WAY.
UM--LIKE THIS?
GOOD.
RIGHT. YOU CAN STOP NOW.
WHAT'S THIS ABOUT, DAD?
OH, YOUR MUM THOUGHT YOU COULD FL--OH, NEVER MIND.
FLY? I SURE CAN. WATCH THIS!
SEE?
KRAK!
WHOOPS!
SORRY, PA!

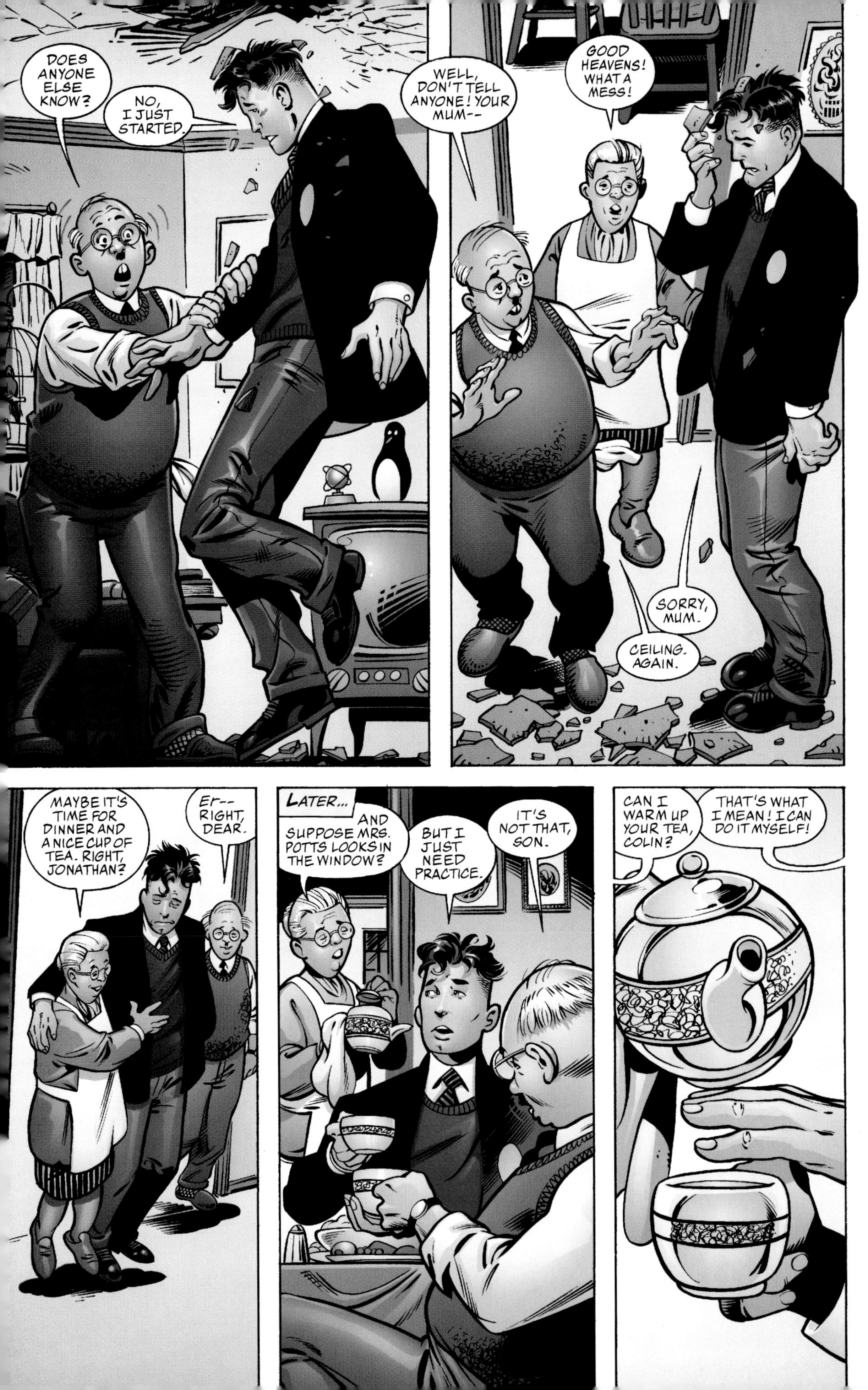
DOES ANYONE ELSE KNOW?
NO, I JUST STARTED.
WELL, DON'T TELL ANYONE! YOUR MUM--
GOOD HEAVENS! WHAT A MESS!
SORRY, MUM.
CEILING. AGAIN.
MAYBE IT'S TIME FOR DINNER AND A NICE CUP OF TEA. RIGHT, JONATHAN?
Er-- RIGHT, DEAR.
LATER...
AND SUPPOSE MRS. POTTS LOOKS IN THE WINDOW?
BUT I JUST NEED PRACTICE.
IT'S NOT THAT, SON.
CAN I WARM UP YOUR TEA, COLIN?
THAT'S WHAT I MEAN! I CAN DO IT MYSELF!

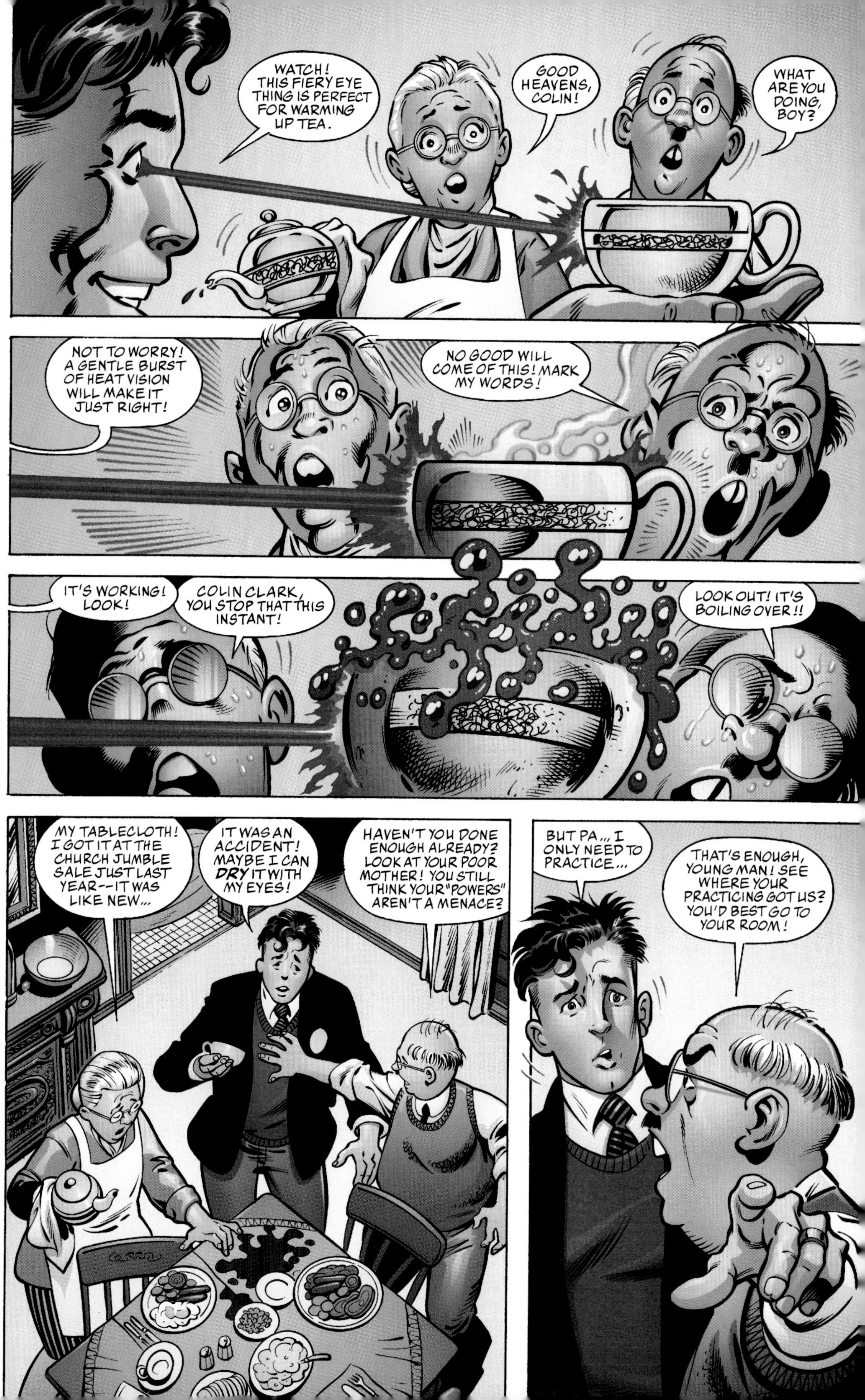
WATCH! THIS FIERY EYE THING IS PERFECT FOR WARMING UP TEA.
GOOD HEAVENS, COLIN!
WHAT ARE YOU DOING, BOY?
NOT TO WORRY! A GENTLE BURST OF HEAT VISION WILL MAKE IT JUST RIGHT!
NO GOOD WILL COME OF THIS! MARK MY WORDS!
IT'S WORKING! LOOK!
COLIN CLARK, YOU STOP THAT THIS INSTANT!
LOOK OUT! IT'S BOILING OVER!!
MY TABLECLOTH! I GOT IT AT THE CHURCH JUMBLE SALE JUST LAST YEAR--IT WAS LIKE NEW...
IT WAS AN ACCIDENT! MAYBE I CAN DRY IT WITH MY EYES!
HAVEN'T YOU DONE ENOUGH ALREADY? LOOK AT YOUR POOR MOTHER! YOU STILL THINK YOUR "POWERS" AREN'T A MENACE?
BUT PA... I ONLY NEED TO PRACTICE...
THAT'S ENOUGH, YOUNG MAN! SEE WHERE YOUR PRACTICING GOT US? YOU'D BEST GO TO YOUR ROOM!

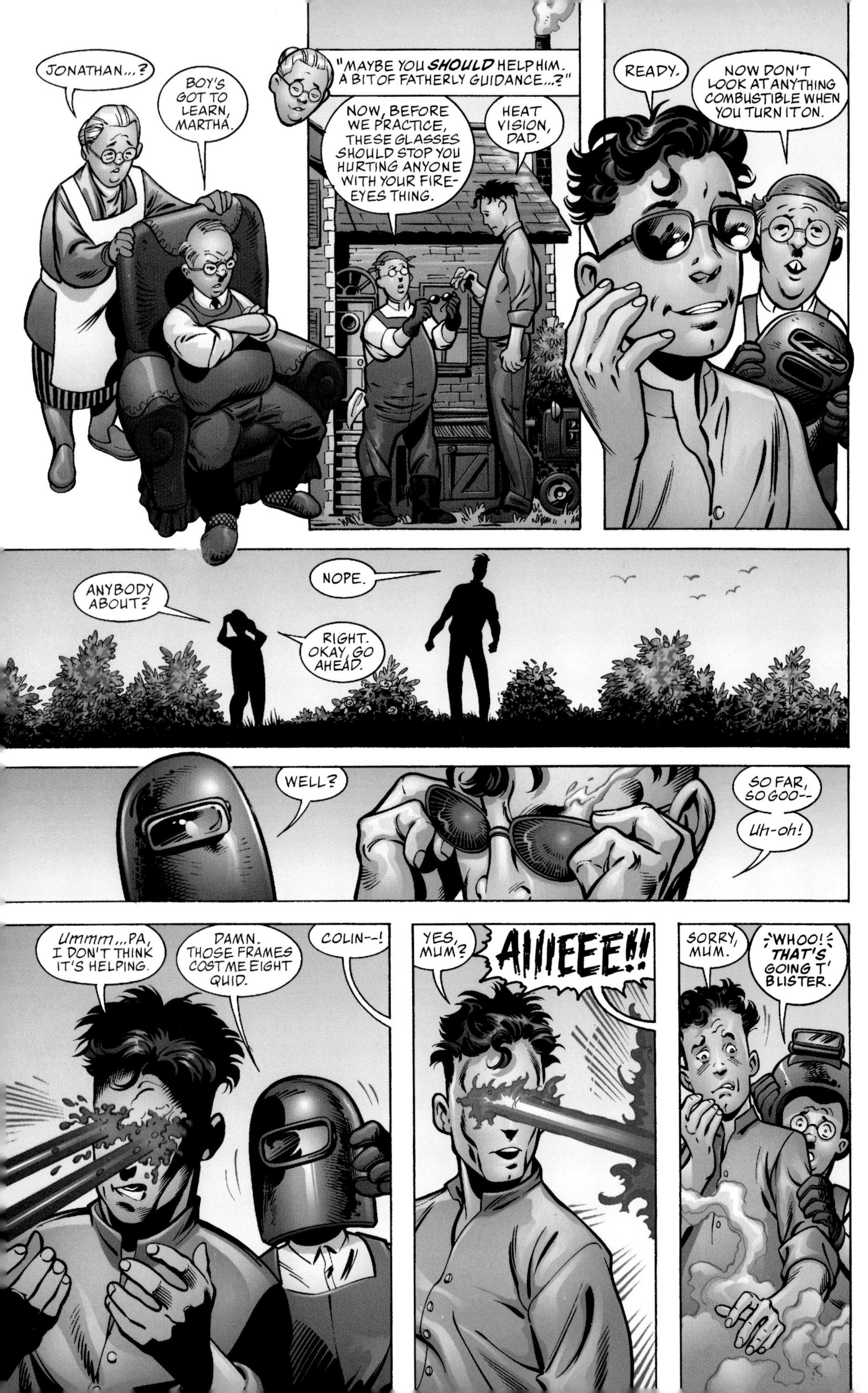
JONATHAN...?
BOY'S GOT TO LEARN, MARTHA.
"MAYBE YOU SHOULD HELP HIM. A BIT OF FATHERLY GUIDANCE...?"
NOW, BEFORE WE PRACTICE, THESE GLASSES SHOULD STOP YOU HURTING ANYONE WITH YOUR FIRE-EYES THING.
HEAT VISION, DAD.
READY.
NOW DON'T LOOK AT ANYTHING COMBUSTIBLE WHEN YOU TURN IT ON.
ANYBODY ABOUT?
NOPE.
RIGHT. OKAY, GO AHEAD.
WELL?
SO FAR, SO GOO--
Uh-oh!
Ummm...PA, I DON'T THINK IT'S HELPING.
DAMN. THOSE FRAMES COST ME EIGHT QUID.
COLIN--!
YES, MUM?
AIIIEEE!!
SORRY, MUM.
WHOO! THAT'S GOING T' BLISTER.

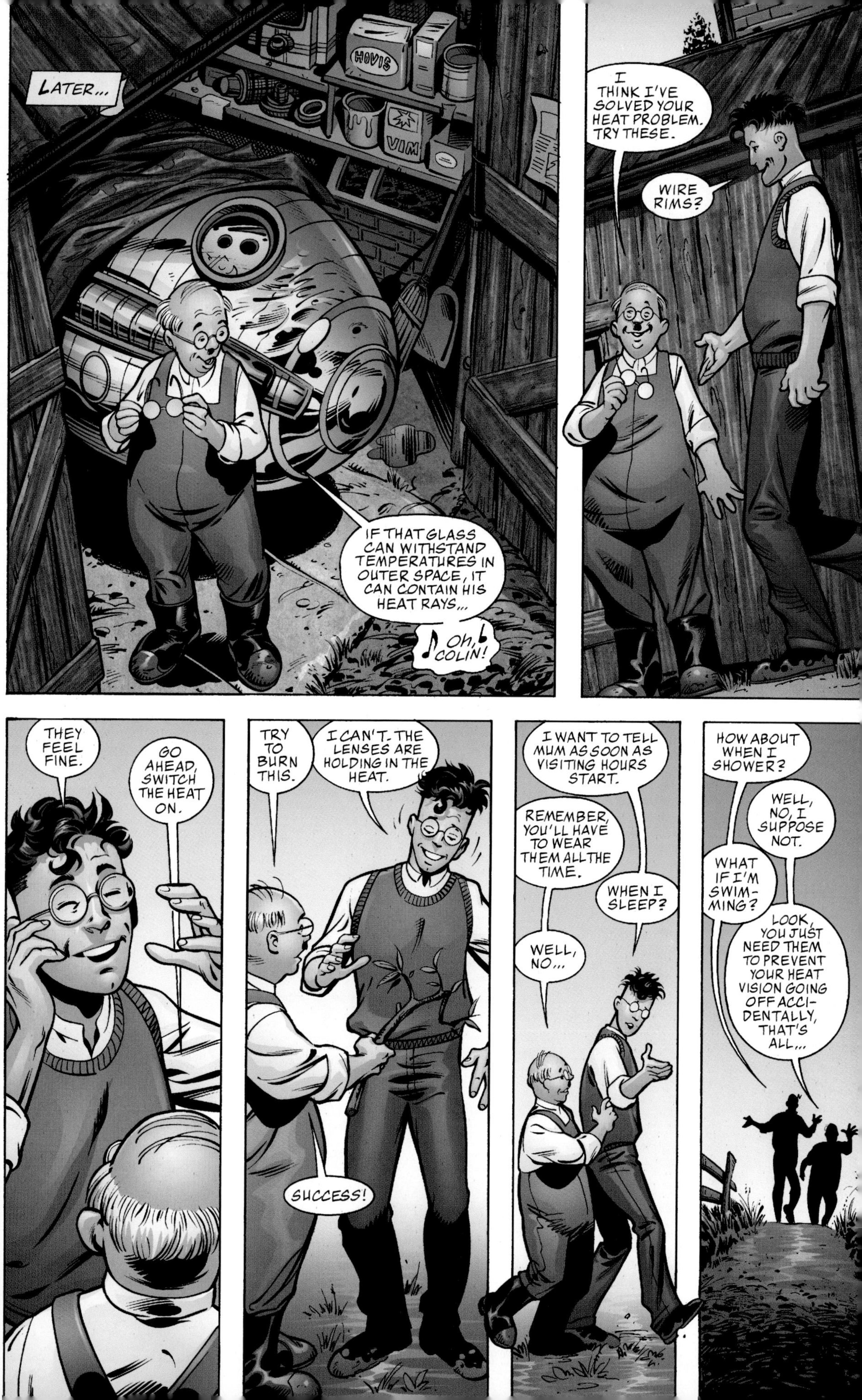
LATER...
IF THAT GLASS CAN WITHSTAND TEMPERATURES IN OUTER SPACE, IT CAN CONTAIN HIS HEAT RAYS...
♪ OH, ♭ COLIN!
I THINK I'VE SOLVED YOUR HEAT PROBLEM. TRY THESE.
WIRE RIMS?
THEY FEEL FINE.
GO AHEAD, SWITCH THE HEAT ON.
TRY TO BURN THIS.
I CAN'T. THE LENSES ARE HOLDING IN THE HEAT.
SUCCESS!
I WANT TO TELL MUM AS SOON AS VISITING HOURS START.
REMEMBER, YOU'LL HAVE TO WEAR THEM ALL THE TIME.
WHEN I SLEEP?
WELL, NO...
HOW ABOUT WHEN I SHOWER?
WELL, NO, I SUPPOSE NOT.
WHAT IF I'M SWIM-MING?
LOOK, YOU JUST NEED THEM TO PREVENT YOUR HEAT VISION GOING OFF ACCI-DENTALLY, THAT'S ALL...

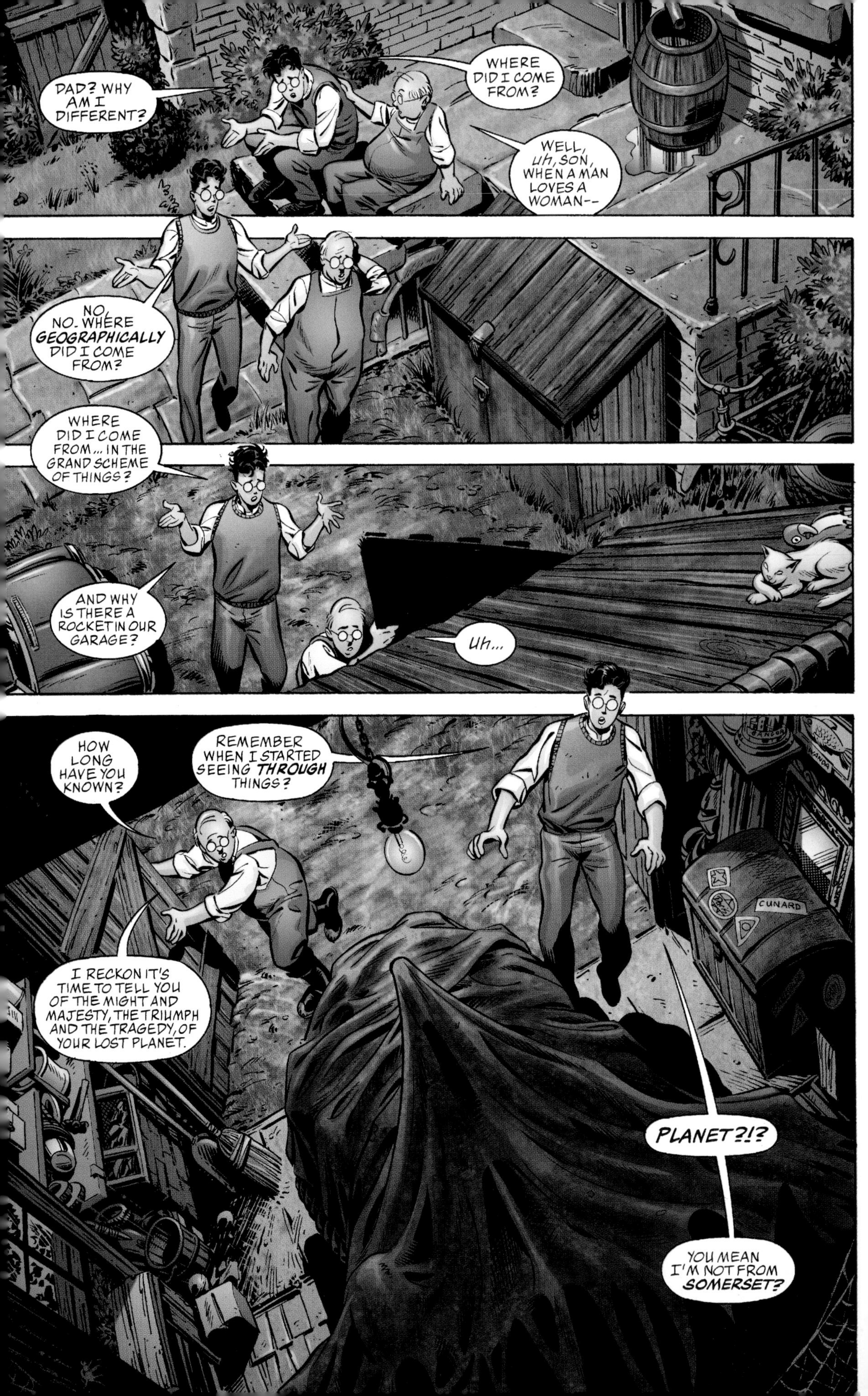
DAD? WHY AM I DIFFERENT?
WHERE DID I COME FROM?
WELL, UH, SON, WHEN A MAN LOVES A WOMAN--
NO, NO. WHERE GEOGRAPHICALLY DID I COME FROM?
WHERE DID I COME FROM... IN THE GRAND SCHEME OF THINGS?
AND WHY IS THERE A ROCKET IN OUR GARAGE?
UH...
HOW LONG HAVE YOU KNOWN?
REMEMBER WHEN I STARTED SEEING THROUGH THINGS?
I RECKON IT'S TIME TO TELL YOU OF THE MIGHT AND MAJESTY, THE TRIUMPH AND THE TRAGEDY, OF YOUR LOST PLANET.
PLANET?!?
YOU MEAN I'M NOT FROM SOMERSET?
CUNARD

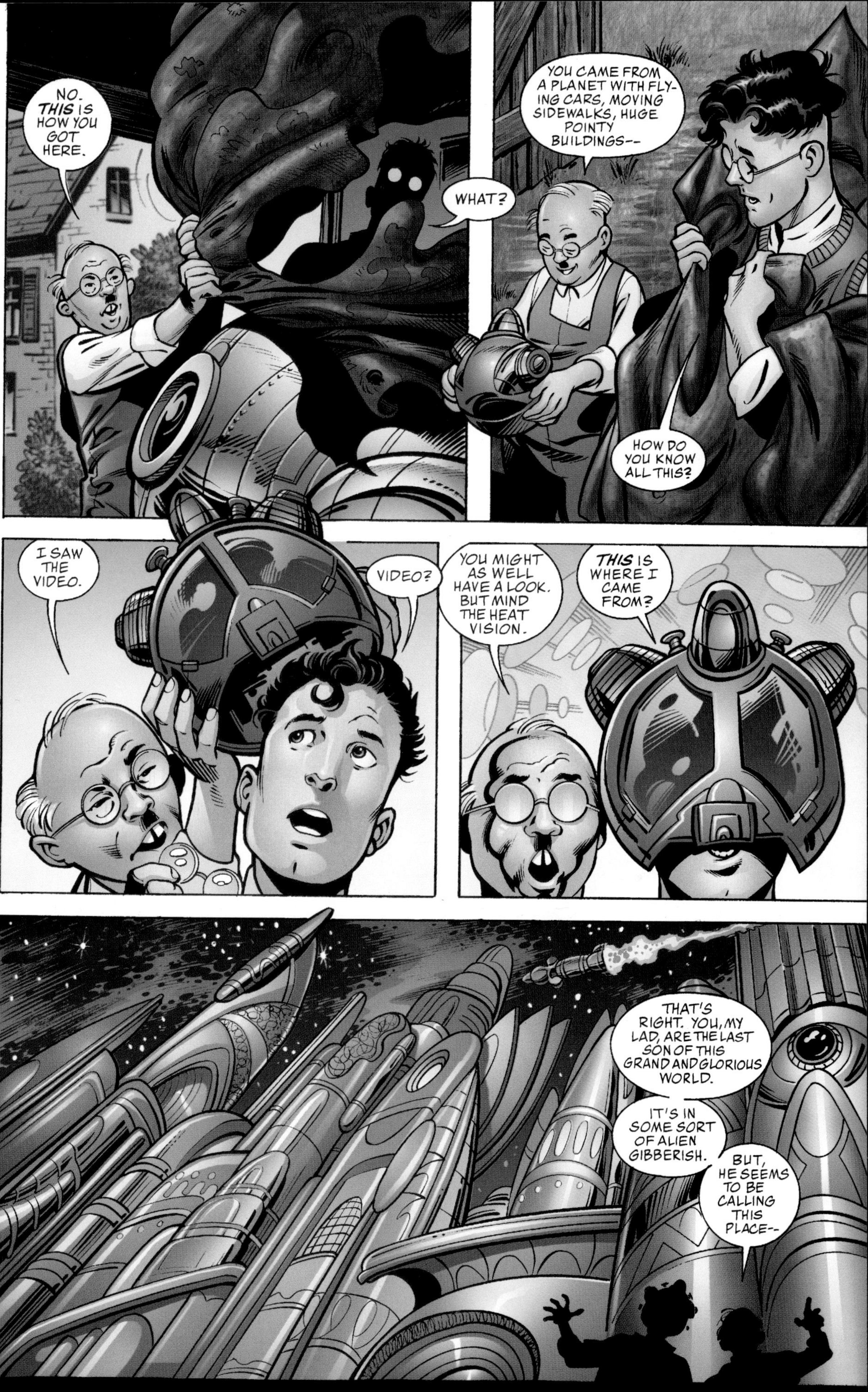
NO. THIS IS HOW YOU GOT HERE.
WHAT?
YOU CAME FROM A PLANET WITH FLYING CARS, MOVING SIDEWALKS, HUGE POINTY BUILDINGS--
HOW DO YOU KNOW ALL THIS?
I SAW THE VIDEO.
VIDEO?
YOU MIGHT AS WELL HAVE A LOOK. BUT MIND THE HEAT VISION.
THIS IS WHERE I CAME FROM?
THAT'S RIGHT. YOU, MY LAD, ARE THE LAST SON OF THIS GRAND AND GLORIOUS WORLD.
IT'S IN SOME SORT OF ALIEN GIBBERISH.
BUT, HE SEEMS TO BE CALLING THIS PLACE--

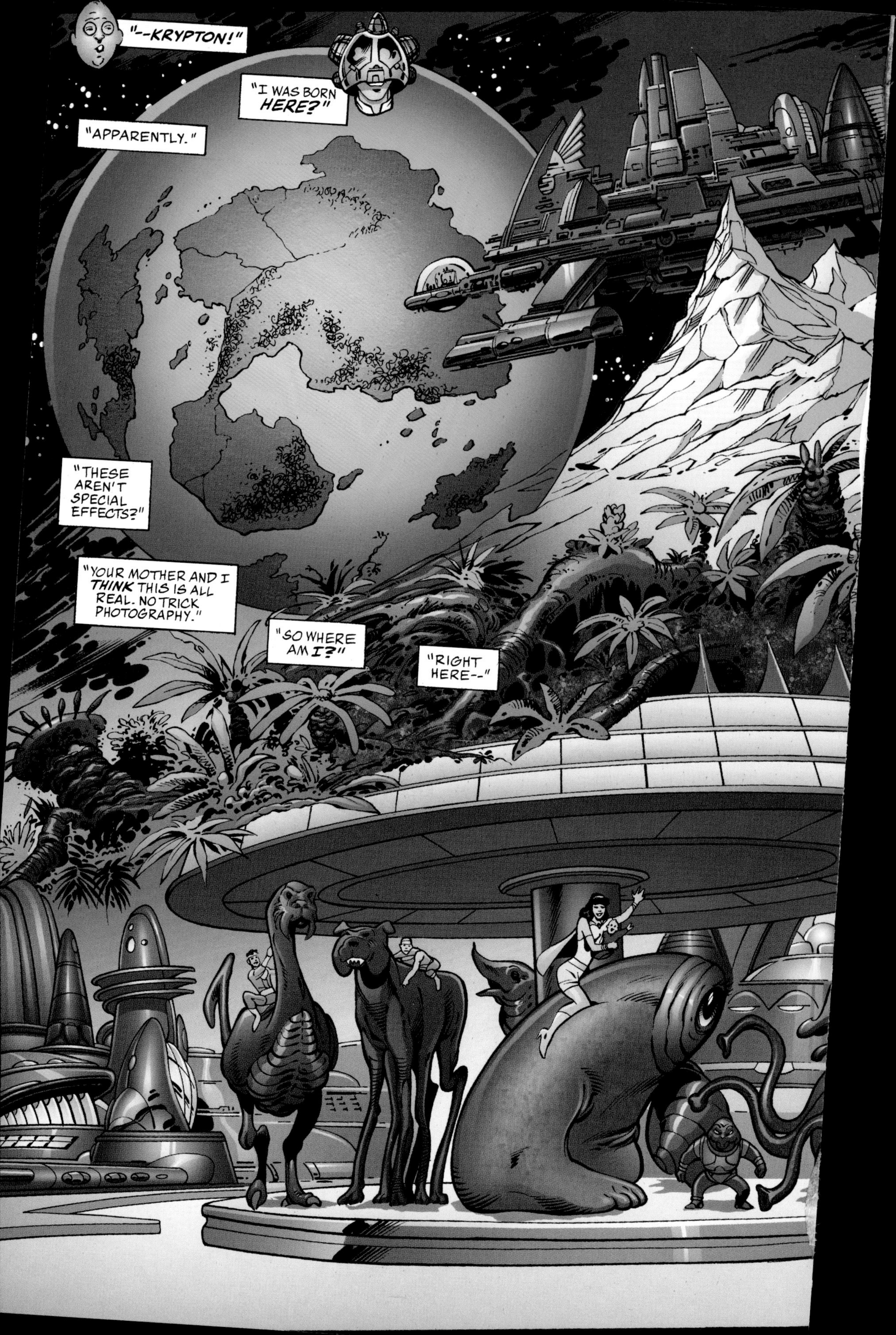
"--KRYPTON!"
"I WAS BORN HERE?"
"APPARENTLY."
"THESE AREN'T SPECIAL EFFECTS?"
"YOUR MOTHER AND I THINK THIS IS ALL REAL. NO TRICK PHOTOGRAPHY."
"SO WHERE AM I?"
"RIGHT HERE--"

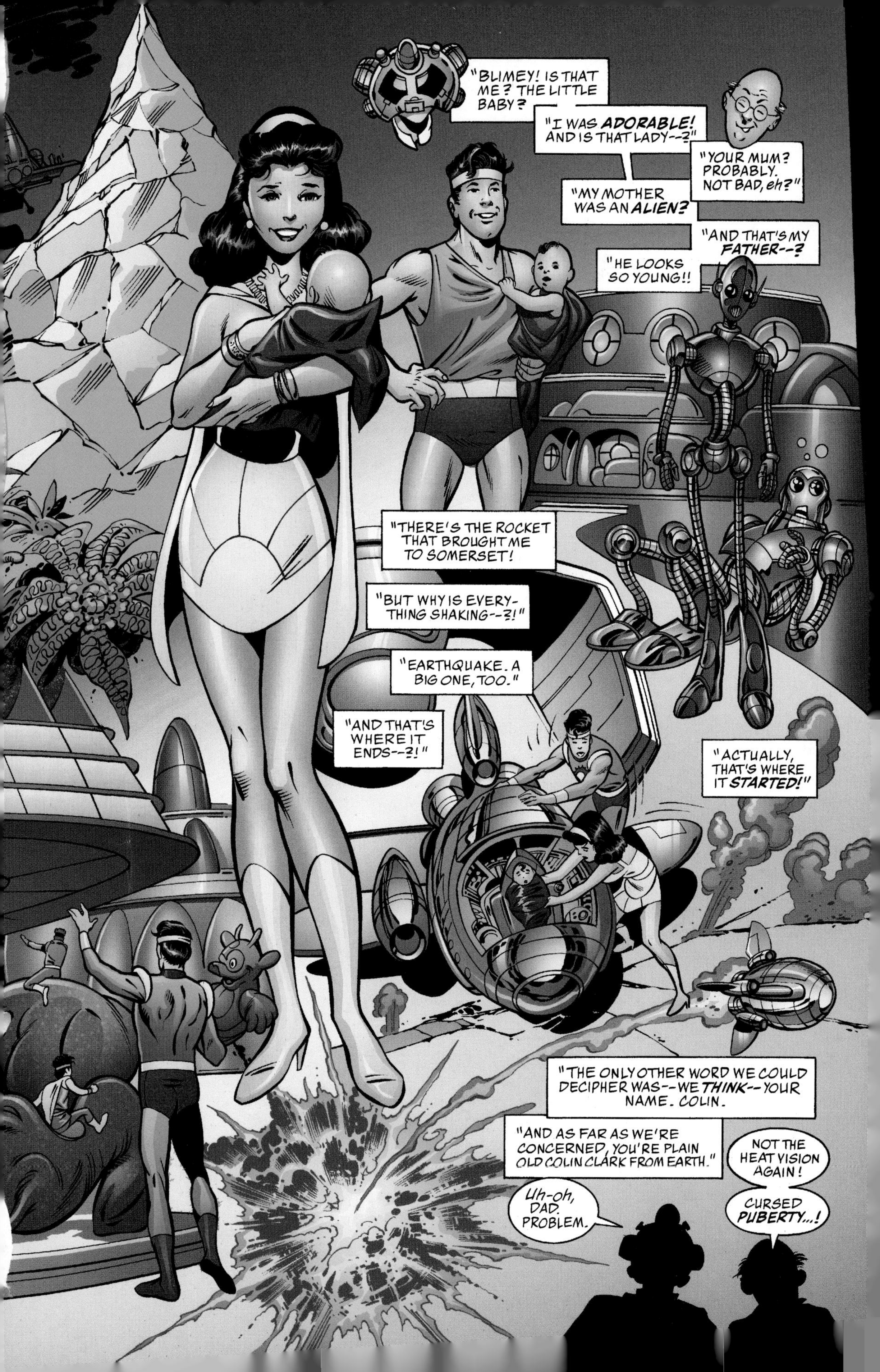
"BLIMEY! IS THAT ME? THE LITTLE BABY?
"I WAS ADORABLE! AND IS THAT LADY--?"
"YOUR MUM? PROBABLY. NOT BAD, eh?"
"MY MOTHER WAS AN ALIEN?
"AND THAT'S MY FATHER--?
"HE LOOKS SO YOUNG!!
"THERE'S THE ROCKET THAT BROUGHT ME TO SOMERSET!
"BUT WHY IS EVERY-THING SHAKING--?!"
"EARTHQUAKE. A BIG ONE, TOO."
"AND THAT'S WHERE IT ENDS--?!"
"ACTUALLY, THAT'S WHERE IT STARTED!"
"THE ONLY OTHER WORD WE COULD DECIPHER WAS--WE THINK--YOUR NAME. COLIN.
"AND AS FAR AS WE'RE CONCERNED, YOU'RE PLAIN OLD COLIN CLARK FROM EARTH."
Uh-oh, DAD. PROBLEM.
NOT THE HEAT VISION AGAIN!
CURSED PUBERTY...!

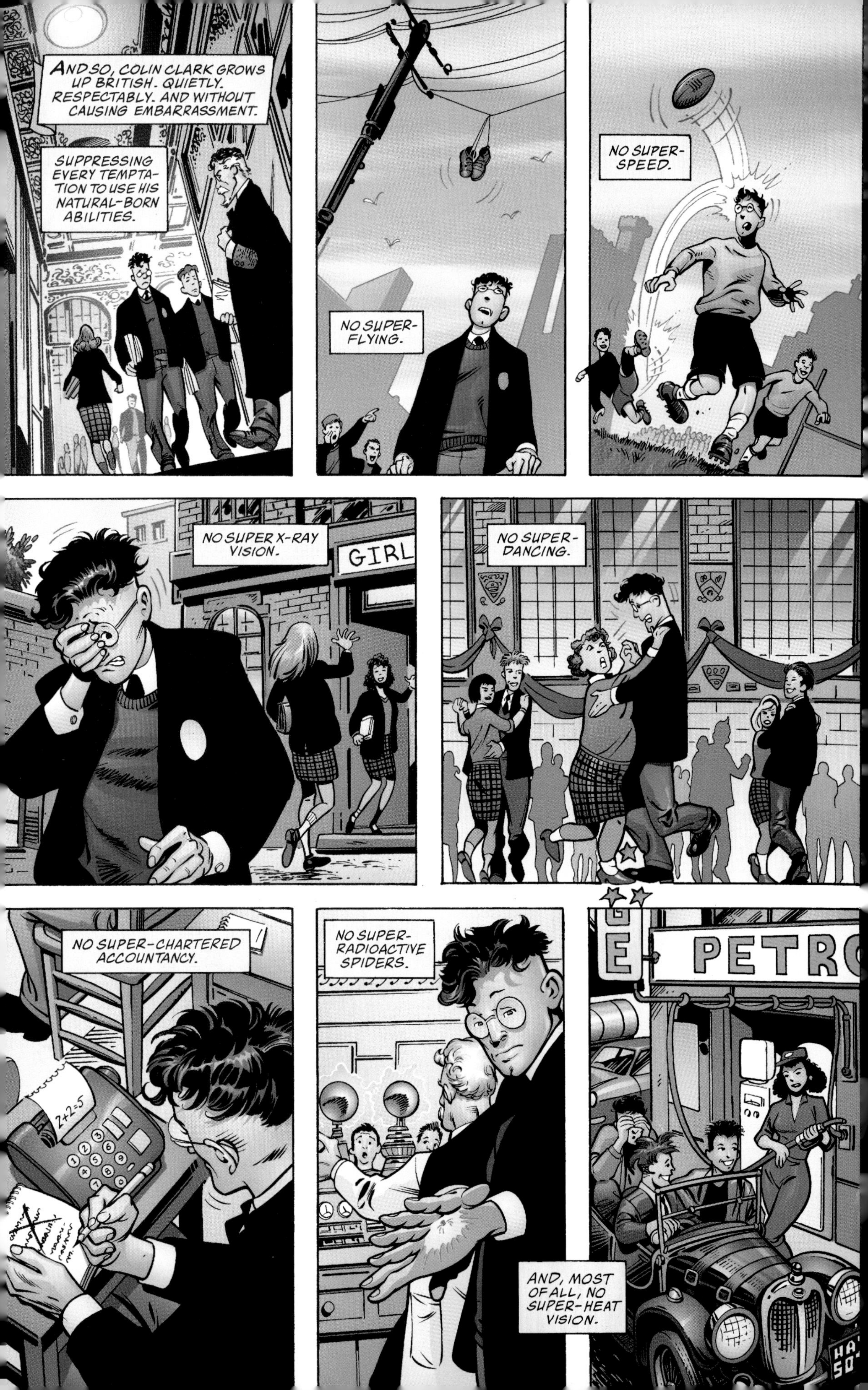
AND SO, COLIN CLARK GROWS UP BRITISH. QUIETLY. RESPECTABLY. AND WITHOUT CAUSING EMBARRASSMENT.
SUPPRESSING EVERY TEMPTATION TO USE HIS NATURAL-BORN ABILITIES.
NO SUPER-FLYING.
NO SUPER-SPEED.
NO SUPER X-RAY VISION.
GIRL
NO SUPER-DANCING.
NO SUPER-CHARTERED ACCOUNTANCY.
2+2=5
NO SUPER-RADIOACTIVE SPIDERS.
PETRO
AND, MOST OF ALL, NO SUPER-HEAT VISION.

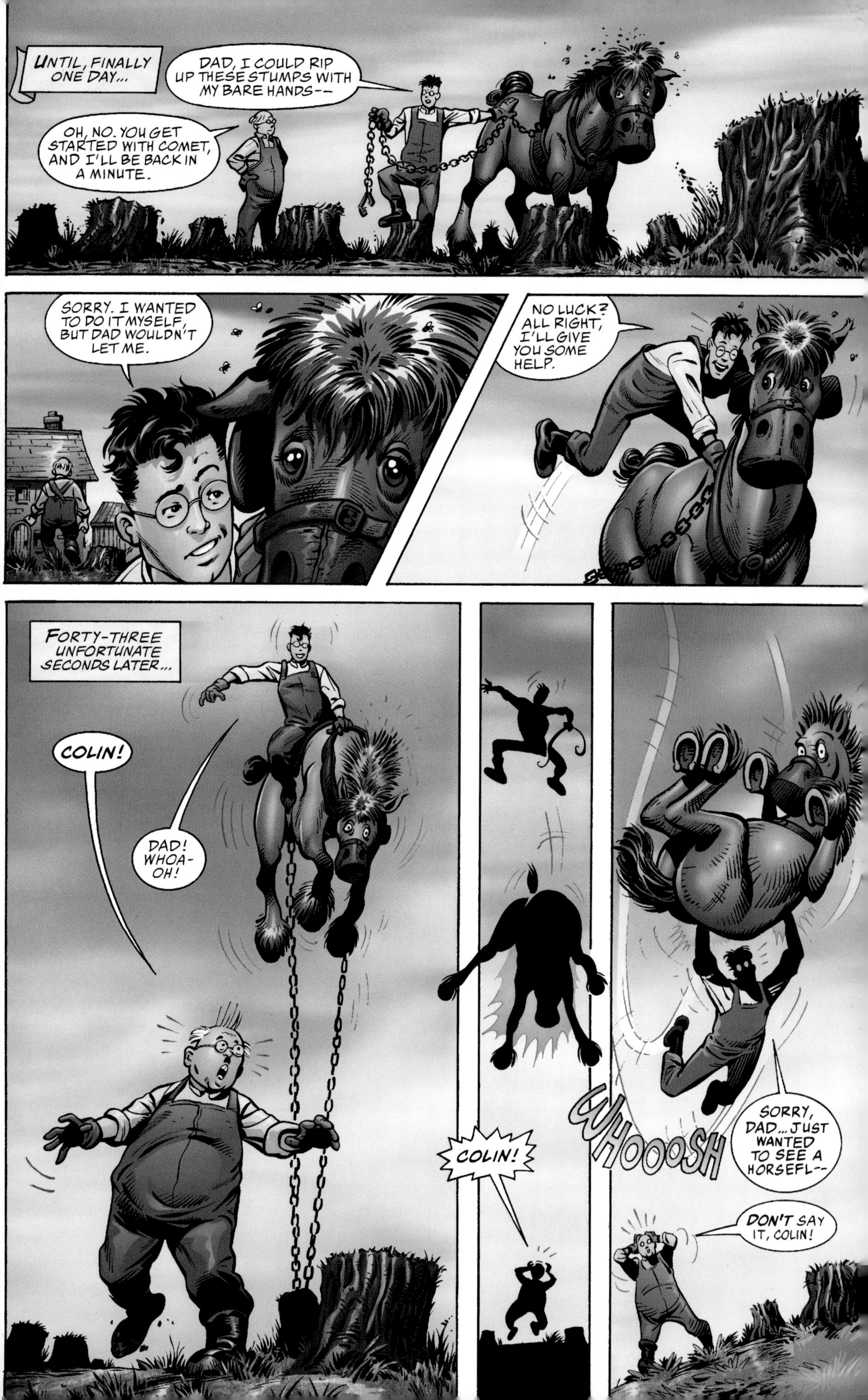
UNTIL, FINALLY ONE DAY...
DAD, I COULD RIP UP THESE STUMPS WITH MY BARE HANDS--
OH, NO. YOU GET STARTED WITH COMET, AND I'LL BE BACK IN A MINUTE.
SORRY. I WANTED TO DO IT MYSELF, BUT DAD WOULDN'T LET ME.
NO LUCK? ALL RIGHT, I'LL GIVE YOU SOME HELP.
FORTY-THREE UNFORTUNATE SECONDS LATER...
COLIN!
DAD! WHOA-OH!
COLIN!
WHOOOSH
SORRY, DAD... JUST WANTED TO SEE A HORSEFL--
DON'T SAY IT, COLIN!

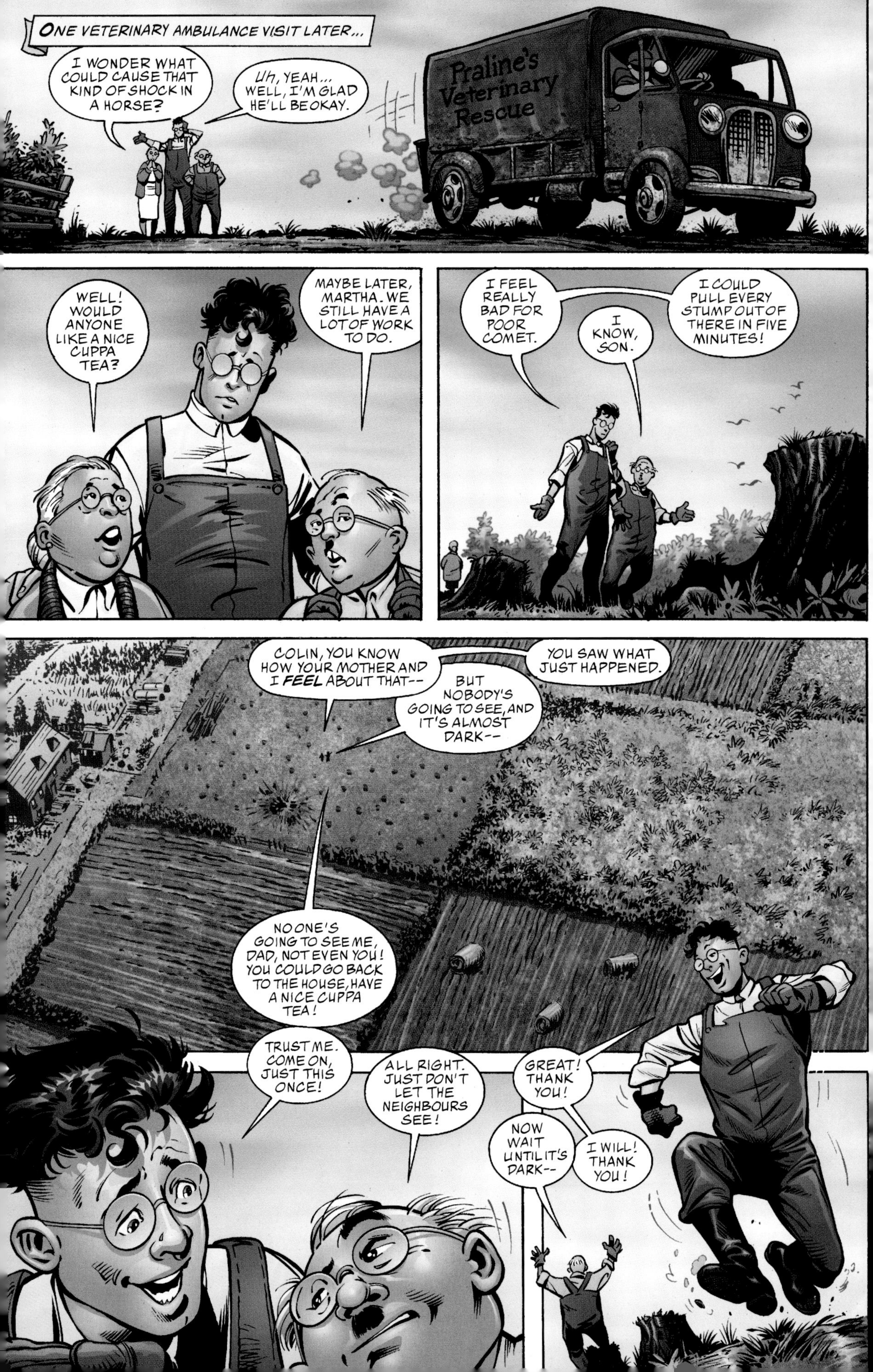
ONE VETERINARY AMBULANCE VISIT LATER...
I WONDER WHAT COULD CAUSE THAT KIND OF SHOCK IN A HORSE?
UH, YEAH... WELL, I'M GLAD HE'LL BE OKAY.
Praline's Veterinary Rescue
WELL! WOULD ANYONE LIKE A NICE CUPPA TEA?
MAYBE LATER, MARTHA. WE STILL HAVE A LOT OF WORK TO DO.
I FEEL REALLY BAD FOR POOR COMET.
I KNOW, SON.
I COULD PULL EVERY STUMP OUT OF THERE IN FIVE MINUTES!
COLIN, YOU KNOW HOW YOUR MOTHER AND I FEEL ABOUT THAT--
YOU SAW WHAT JUST HAPPENED.
BUT NOBODY'S GOING TO SEE, AND IT'S ALMOST DARK--
NO ONE'S GOING TO SEE ME, DAD, NOT EVEN YOU! YOU COULD GO BACK TO THE HOUSE, HAVE A NICE CUPPA TEA!
TRUST ME. COME ON, JUST THIS ONCE!
ALL RIGHT. JUST DON'T LET THE NEIGHBOURS SEE!
GREAT! THANK YOU!
NOW WAIT UNTIL IT'S DARK--
I WILL! THANK YOU!

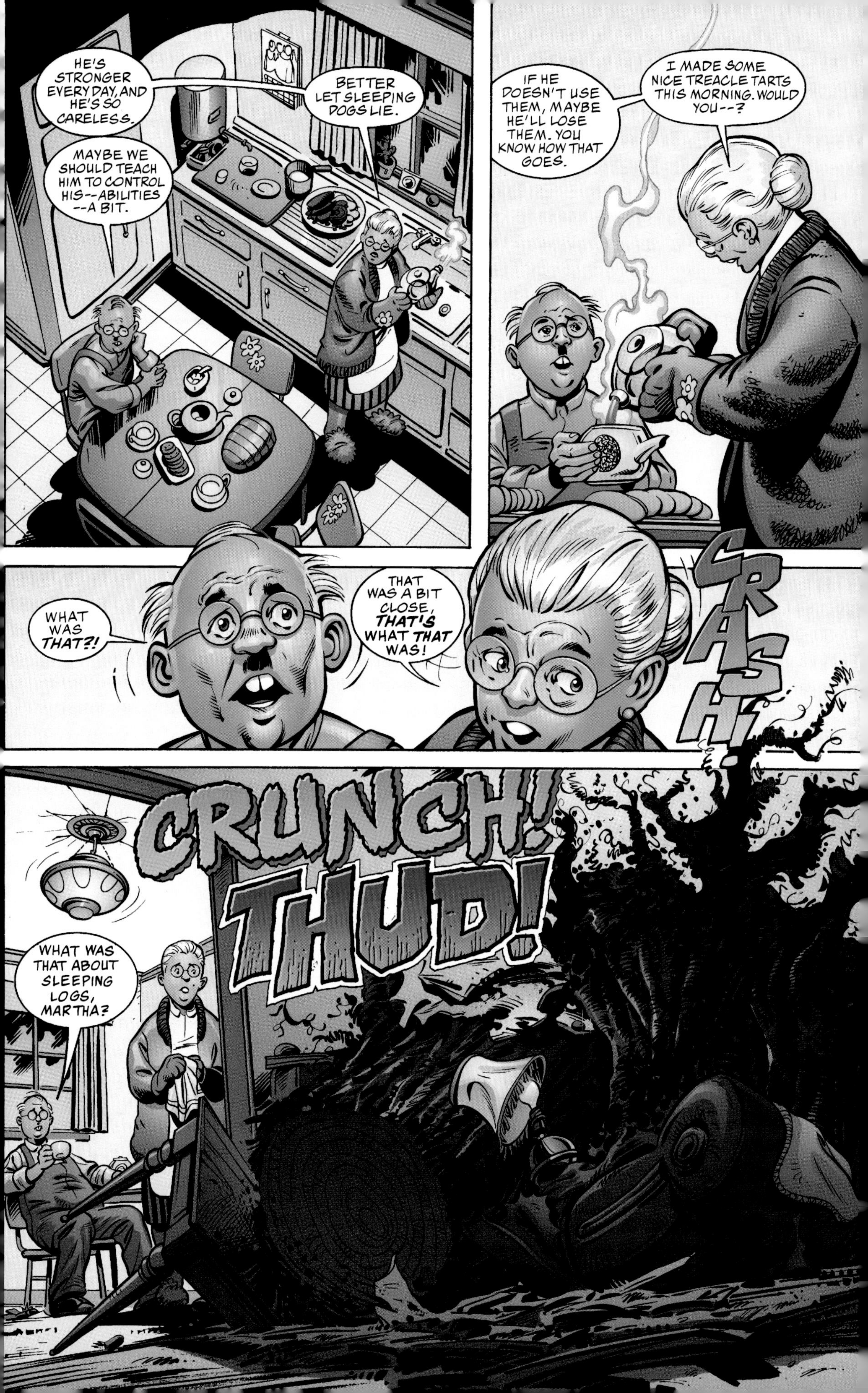
HE'S STRONGER EVERY DAY, AND HE'S SO CARELESS.
BETTER LET SLEEPING DOGS LIE.
MAYBE WE SHOULD TEACH HIM TO CONTROL HIS--ABILITIES --A BIT.
IF HE DOESN'T USE THEM, MAYBE HE'LL LOSE THEM. YOU KNOW HOW THAT GOES.
I MADE SOME NICE TREACLE TARTS THIS MORNING. WOULD YOU--?
CRASH!
WHAT WAS THAT?!
THAT WAS A BIT CLOSE, THAT'S WHAT THAT WAS!
CRUNCH!
THUD!
WHAT WAS THAT ABOUT SLEEPING LOGS, MARTHA?

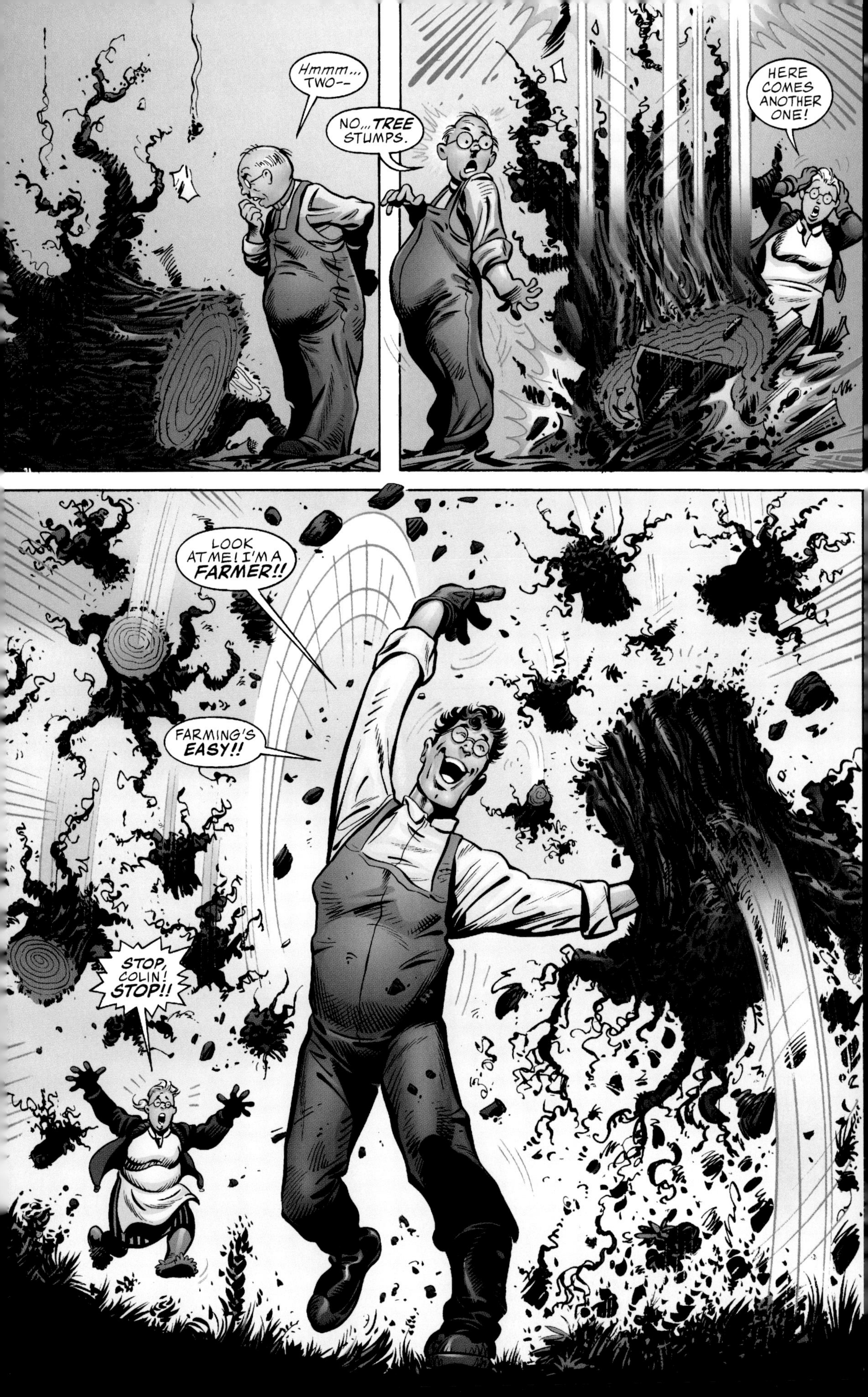

Hmmm... TWO--
NO... TREE STUMPS.
HERE COMES ANOTHER ONE!
LOOK AT ME! I'M A FARMER!!
FARMING'S EASY!!
STOP, COLIN! STOP!!

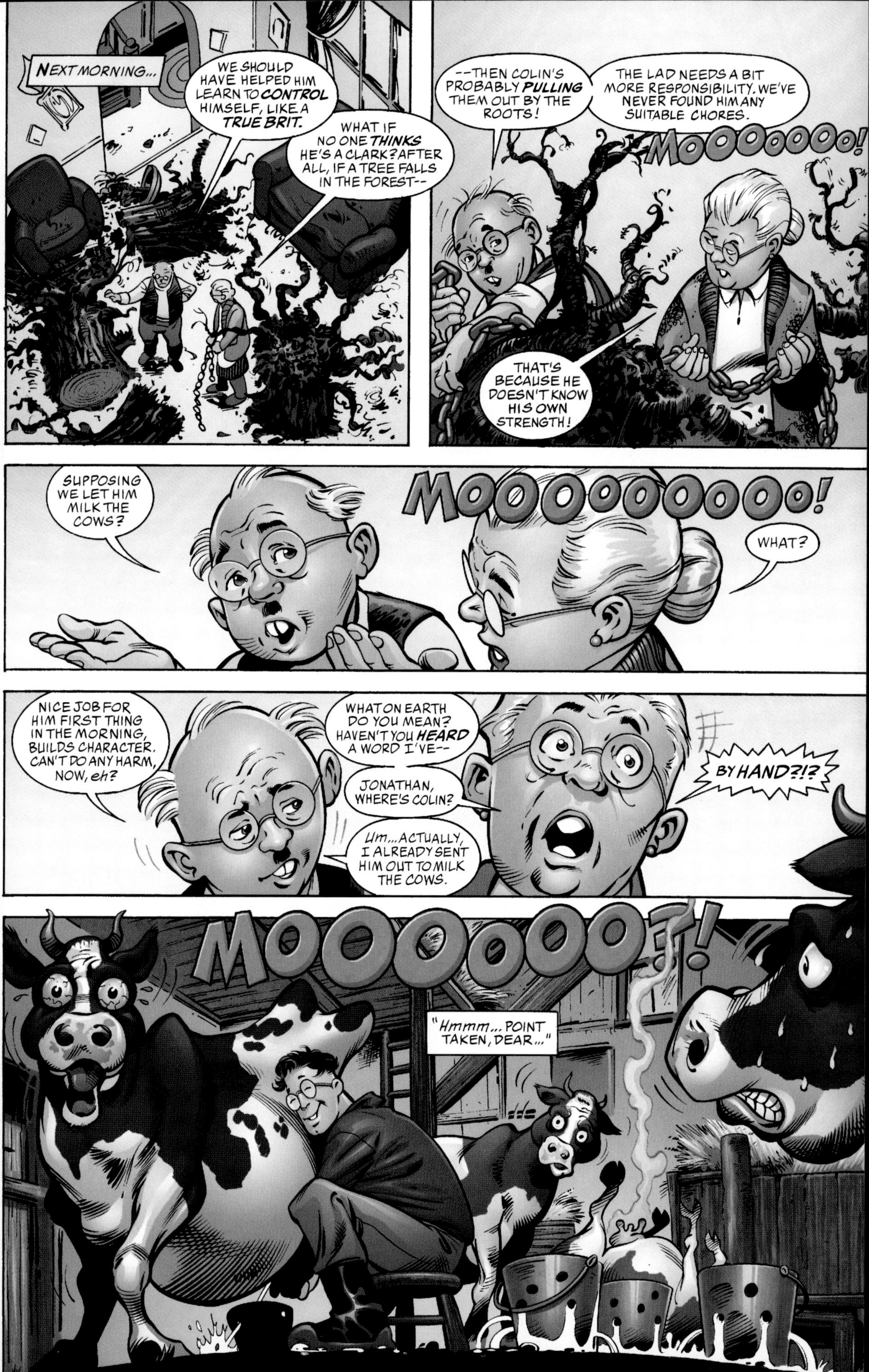
NEXT MORNING...
WE SHOULD HAVE HELPED HIM LEARN TO CONTROL HIMSELF, LIKE A TRUE BRIT.
WHAT IF NO ONE THINKS HE'S A CLARK? AFTER ALL, IF A TREE FALLS IN THE FOREST--
--THEN COLIN'S PROBABLY PULLING THEM OUT BY THE ROOTS!
THE LAD NEEDS A BIT MORE RESPONSIBILITY. WE'VE NEVER FOUND HIM ANY SUITABLE CHORES.
MOOOooooo!
THAT'S BECAUSE HE DOESN'T KNOW HIS OWN STRENGTH!
SUPPOSING WE LET HIM MILK THE COWS?
MOOOOOOOOOo!
WHAT?
NICE JOB FOR HIM FIRST THING IN THE MORNING, BUILDS CHARACTER. CAN'T DO ANY HARM, NOW, eh?
WHAT ON EARTH DO YOU MEAN? HAVEN'T YOU HEARD A WORD I'VE--
JONATHAN, WHERE'S COLIN?
Um... ACTUALLY, I ALREADY SENT HIM OUT TO MILK THE COWS.
BY HAND?!?
MOOOOOOO?!
"Hmmm... POINT TAKEN, DEAR..."

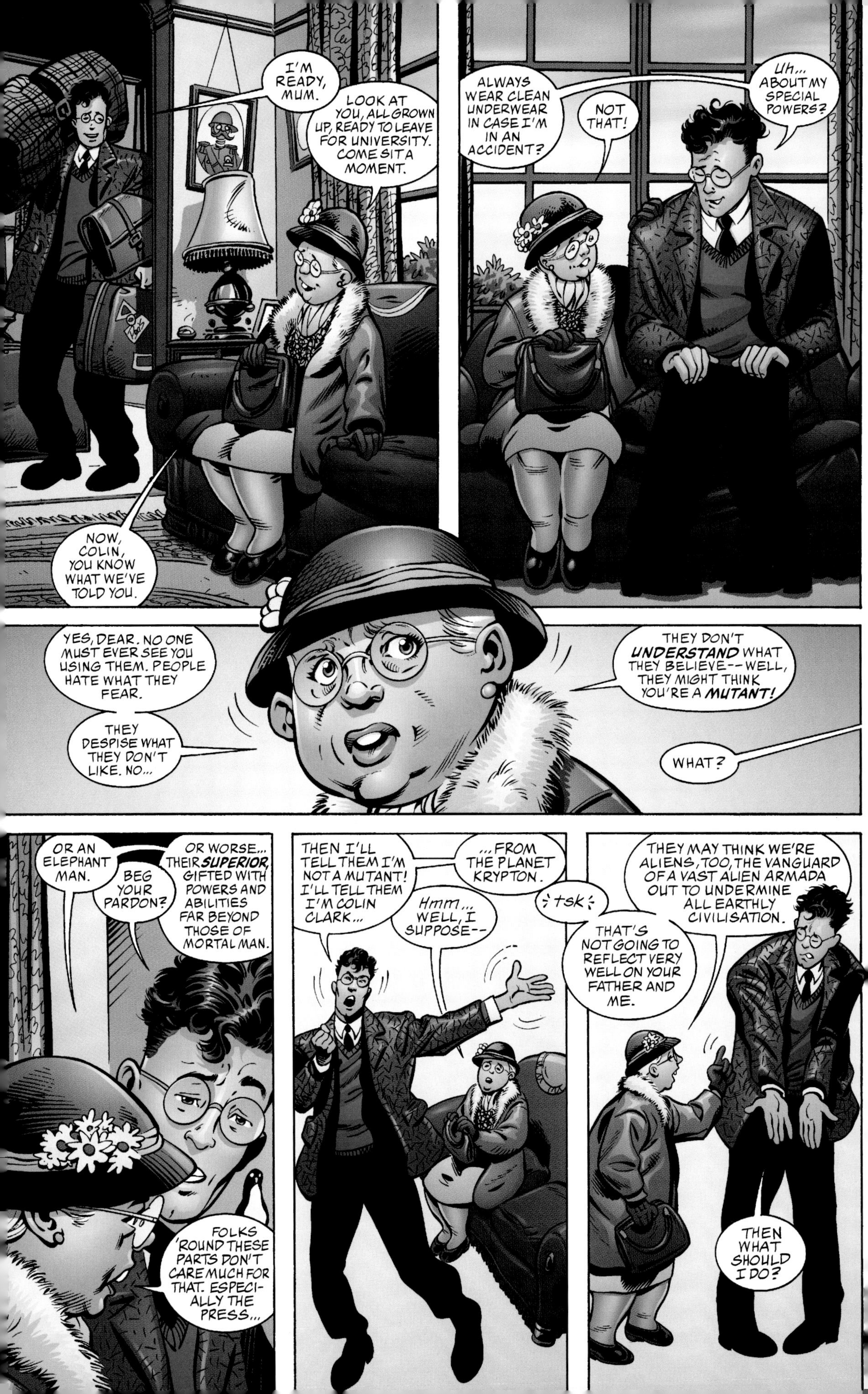
I'M READY, MUM.
LOOK AT YOU, ALL GROWN UP, READY TO LEAVE FOR UNIVERSITY. COME SIT A MOMENT.
NOW, COLIN, YOU KNOW WHAT WE'VE TOLD YOU.
ALWAYS WEAR CLEAN UNDERWEAR IN CASE I'M IN AN ACCIDENT?
NOT THAT!
Uh... ABOUT MY SPECIAL POWERS?
YES, DEAR. NO ONE MUST EVER SEE YOU USING THEM. PEOPLE HATE WHAT THEY FEAR.
THEY DESPISE WHAT THEY DON'T LIKE. NO...
THEY DON'T UNDERSTAND WHAT THEY BELIEVE--WELL, THEY MIGHT THINK YOU'RE A MUTANT!
WHAT?
OR AN ELEPHANT MAN.
BEG YOUR PARDON?
OR WORSE... THEIR SUPERIOR, GIFTED WITH POWERS AND ABILITIES FAR BEYOND THOSE OF MORTAL MAN.
FOLKS 'ROUND THESE PARTS DON'T CARE MUCH FOR THAT. ESPECIALLY THE PRESS...
THEN I'LL TELL THEM I'M NOT A MUTANT! I'LL TELL THEM I'M COLIN CLARK...
...FROM THE PLANET KRYPTON.
Hmm... WELL, I SUPPOSE--
tsk
THAT'S NOT GOING TO REFLECT VERY WELL ON YOUR FATHER AND ME.
THEY MAY THINK WE'RE ALIENS, TOO, THE VANGUARD OF A VAST ALIEN ARMADA OUT TO UNDERMINE ALL EARTHLY CIVILISATION.
THEN WHAT SHOULD I DO?

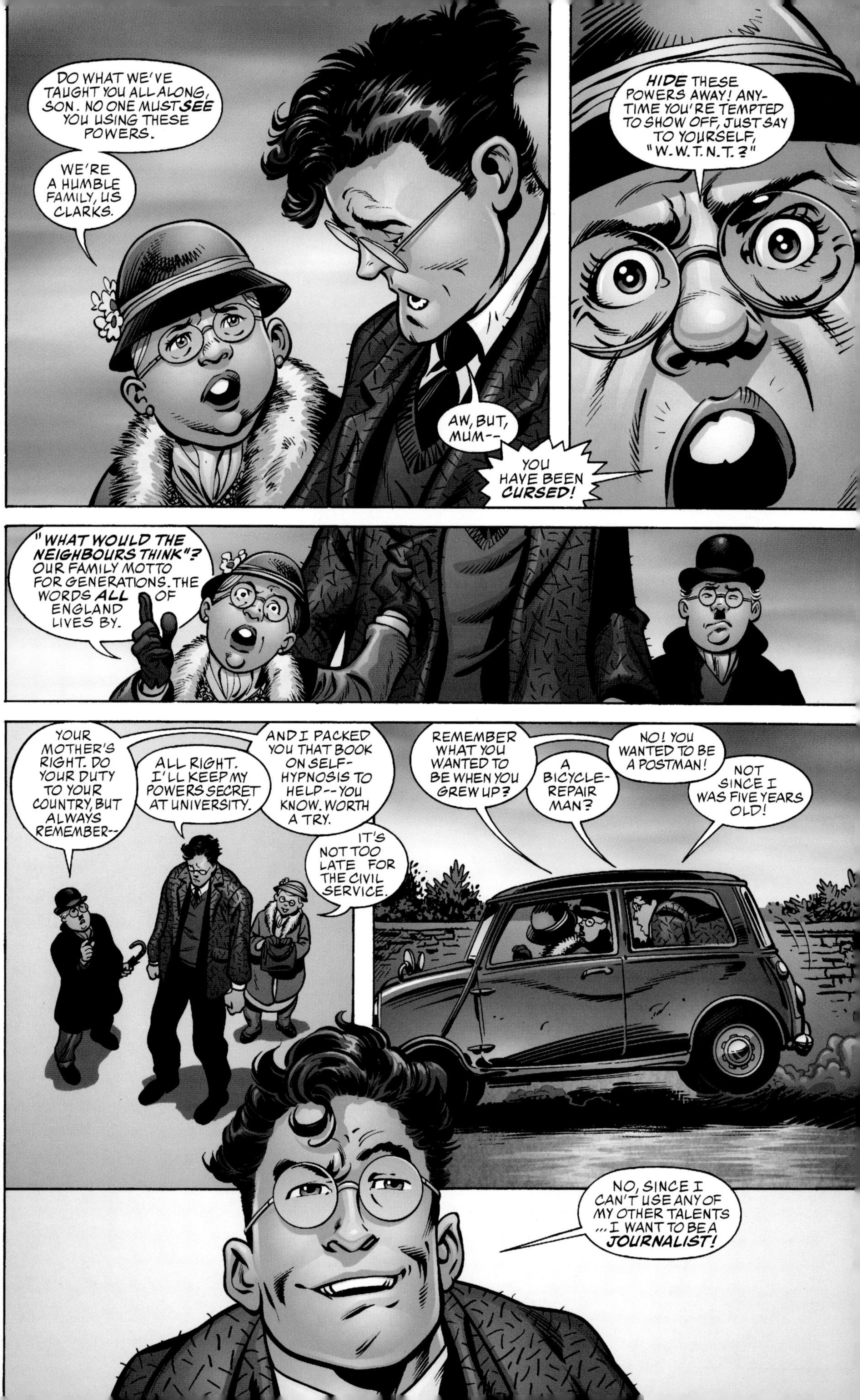
DO WHAT WE'VE TAUGHT YOU ALL ALONG, SON. NO ONE MUST SEE YOU USING THESE POWERS.
WE'RE A HUMBLE FAMILY, US CLARKS.
AW, BUT, MUM--
HIDE THESE POWERS AWAY! ANY-TIME YOU'RE TEMPTED TO SHOW OFF, JUST SAY TO YOURSELF, "W.W.T.N.T.?"
YOU HAVE BEEN CURSED!
"WHAT WOULD THE NEIGHBOURS THINK"? OUR FAMILY MOTTO FOR GENERATIONS. THE WORDS ALL OF ENGLAND LIVES BY.
YOUR MOTHER'S RIGHT. DO YOUR DUTY TO YOUR COUNTRY, BUT ALWAYS REMEMBER--
ALL RIGHT. I'LL KEEP MY POWERS SECRET AT UNIVERSITY.
AND I PACKED YOU THAT BOOK ON SELF-HYPNOSIS TO HELP--YOU KNOW. WORTH A TRY.
IT'S NOT TOO LATE FOR THE CIVIL SERVICE.
REMEMBER WHAT YOU WANTED TO BE WHEN YOU GREW UP?
A BICYCLE-REPAIR MAN?
NO! YOU WANTED TO BE A POSTMAN!
NOT SINCE I WAS FIVE YEARS OLD!
NO, SINCE I CAN'T USE ANY OF MY OTHER TALENTS ...I WANT TO BE A JOURNALIST!

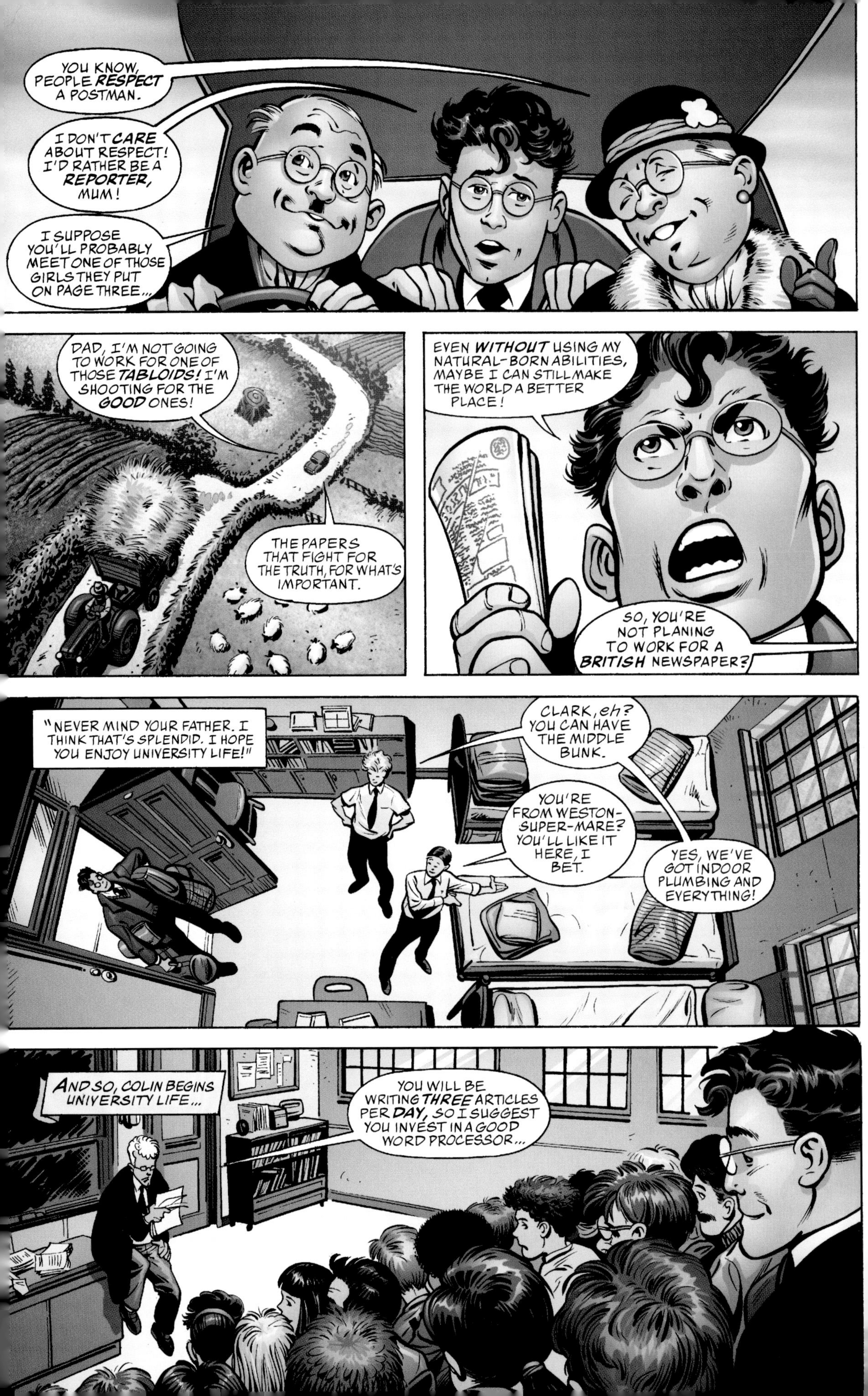
YOU KNOW, PEOPLE RESPECT A POSTMAN.
I DON'T CARE ABOUT RESPECT! I'D RATHER BE A REPORTER, MUM!
I SUPPOSE YOU'LL PROBABLY MEET ONE OF THOSE GIRLS THEY PUT ON PAGE THREE...
DAD, I'M NOT GOING TO WORK FOR ONE OF THOSE TABLOIDS! I'M SHOOTING FOR THE GOOD ONES!
THE PAPERS THAT FIGHT FOR THE TRUTH, FOR WHAT'S IMPORTANT.
EVEN WITHOUT USING MY NATURAL-BORN ABILITIES, MAYBE I CAN STILL MAKE THE WORLD A BETTER PLACE!
SO, YOU'RE NOT PLANING TO WORK FOR A BRITISH NEWSPAPER?
"NEVER MIND YOUR FATHER. I THINK THAT'S SPLENDID. I HOPE YOU ENJOY UNIVERSITY LIFE!"
CLARK, eh? YOU CAN HAVE THE MIDDLE BUNK.
YOU'RE FROM WESTON-SUPER-MARE? YOU'LL LIKE IT HERE, I BET.
YES, WE'VE GOT INDOOR PLUMBING AND EVERYTHING!
AND SO, COLIN BEGINS UNIVERSITY LIFE...
YOU WILL BE WRITING THREE ARTICLES PER DAY, SO I SUGGEST YOU INVEST IN A GOOD WORD PROCESSOR...

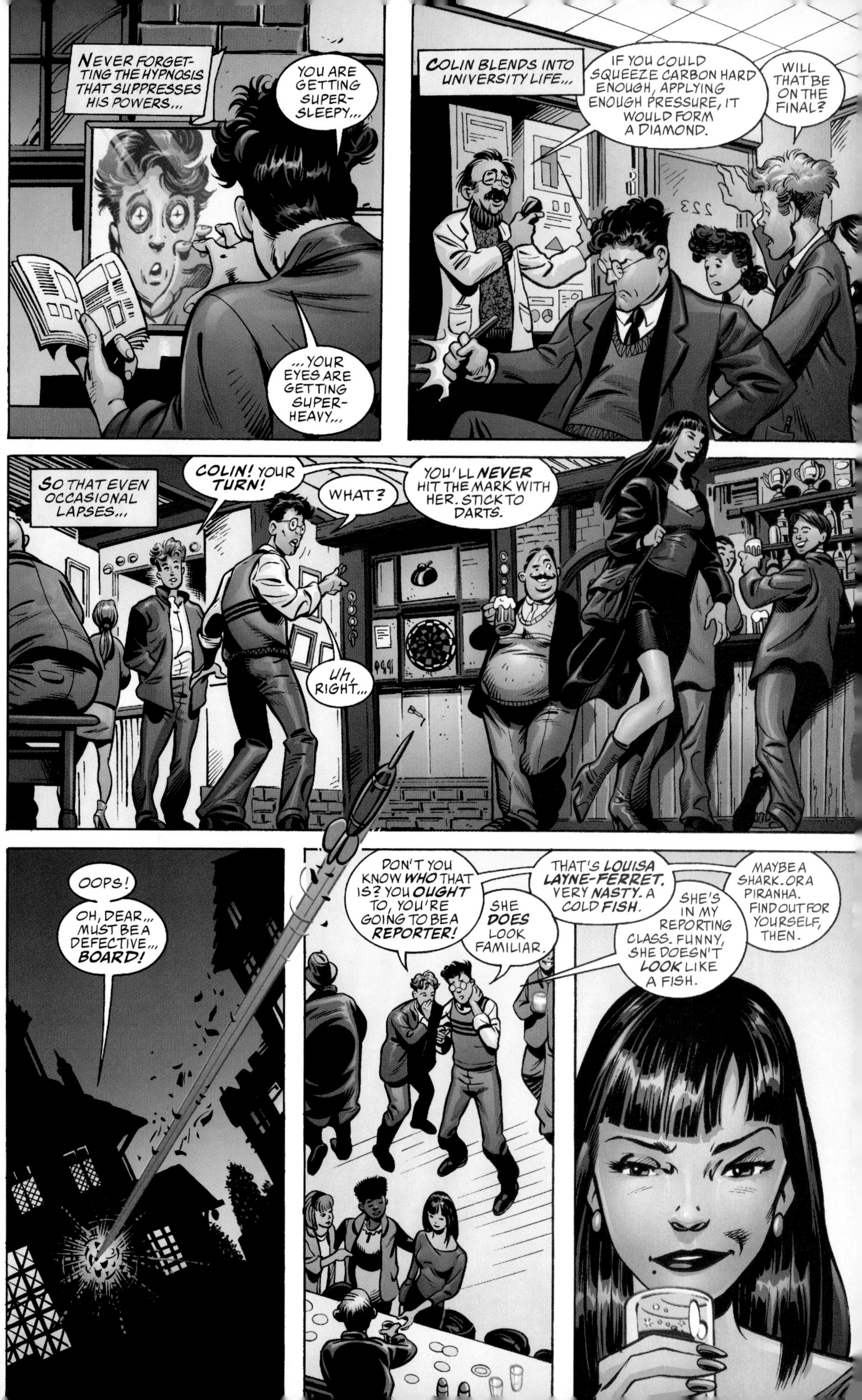
NEVER FORGETTING THE HYPNOSIS THAT SUPPRESSES HIS POWERS...
YOU ARE GETTING SUPER-SLEEPY...
...YOUR EYES ARE GETTING SUPER-HEAVY...
COLIN BLENDS INTO UNIVERSITY LIFE...
IF YOU COULD SQUEEZE CARBON HARD ENOUGH, APPLYING ENOUGH PRESSURE, IT WOULD FORM A DIAMOND.
WILL THAT BE ON THE FINAL?
SO THAT EVEN OCCASIONAL LAPSES...
COLIN! YOUR TURN!
WHAT?
YOU'LL NEVER HIT THE MARK WITH HER. STICK TO DARTS.
UH, RIGHT...
OOPS!
OH, DEAR... MUST BE A DEFECTIVE... BOARD!
DON'T YOU KNOW WHO THAT IS? YOU OUGHT TO, YOU'RE GOING TO BE A REPORTER!
SHE DOES LOOK FAMILIAR.
THAT'S LOUISA LAYNE-FERRET. VERY NASTY. A COLD FISH.
SHE'S IN MY REPORTING CLASS. FUNNY, SHE DOESN'T LOOK LIKE A FISH.
MAYBE A SHARK. OR A PIRANHA. FIND OUT FOR YOURSELF, THEN.

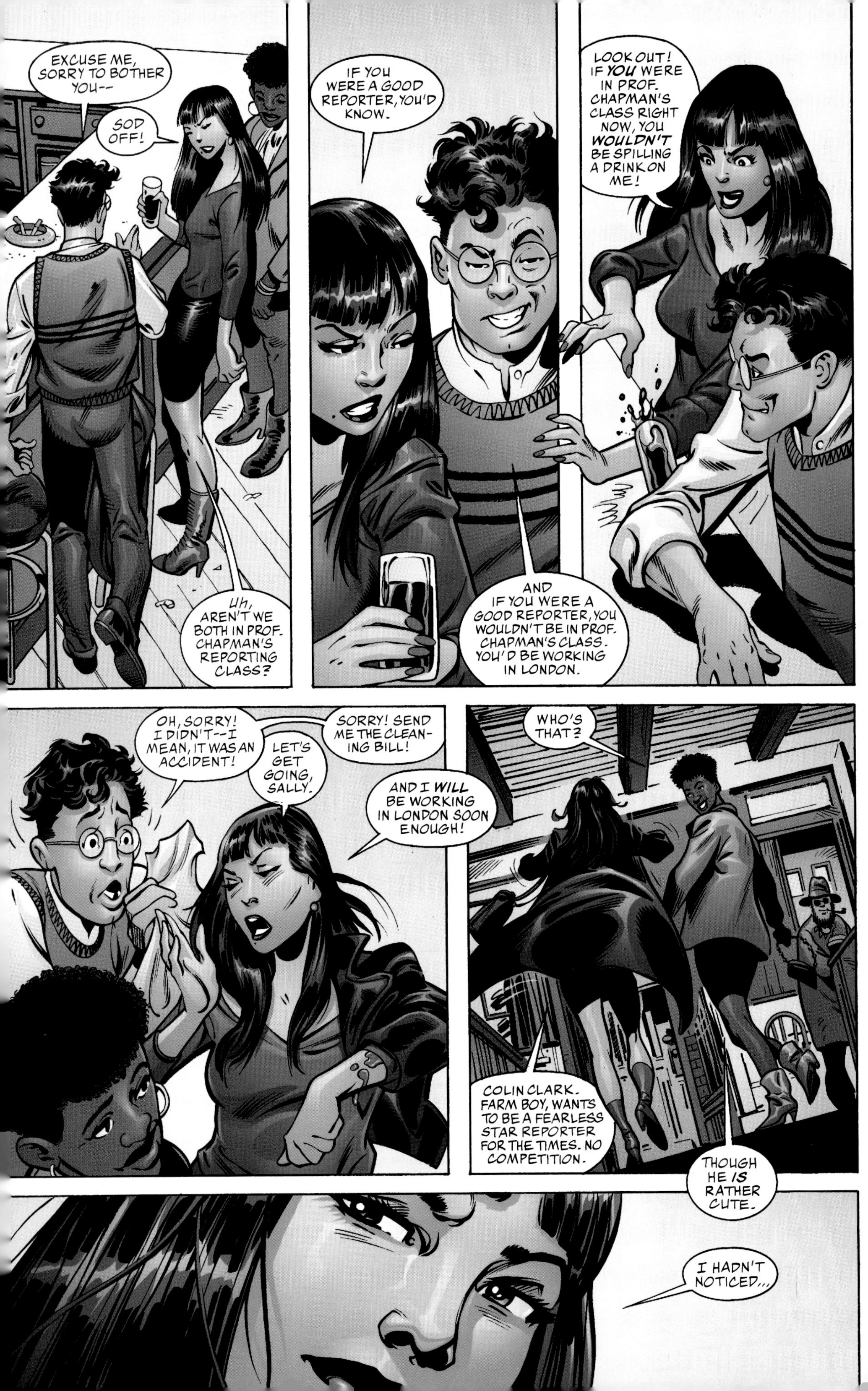

EXCUSE ME, SORRY TO BOTHER YOU--
SOD OFF!
Uh, AREN'T WE BOTH IN PROF. CHAPMAN'S REPORTING CLASS?
IF YOU WERE A GOOD REPORTER, YOU'D KNOW.
AND IF YOU WERE A GOOD REPORTER, YOU WOULDN'T BE IN PROF. CHAPMAN'S CLASS. YOU'D BE WORKING IN LONDON.
LOOK OUT! IF YOU WERE IN PROF. CHAPMAN'S CLASS RIGHT NOW, YOU WOULDN'T BE SPILLING A DRINK ON ME!
OH, SORRY! I DIDN'T--I MEAN, IT WAS AN ACCIDENT!
SORRY! SEND ME THE CLEANING BILL!
LET'S GET GOING, SALLY.
AND I WILL BE WORKING IN LONDON SOON ENOUGH!
WHO'S THAT?
COLIN CLARK. FARM BOY, WANTS TO BE A FEARLESS STAR REPORTER FOR THE TIMES. NO COMPETITION.
THOUGH HE IS RATHER CUTE.
I HADN'T NOTICED...

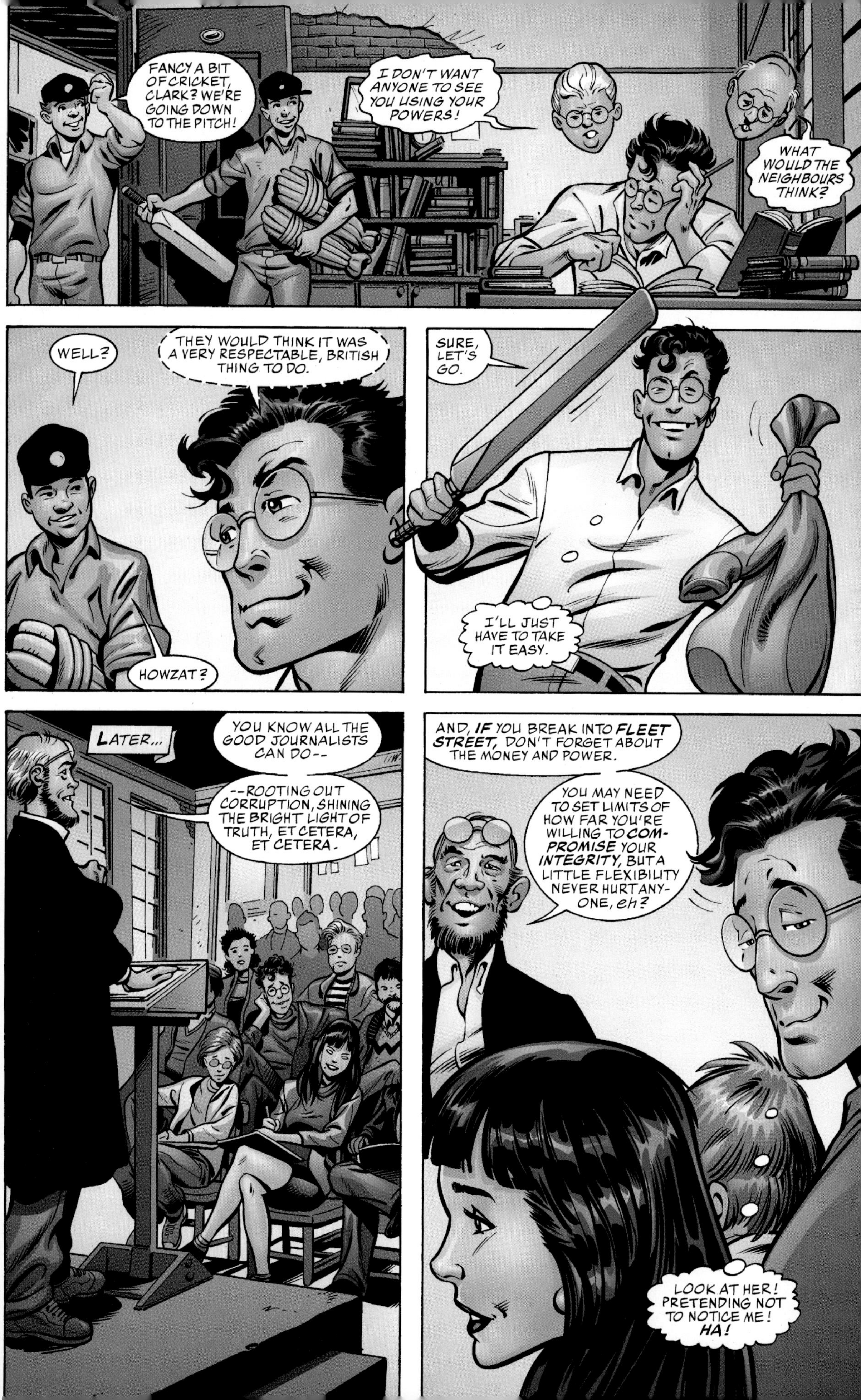
FANCY A BIT OF CRICKET, CLARK? WE'RE GOING DOWN TO THE PITCH!
I DON'T WANT ANYONE TO SEE YOU USING YOUR POWERS!
WHAT WOULD THE NEIGHBOURS THINK?
WELL?
THEY WOULD THINK IT WAS A VERY RESPECTABLE, BRITISH THING TO DO.
HOWZAT?
SURE, LET'S GO.
I'LL JUST HAVE TO TAKE IT EASY.
LATER...
YOU KNOW ALL THE GOOD JOURNALISTS CAN DO--
--ROOTING OUT CORRUPTION, SHINING THE BRIGHT LIGHT OF TRUTH, ET CETERA, ET CETERA.
AND, IF YOU BREAK INTO FLEET STREET, DON'T FORGET ABOUT THE MONEY AND POWER.
YOU MAY NEED TO SET LIMITS OF HOW FAR YOU'RE WILLING TO COMPROMISE YOUR INTEGRITY, BUT A LITTLE FLEXIBILITY NEVER HURT ANYONE, eh?
LOOK AT HER! PRETENDING NOT TO NOTICE ME! HA!

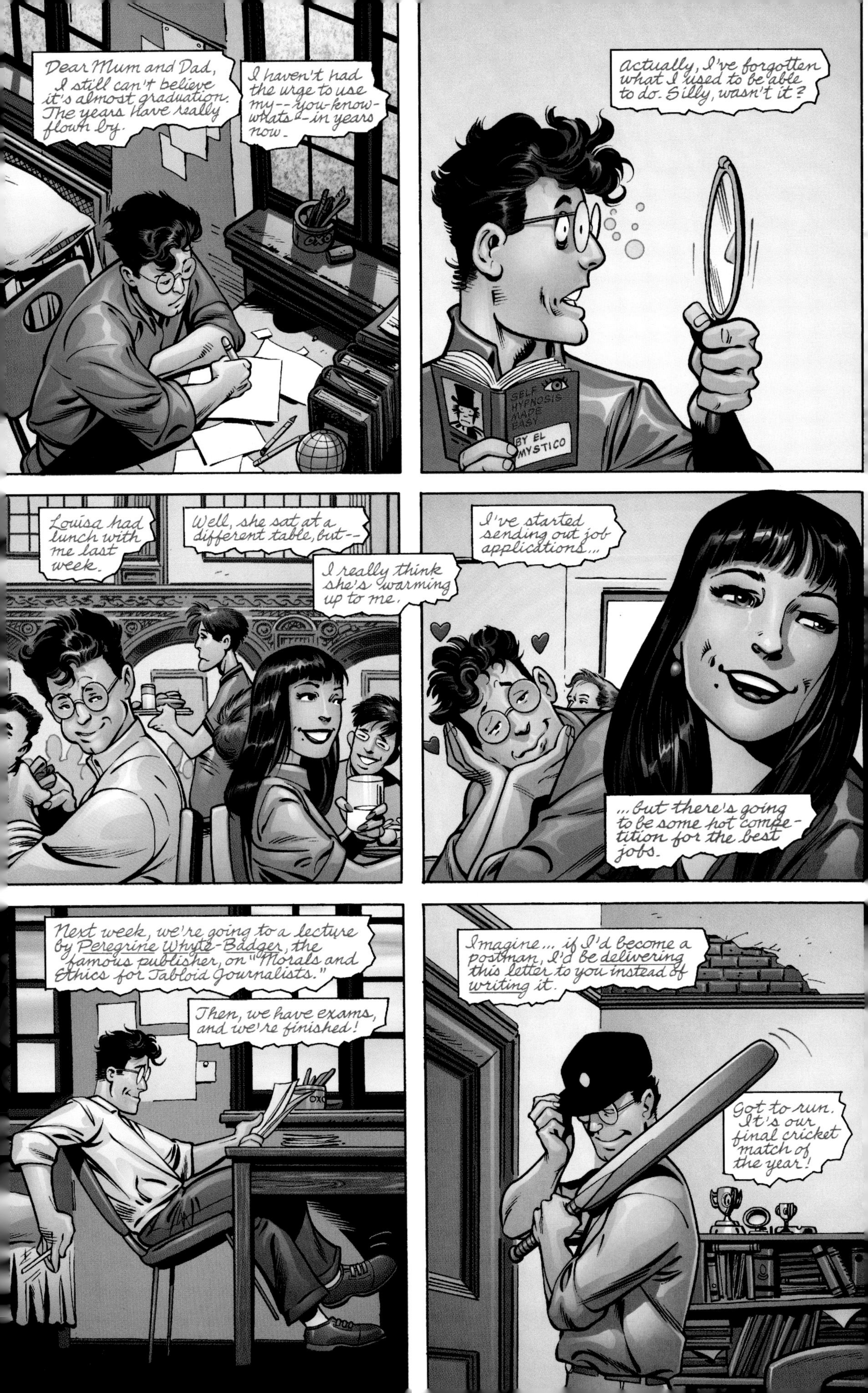
Dear Mum and Dad, I still can't believe it's almost graduation. The years have really flown by.
I haven't had the urge to use my--you-know-whats--in years now.
Actually, I've forgotten what I used to be able to do. Silly, wasn't it?
SELF HYPNOSIS MADE EASY
BY EL MYSTICO
Louisa had lunch with me last week.
Well, she sat at a different table, but--
I really think she's warming up to me.
I've started sending out job applications...
...but there's going to be some hot competition for the best jobs.
Next week, we're going to a lecture by Peregrine Whyte-Badger, the famous publisher, on "Morals and Ethics for Tabloid Journalists."
Then, we have exams, and we're finished!
Imagine... if I'd become a postman, I'd be delivering this letter to you instead of writing it.
Got to run. It's our final cricket match of the year!

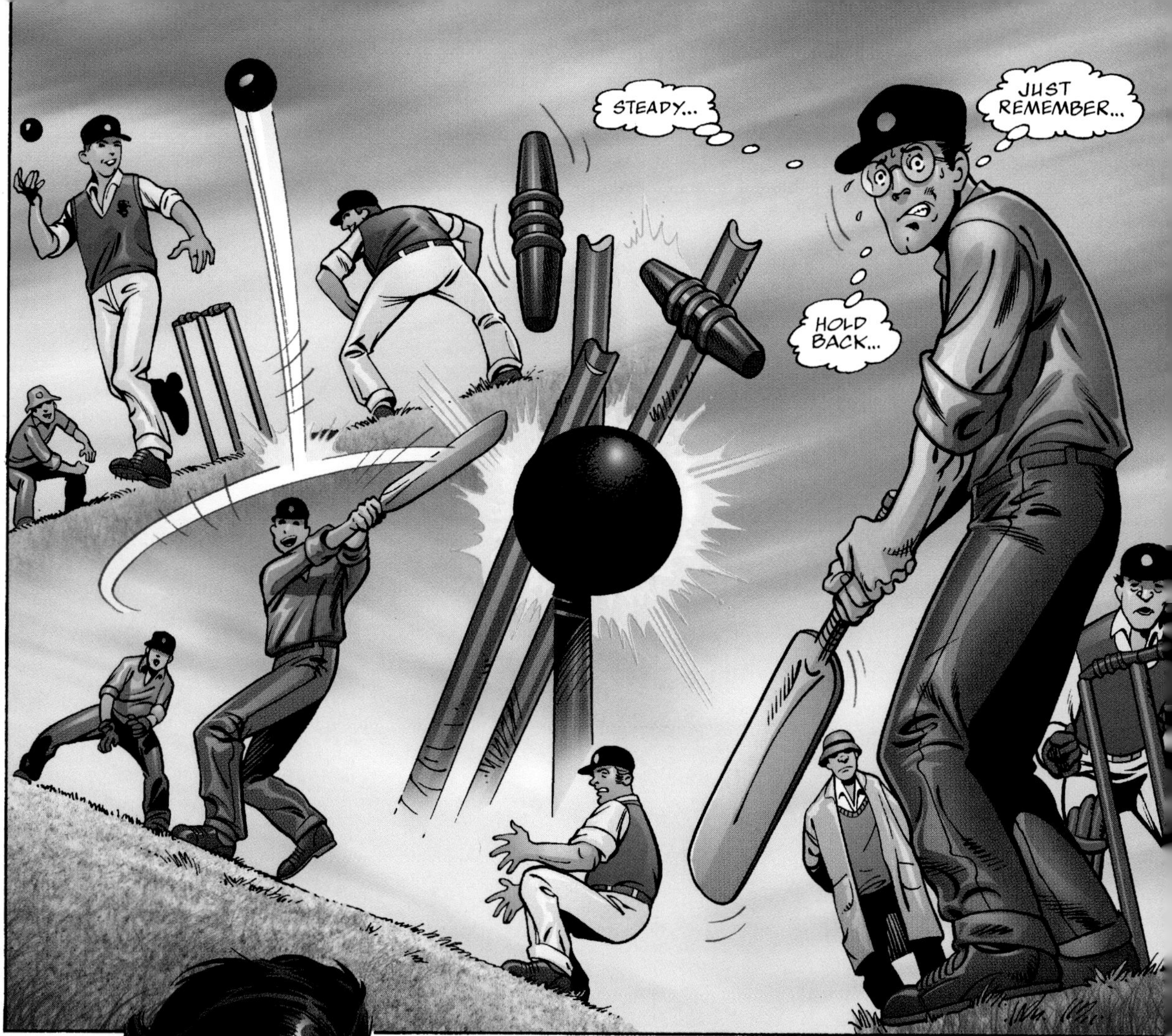
STEADY...
JUST REMEMBER...
HOLD BACK...

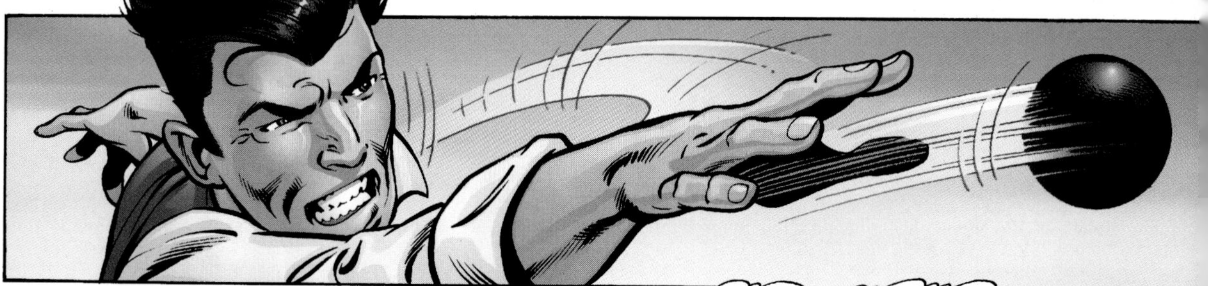

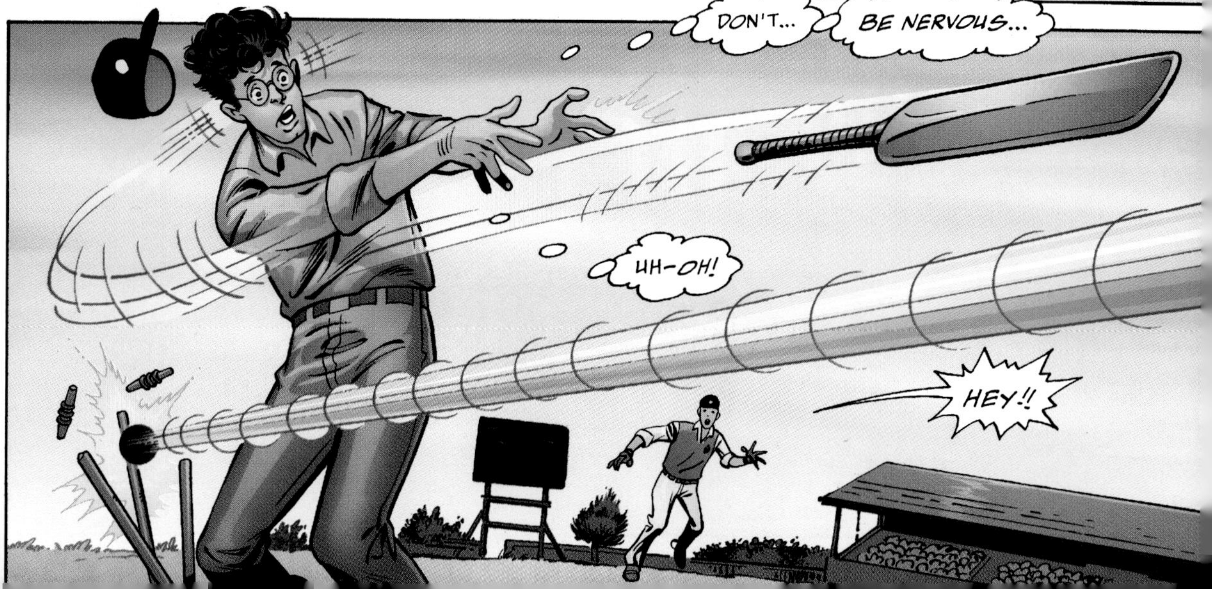
DON'T...
BE NERVOUS...
UH-OH!
HEY!!

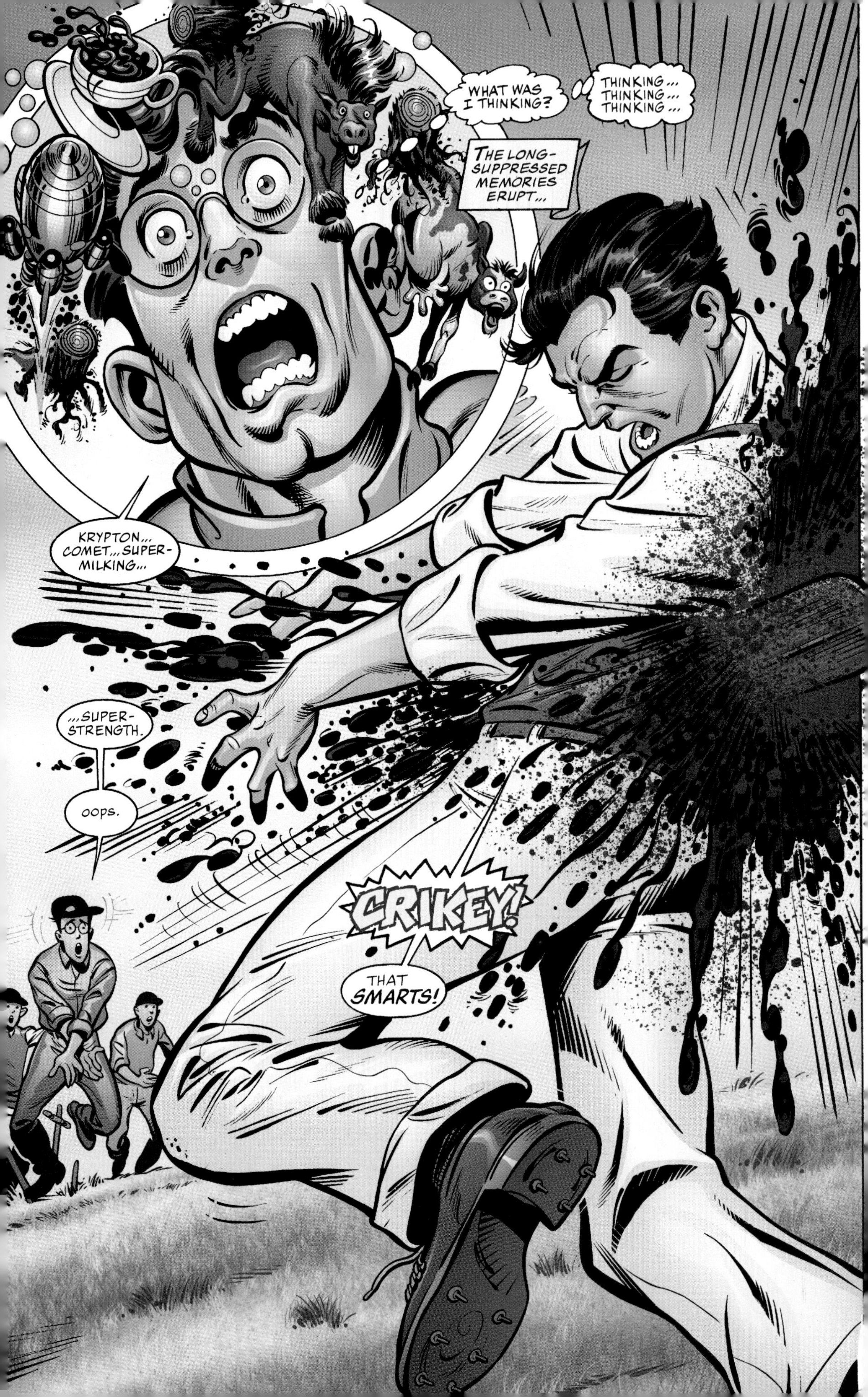

WHAT WAS I THINKING?
THINKING... THINKING... THINKING...
THE LONG-SUPPRESSED MEMORIES ERUPT...
KRYPTON... COMET... SUPER-MILKING...
...SUPER-STRENGTH.
OOPS.
CRIKEY!
THAT SMARTS!

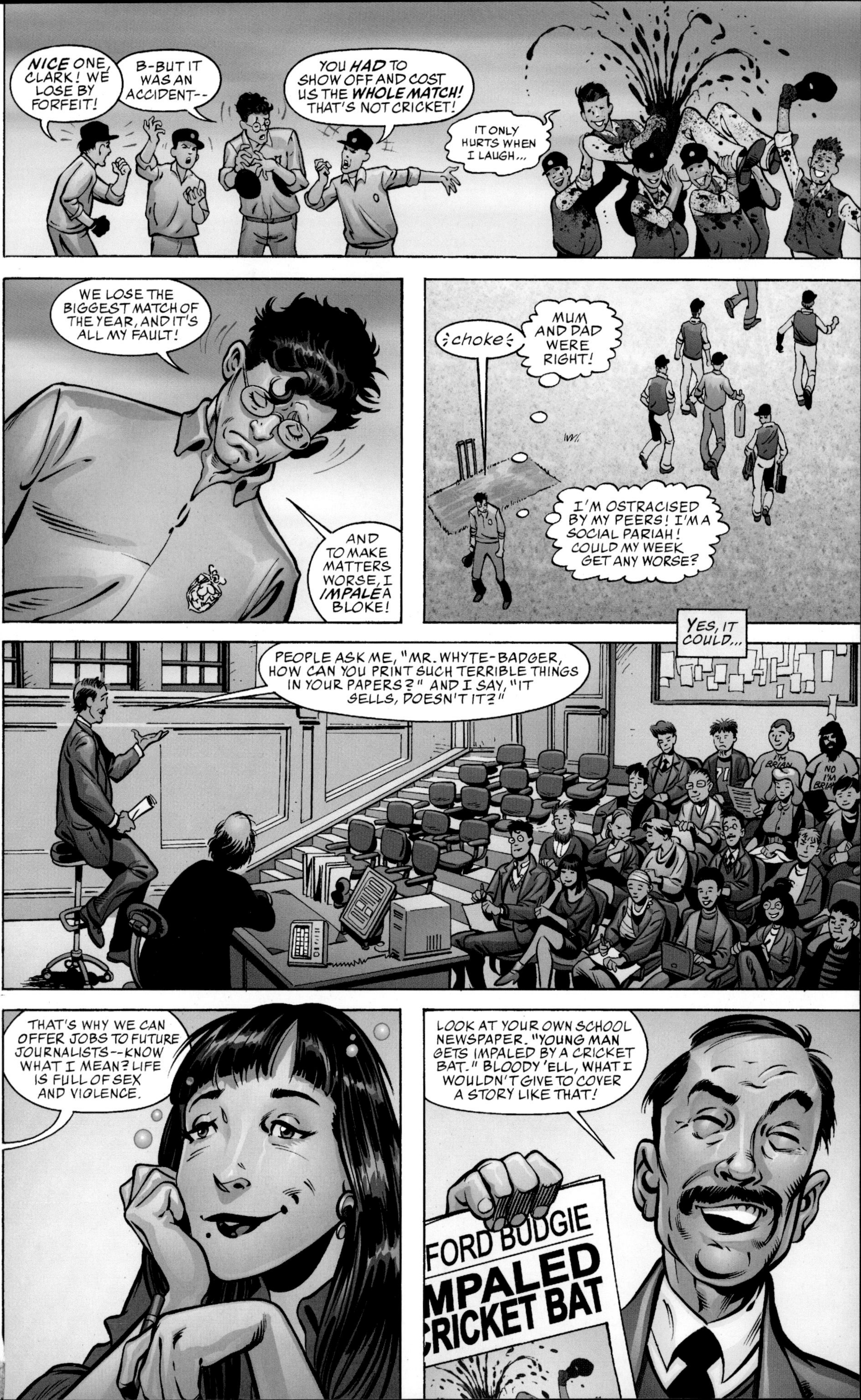

NICE ONE, CLARK! WE LOSE BY FORFEIT!
B-BUT IT WAS AN ACCIDENT--
YOU HAD TO SHOW OFF AND COST US THE WHOLE MATCH! THAT'S NOT CRICKET!
IT ONLY HURTS WHEN I LAUGH...
WE LOSE THE BIGGEST MATCH OF THE YEAR, AND IT'S ALL MY FAULT!
AND TO MAKE MATTERS WORSE, I IMPALE A BLOKE!
choke
MUM AND DAD WERE RIGHT!
I'M OSTRACISED BY MY PEERS! I'M A SOCIAL PARIAH! COULD MY WEEK GET ANY WORSE?
YES, IT COULD...
PEOPLE ASK ME, "MR. WHYTE-BADGER, HOW CAN YOU PRINT SUCH TERRIBLE THINGS IN YOUR PAPERS?" AND I SAY, "IT SELLS, DOESN'T IT?"
I'M BRIAN
NO I'M BRIAN
THAT'S WHY WE CAN OFFER JOBS TO FUTURE JOURNALISTS--KNOW WHAT I MEAN? LIFE IS FULL OF SEX AND VIOLENCE.
LOOK AT YOUR OWN SCHOOL NEWSPAPER. "YOUNG MAN GETS IMPALED BY A CRICKET BAT." BLOODY 'ELL, WHAT I WOULDN'T GIVE TO COVER A STORY LIKE THAT!
FORD BUDGIE
MPALED
CRICKET BAT

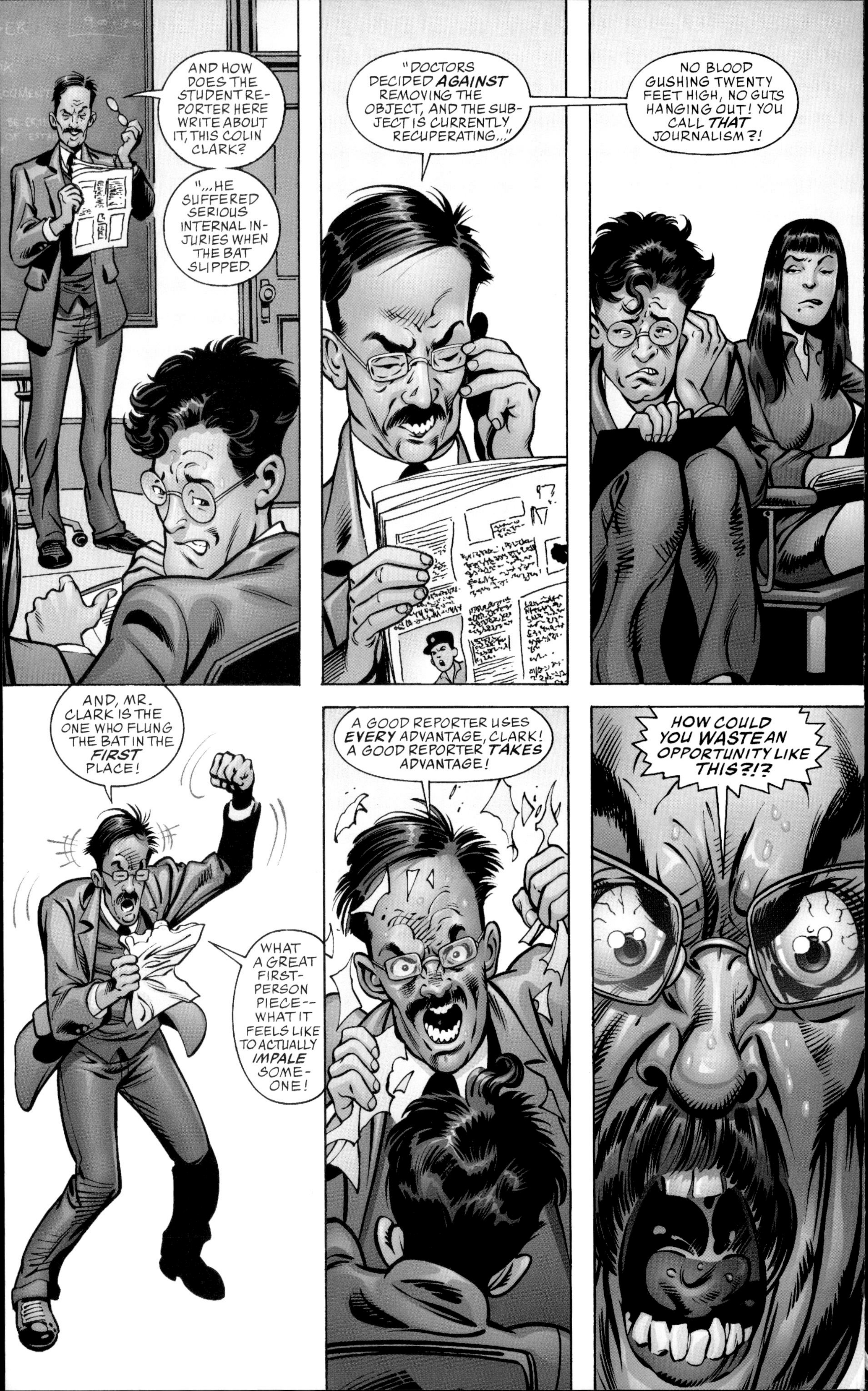
AND HOW DOES THE STUDENT REPORTER HERE WRITE ABOUT IT, THIS COLIN CLARK?
"...HE SUFFERED SERIOUS INTERNAL INJURIES WHEN THE BAT SLIPPED.
"DOCTORS DECIDED AGAINST REMOVING THE OBJECT, AND THE SUBJECT IS CURRENTLY RECUPERATING..."
NO BLOOD GUSHING TWENTY FEET HIGH, NO GUTS HANGING OUT! YOU CALL THAT JOURNALISM?!
AND, MR. CLARK IS THE ONE WHO FLUNG THE BAT IN THE FIRST PLACE!
WHAT A GREAT FIRST-PERSON PIECE--WHAT IT FEELS LIKE TO ACTUALLY IMPALE SOMEONE!
A GOOD REPORTER USES EVERY ADVANTAGE, CLARK! A GOOD REPORTER TAKES ADVANTAGE!
HOW COULD YOU WASTE AN OPPORTUNITY LIKE THIS?!?

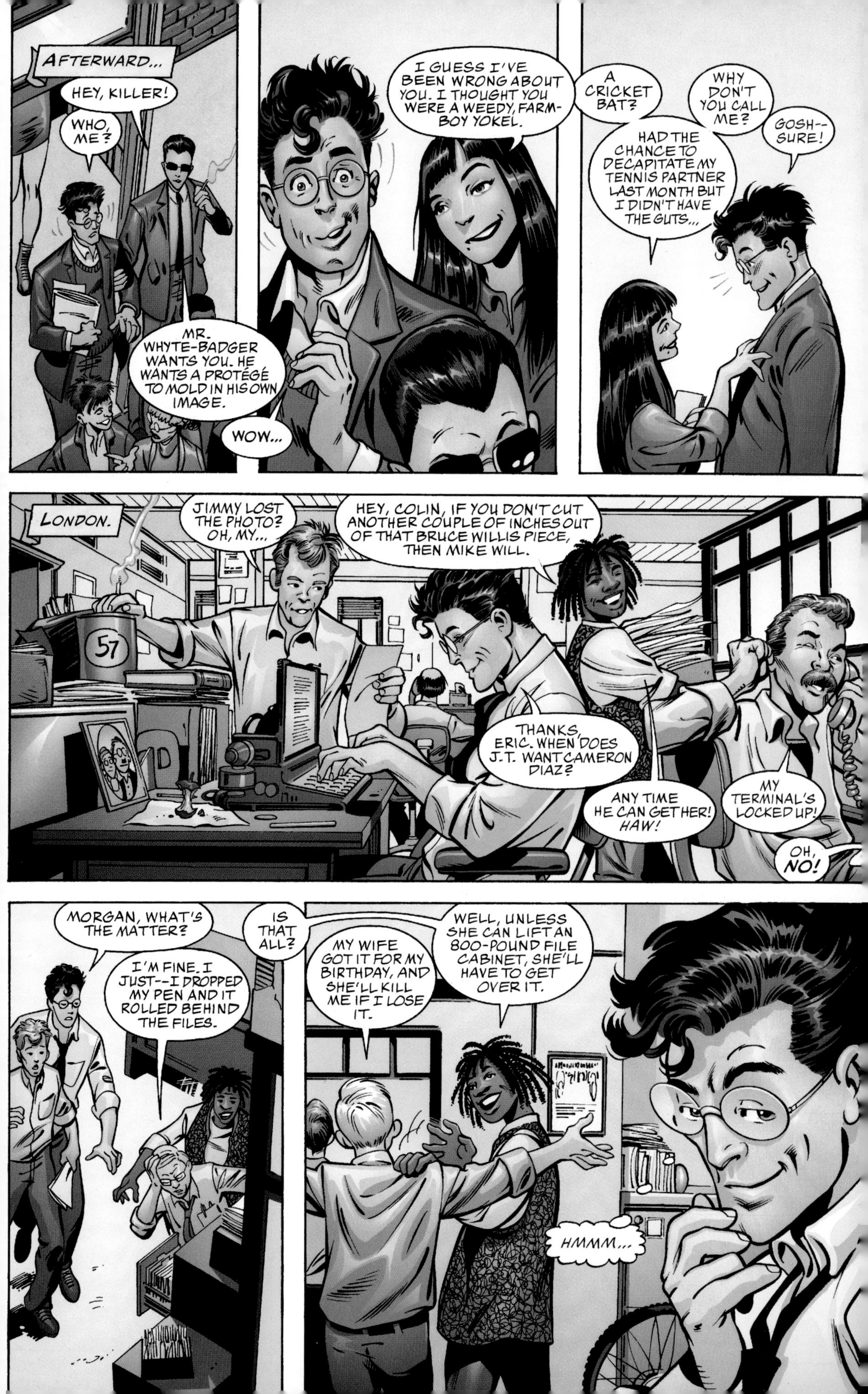
AFTERWARD...
HEY, KILLER!
WHO, ME?
MR. WHYTE-BADGER WANTS YOU. HE WANTS A PROTÉGÉ TO MOLD IN HIS OWN IMAGE.
WOW...
I GUESS I'VE BEEN WRONG ABOUT YOU. I THOUGHT YOU WERE A WEEDY, FARM-BOY YOKEL.
A CRICKET BAT?
HAD THE CHANCE TO DECAPITATE MY TENNIS PARTNER LAST MONTH BUT I DIDN'T HAVE THE GUTS...
WHY DON'T YOU CALL ME?
GOSH--SURE!
LONDON.
JIMMY LOST THE PHOTO? OH, MY...
HEY, COLIN, IF YOU DON'T CUT ANOTHER COUPLE OF INCHES OUT OF THAT BRUCE WILLIS PIECE, THEN MIKE WILL.
57
THANKS, ERIC. WHEN DOES J.T. WANT CAMERON DIAZ?
ANY TIME HE CAN GET HER! HAW!
MY TERMINAL'S LOCKED UP!
OH, NO!
MORGAN, WHAT'S THE MATTER?
I'M FINE. I JUST--I DROPPED MY PEN AND IT ROLLED BEHIND THE FILES.
IS THAT ALL?
MY WIFE GOT IT FOR MY BIRTHDAY, AND SHE'LL KILL ME IF I LOSE IT.
WELL, UNLESS SHE CAN LIFT AN 800-POUND FILE CABINET, SHE'LL HAVE TO GET OVER IT.
HMMM...

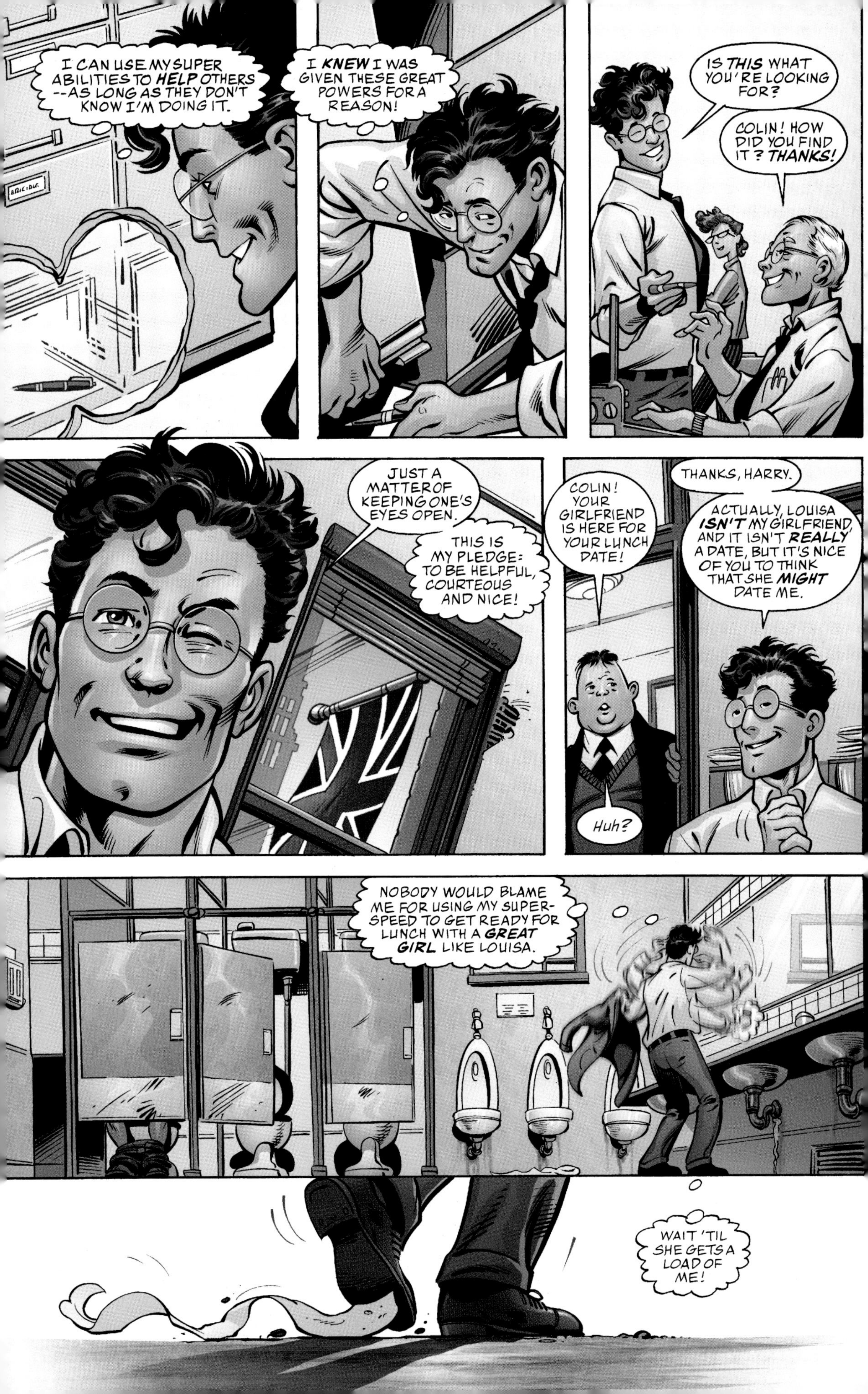
I CAN USE MY SUPER ABILITIES TO HELP OTHERS --AS LONG AS THEY DON'T KNOW I'M DOING IT.
I KNEW I WAS GIVEN THESE GREAT POWERS FOR A REASON!
IS THIS WHAT YOU'RE LOOKING FOR?
COLIN! HOW DID YOU FIND IT? THANKS!
JUST A MATTER OF KEEPING ONE'S EYES OPEN.
THIS IS MY PLEDGE: TO BE HELPFUL, COURTEOUS AND NICE!
COLIN! YOUR GIRLFRIEND IS HERE FOR YOUR LUNCH DATE!
THANKS, HARRY.
ACTUALLY, LOUISA ISN'T MY GIRLFRIEND, AND IT ISN'T REALLY A DATE, BUT IT'S NICE OF YOU TO THINK THAT SHE MIGHT DATE ME.
Huh?
NOBODY WOULD BLAME ME FOR USING MY SUPER-SPEED TO GET READY FOR LUNCH WITH A GREAT GIRL LIKE LOUISA.
WAIT 'TIL SHE GETS A LOAD OF ME!

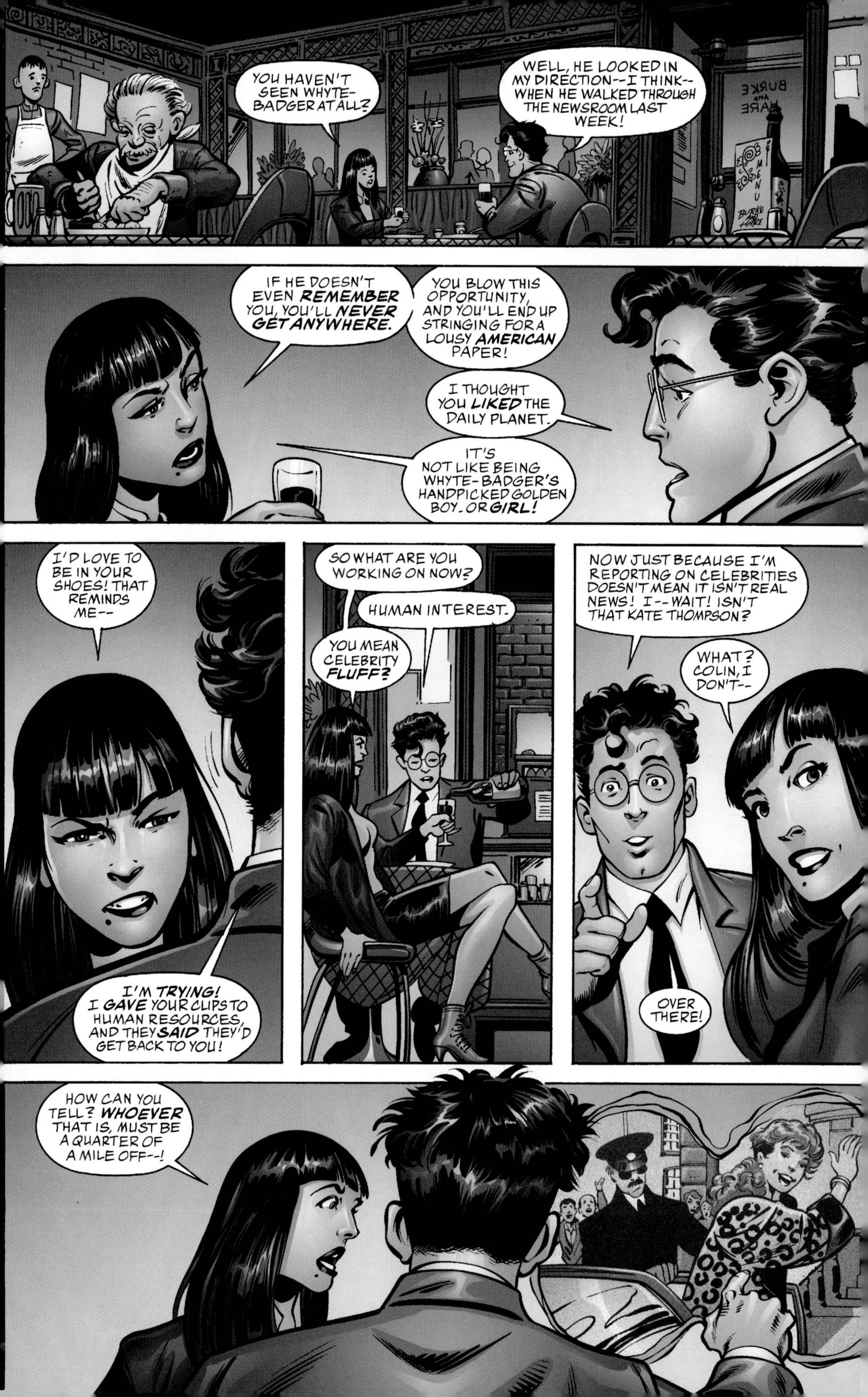

YOU HAVEN'T SEEN WHYTE-BADGER AT ALL?
WELL, HE LOOKED IN MY DIRECTION--I THINK--WHEN HE WALKED THROUGH THE NEWSROOM LAST WEEK!
BURKE AND HARE
MENU
IF HE DOESN'T EVEN REMEMBER YOU, YOU'LL NEVER GET ANYWHERE.
YOU BLOW THIS OPPORTUNITY, AND YOU'LL END UP STRINGING FOR A LOUSY AMERICAN PAPER!
I THOUGHT YOU LIKED THE DAILY PLANET.
IT'S NOT LIKE BEING WHYTE-BADGER'S HANDPICKED GOLDEN BOY. OR GIRL!
I'D LOVE TO BE IN YOUR SHOES! THAT REMINDS ME--
I'M TRYING! I GAVE YOUR CLIPS TO HUMAN RESOURCES, AND THEY SAID THEY'D GET BACK TO YOU!
SO WHAT ARE YOU WORKING ON NOW?
HUMAN INTEREST.
YOU MEAN CELEBRITY FLUFF?
NOW JUST BECAUSE I'M REPORTING ON CELEBRITIES DOESN'T MEAN IT ISN'T REAL NEWS! I--WAIT! ISN'T THAT KATE THOMPSON?
WHAT? COLIN, I DON'T--
OVER THERE!
HOW CAN YOU TELL? WHOEVER THAT IS, MUST BE A QUARTER OF A MILE OFF--!

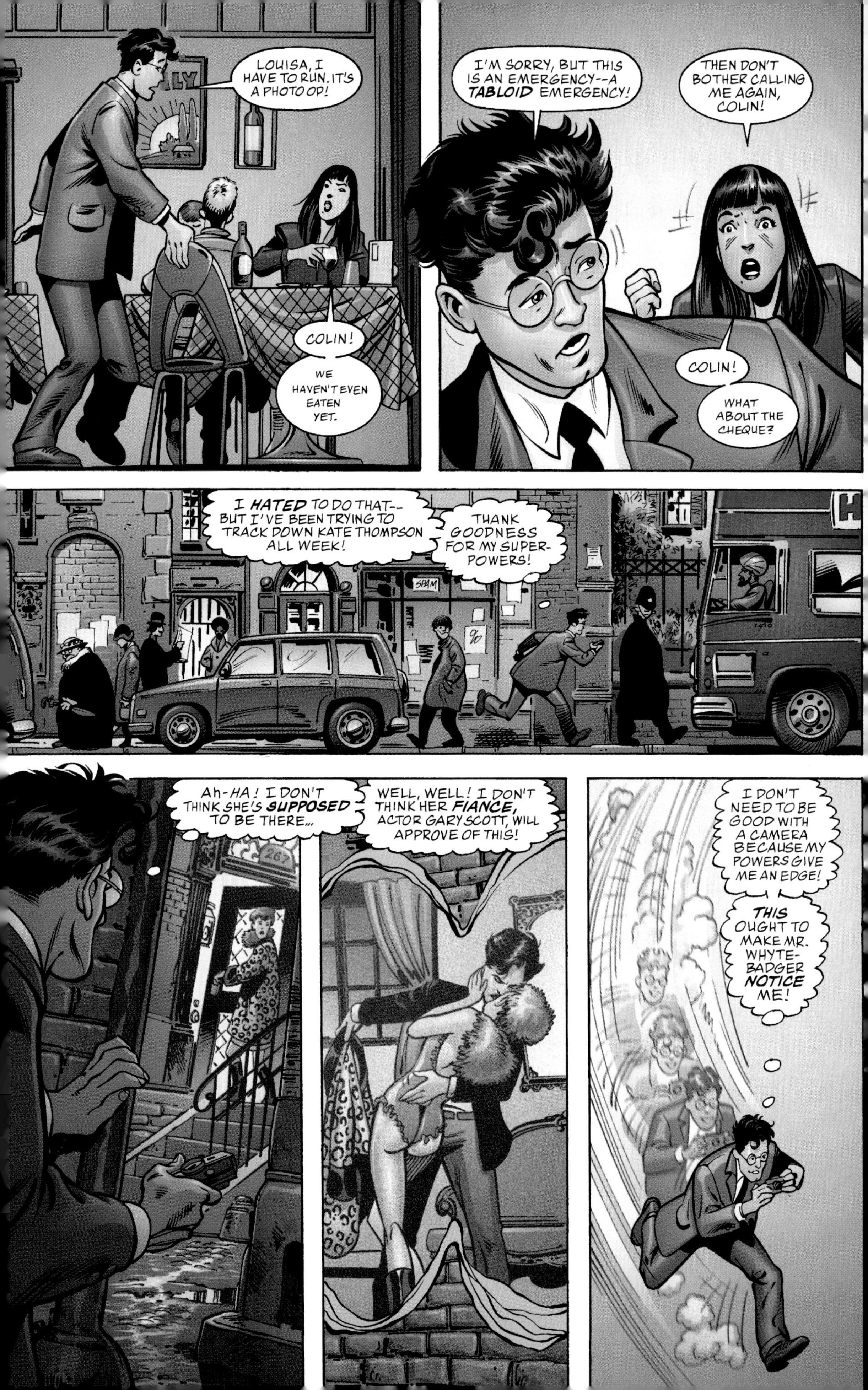
LOUISA, I HAVE TO RUN. IT'S A PHOTO OP!
COLIN!
WE HAVEN'T EVEN EATEN YET.
I'M SORRY, BUT THIS IS AN EMERGENCY--A TABLOID EMERGENCY!
THEN DON'T BOTHER CALLING ME AGAIN, COLIN!
COLIN!
WHAT ABOUT THE CHEQUE?
I HATED TO DO THAT-- BUT I'VE BEEN TRYING TO TRACK DOWN KATE THOMPSON ALL WEEK!
THANK GOODNESS FOR MY SUPER-POWERS!
SPAM
AH-HA! I DON'T THINK SHE'S SUPPOSED TO BE THERE...
267
WELL, WELL! I DON'T THINK HER FIANCE, ACTOR GARY SCOTT, WILL APPROVE OF THIS!
I DON'T NEED TO BE GOOD WITH A CAMERA BECAUSE MY POWERS GIVE ME AN EDGE!
THIS OUGHT TO MAKE MR. WHYTE-BADGER NOTICE ME!

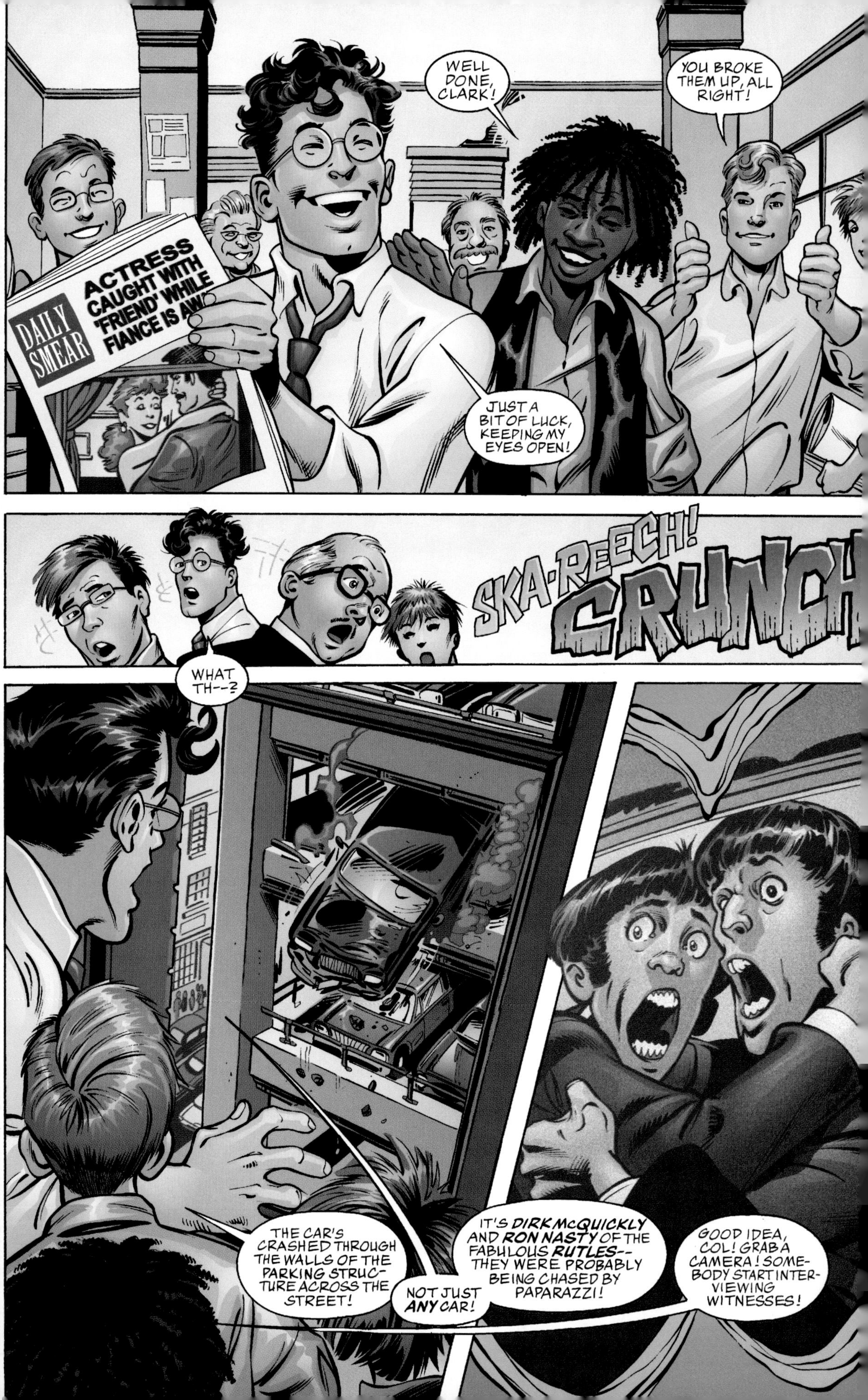
DAILY SMEAR
ACTRESS CAUGHT WITH 'FRIEND' WHILE FIANCE IS AW
WELL DONE, CLARK!
YOU BROKE THEM UP, ALL RIGHT!
JUST A BIT OF LUCK, KEEPING MY EYES OPEN!
SKA-REECH! CRUNCH
WHAT TH--?
THE CAR'S CRASHED THROUGH THE WALLS OF THE PARKING STRUC-TURE ACROSS THE STREET!
NOT JUST ANY CAR!
IT'S DIRK McQUICKLY AND RON NASTY OF THE FABULOUS RUTLES-- THEY WERE PROBABLY BEING CHASED BY PAPARAZZI!
GOOD IDEA, COL! GRAB A CAMERA! SOME-BODY START INTER-VIEWING WITNESSES!

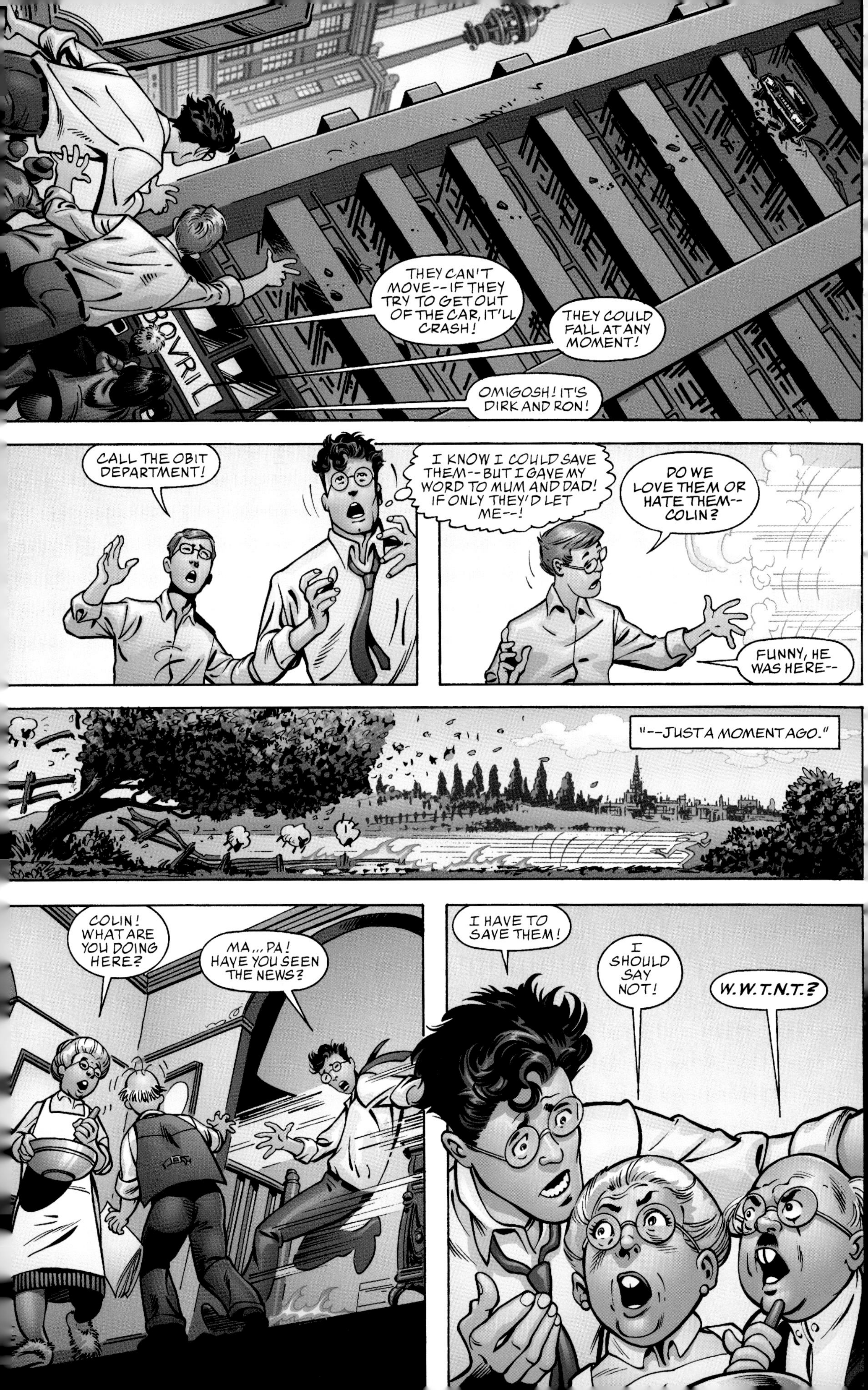
BOVRIL
OMIGOSH! IT'S DIRK AND RON!
THEY COULD FALL AT ANY MOMENT!
THEY CAN'T MOVE--IF THEY TRY TO GET OUT OF THE CAR, IT'LL CRASH!
CALL THE OBIT DEPARTMENT!
I KNOW I COULD SAVE THEM--BUT I GAVE MY WORD TO MUM AND DAD! IF ONLY THEY'D LET ME--!
DO WE LOVE THEM OR HATE THEM--COLIN?
FUNNY, HE WAS HERE--
"--JUST A MOMENT AGO."
COLIN! WHAT ARE YOU DOING HERE?
MA... PA! HAVE YOU SEEN THE NEWS?
I HAVE TO SAVE THEM!
I SHOULD SAY NOT!
W.W.T.N.T.?

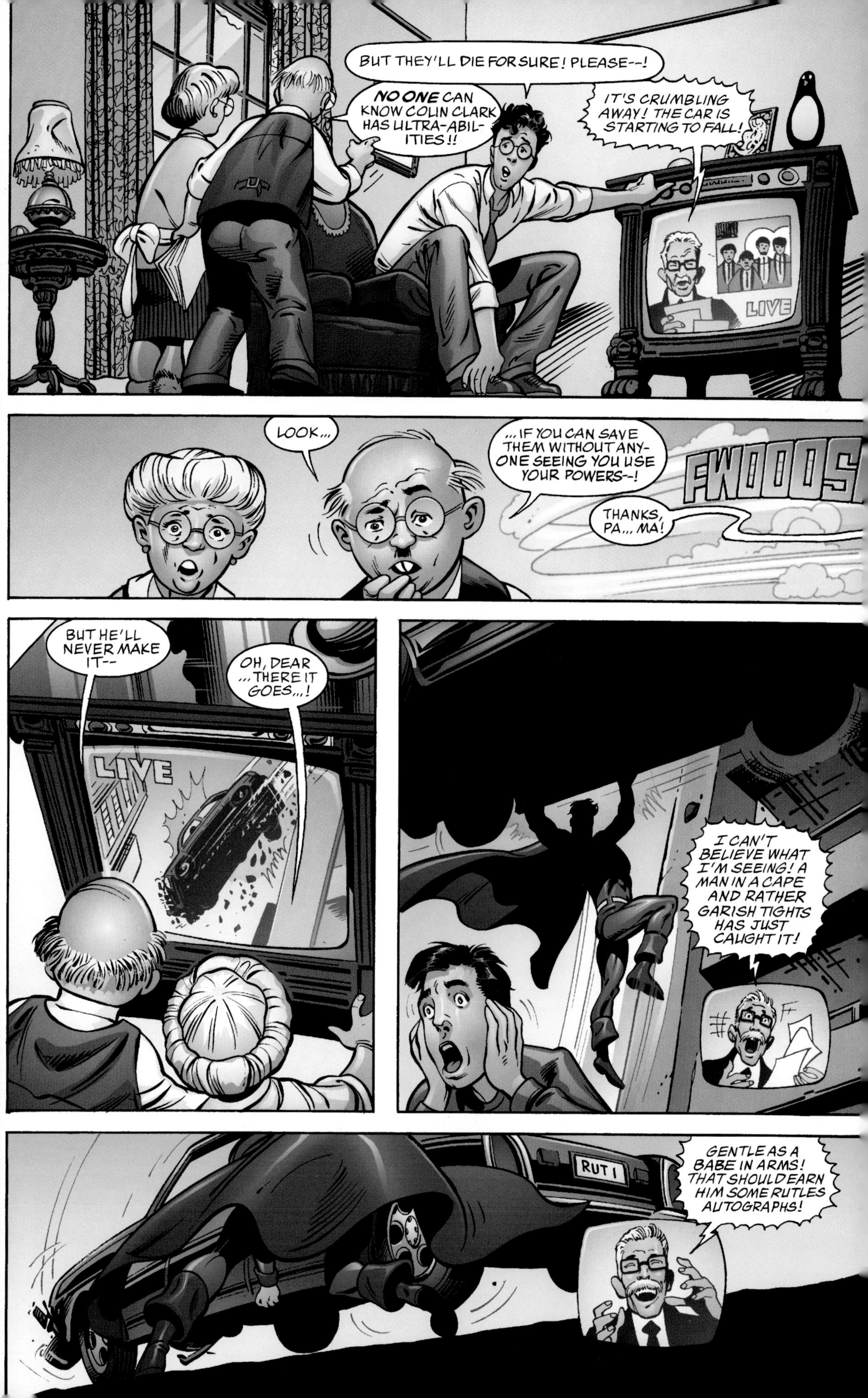

BUT THEY'LL DIE FOR SURE! PLEASE--!
NO ONE CAN KNOW COLIN CLARK HAS ULTRA-ABILITIES!!
IT'S CRUMBLING AWAY! THE CAR IS STARTING TO FALL!
LIVE
LOOK...
...IF YOU CAN SAVE THEM WITHOUT ANYONE SEEING YOU USE YOUR POWERS--!
FWOOOS
THANKS, PA... MA!
BUT HE'LL NEVER MAKE IT--
OH, DEAR ...THERE IT GOES...!
LIVE
I CAN'T BELIEVE WHAT I'M SEEING! A MAN IN A CAPE AND RATHER GARISH TIGHTS HAS JUST CAUGHT IT!
RUT 1
GENTLE AS A BABE IN ARMS! THAT SHOULD EARN HIM SOME RUTLES AUTOGRAPHS!

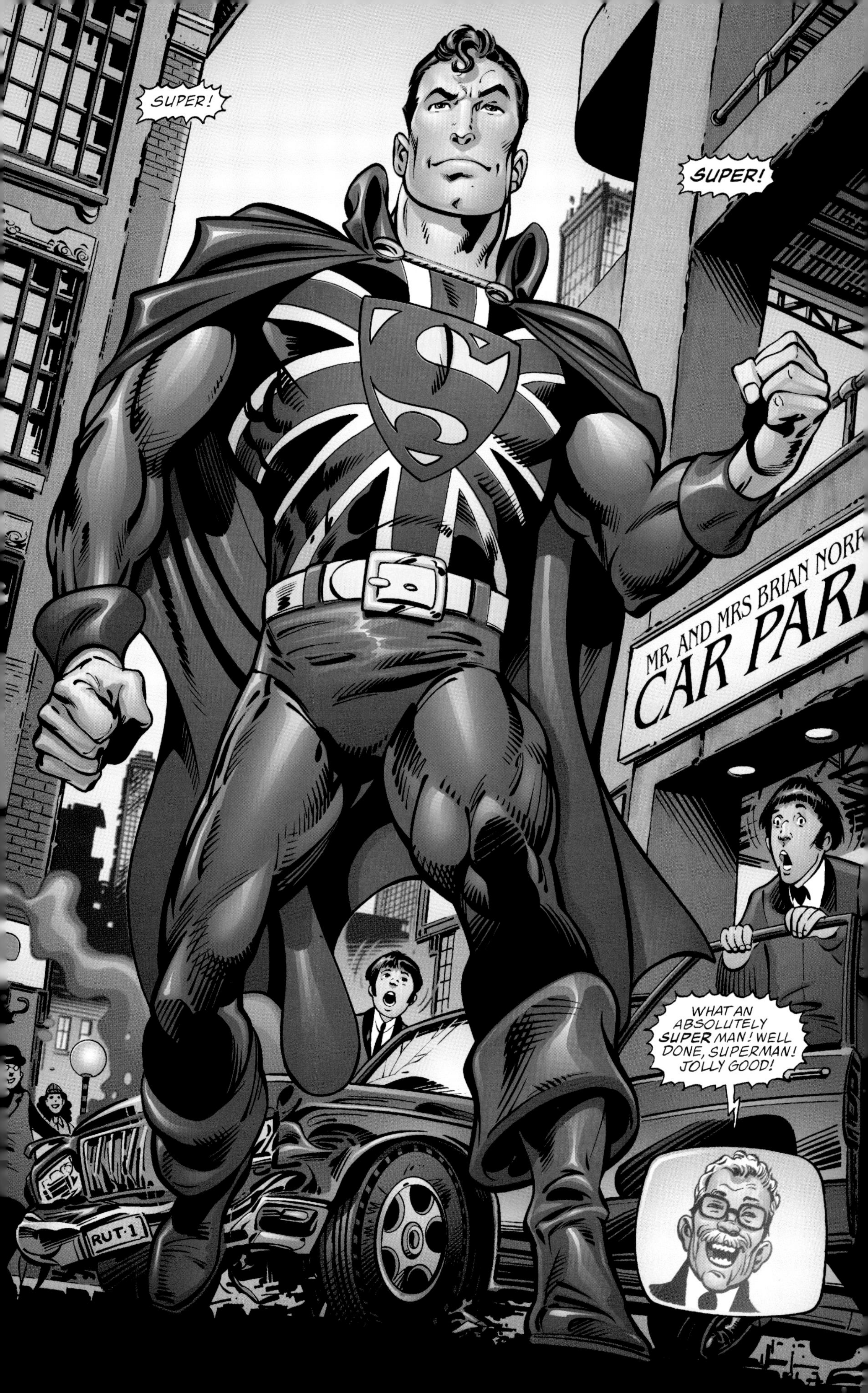
SUPER!
SUPER!
MR. AND MRS BRIAN NORR
CAR PAR
WHAT AN ABSOLUTELY SUPER MAN! WELL DONE, SUPERMAN! JOLLY GOOD!
RUT·1

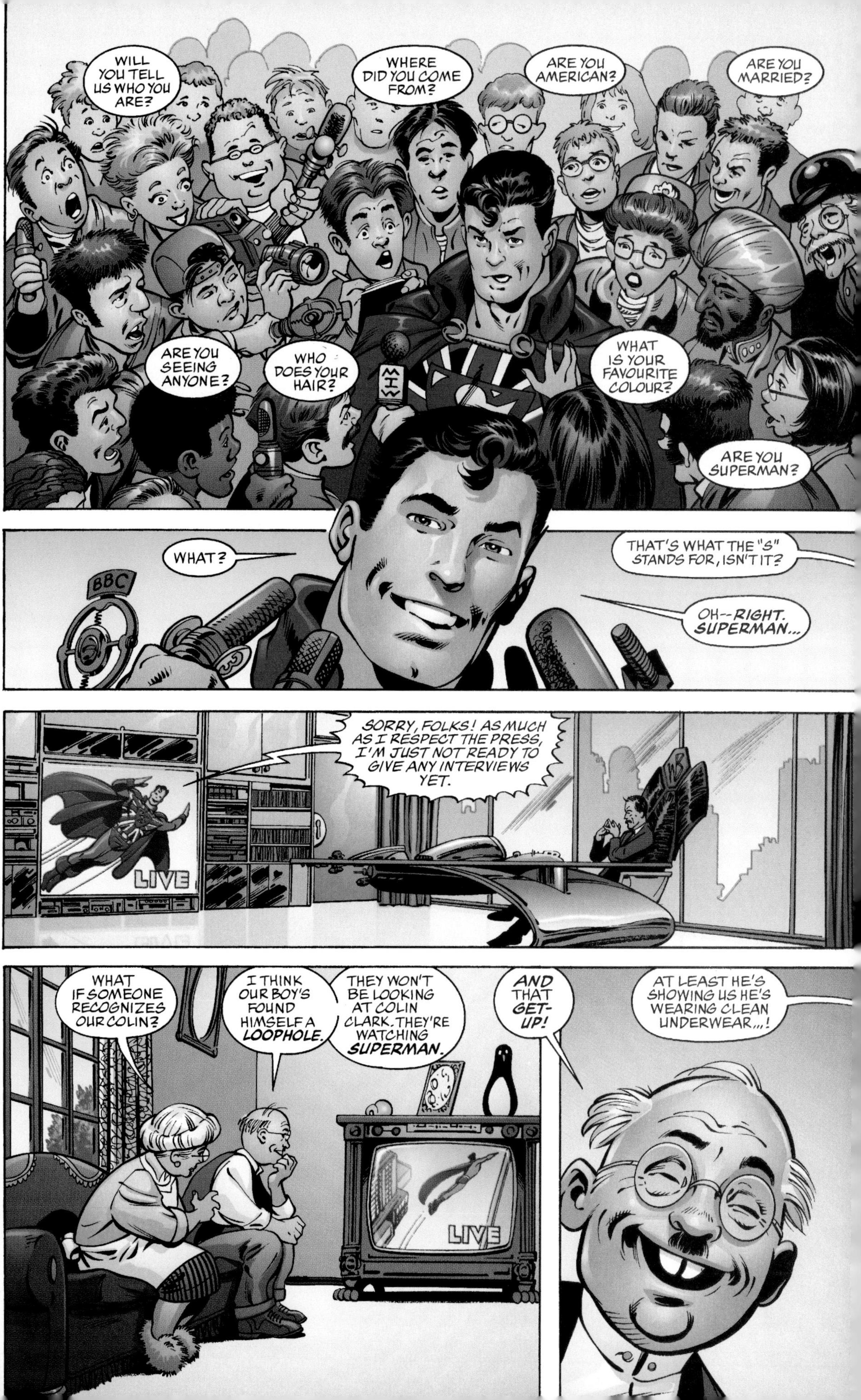

WILL YOU TELL US WHO YOU ARE?
WHERE DID YOU COME FROM?
ARE YOU AMERICAN?
ARE YOU MARRIED?
ARE YOU SEEING ANYONE?
WHO DOES YOUR HAIR?
WHAT IS YOUR FAVOURITE COLOUR?
ARE YOU SUPERMAN?
WHAT?
THAT'S WHAT THE "S" STANDS FOR, ISN'T IT?
OH-- RIGHT. SUPERMAN...
BBC
SORRY, FOLKS! AS MUCH AS I RESPECT THE PRESS, I'M JUST NOT READY TO GIVE ANY INTERVIEWS YET.
LIVE
WHAT IF SOMEONE RECOGNIZES OUR COLIN?
I THINK OUR BOY'S FOUND HIMSELF A LOOPHOLE.
THEY WON'T BE LOOKING AT COLIN CLARK. THEY'RE WATCHING SUPERMAN.
AND THAT GET-UP!
AT LEAST HE'S SHOWING US HE'S WEARING CLEAN UNDERWEAR...!
LIVE

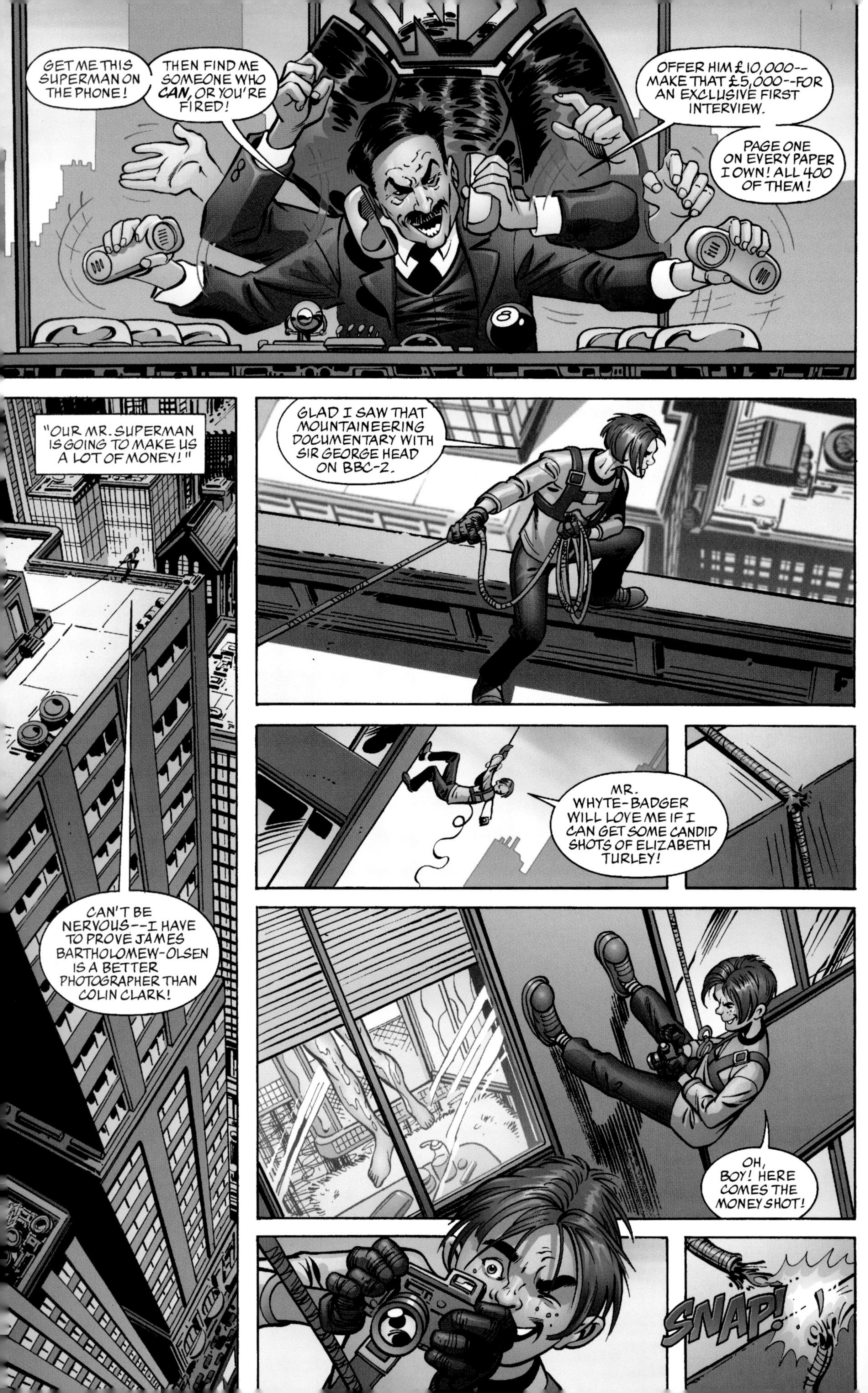
GET ME THIS SUPERMAN ON THE PHONE!
THEN FIND ME SOMEONE WHO CAN, OR YOU'RE FIRED!
OFFER HIM £10,000--MAKE THAT £5,000--FOR AN EXCLUSIVE FIRST INTERVIEW.
PAGE ONE ON EVERY PAPER I OWN! ALL 400 OF THEM!
"OUR MR. SUPERMAN IS GOING TO MAKE US A LOT OF MONEY!"
CAN'T BE NERVOUS--I HAVE TO PROVE JAMES BARTHOLOMEW-OLSEN IS A BETTER PHOTOGRAPHER THAN COLIN CLARK!
GLAD I SAW THAT MOUNTAINEERING DOCUMENTARY WITH SIR GEORGE HEAD ON BBC-2.
MR. WHYTE-BADGER WILL LOVE ME IF I CAN GET SOME CANDID SHOTS OF ELIZABETH TURLEY!
OH, BOY! HERE COMES THE MONEY SHOT!
SNAP!

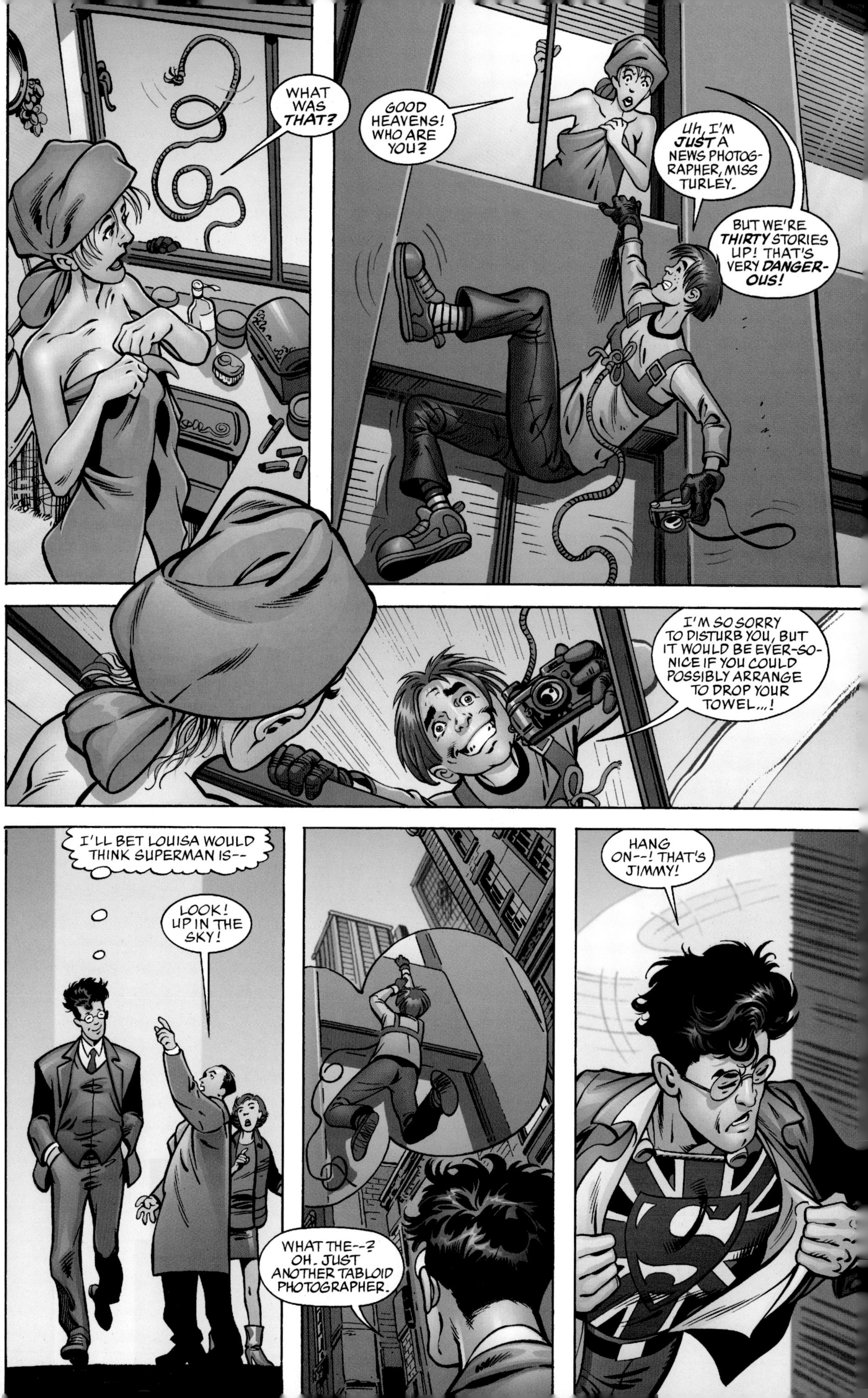
WHAT WAS THAT?
GOOD HEAVENS! WHO ARE YOU?
UH, I'M JUST A NEWS PHOTOG-RAPHER, MISS TURLEY.
BUT WE'RE THIRTY STORIES UP! THAT'S VERY DANGER-OUS!
I'M SO SORRY TO DISTURB YOU, BUT IT WOULD BE EVER-SO-NICE IF YOU COULD POSSIBLY ARRANGE TO DROP YOUR TOWEL...!
I'LL BET LOUISA WOULD THINK SUPERMAN IS--
LOOK! UP IN THE SKY!
WHAT THE--? OH. JUST ANOTHER TABLOID PHOTOGRAPHER.
HANG ON--! THAT'S JIMMY!

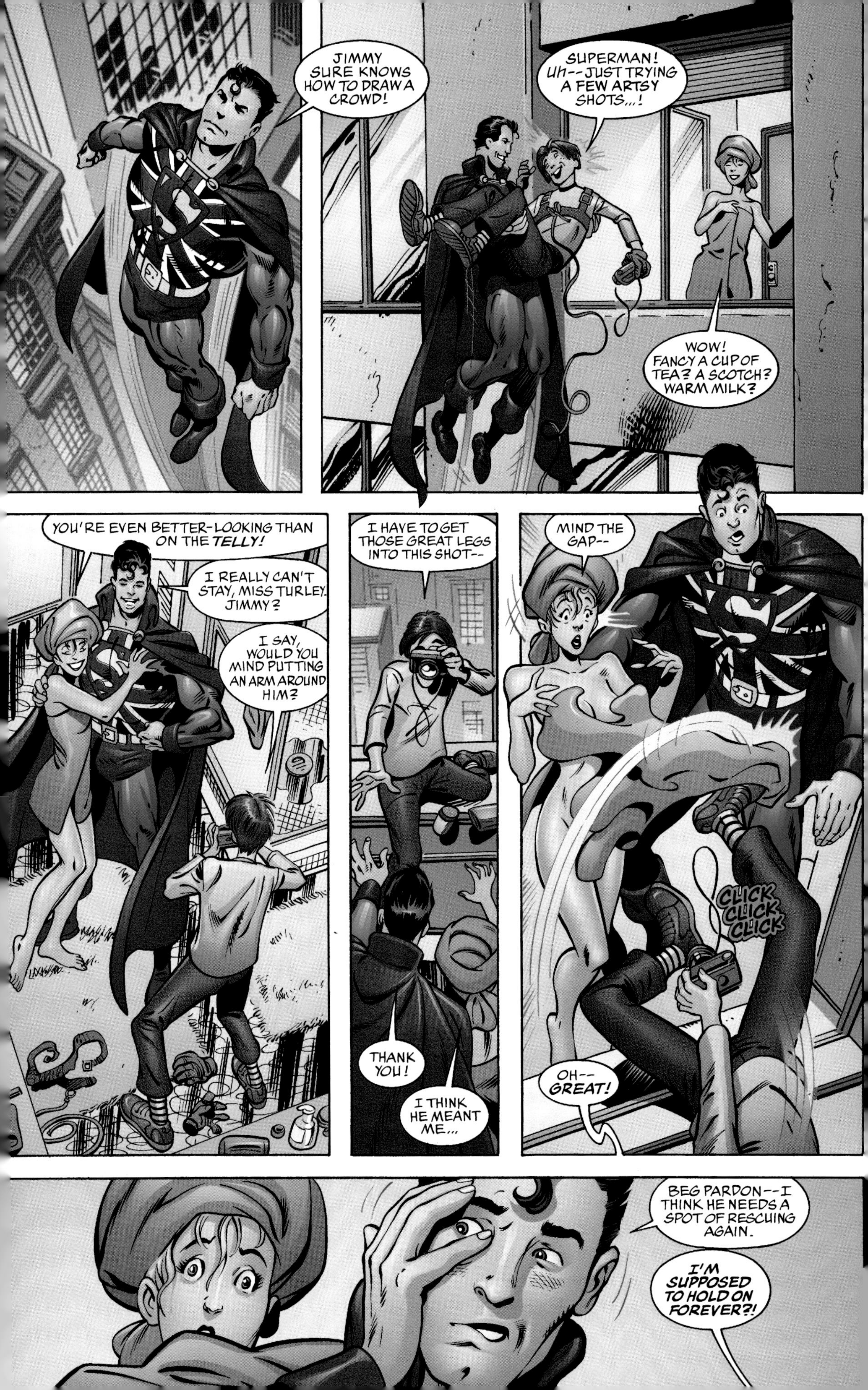
JIMMY SURE KNOWS HOW TO DRAW A CROWD!
SUPERMAN! UH-- JUST TRYING A FEW ARTSY SHOTS...!
WOW! FANCY A CUP OF TEA? A SCOTCH? WARM MILK?
YOU'RE EVEN BETTER-LOOKING THAN ON THE TELLY!
I REALLY CAN'T STAY, MISS TURLEY. JIMMY?
I SAY, WOULD YOU MIND PUTTING AN ARM AROUND HIM?
I HAVE TO GET THOSE GREAT LEGS INTO THIS SHOT--
THANK YOU!
I THINK HE MEANT ME...
MIND THE GAP--
CLICK CLICK CLICK
OH-- GREAT!
BEG PARDON--I THINK HE NEEDS A SPOT OF RESCUING AGAIN.
I'M SUPPOSED TO HOLD ON FOREVER?!

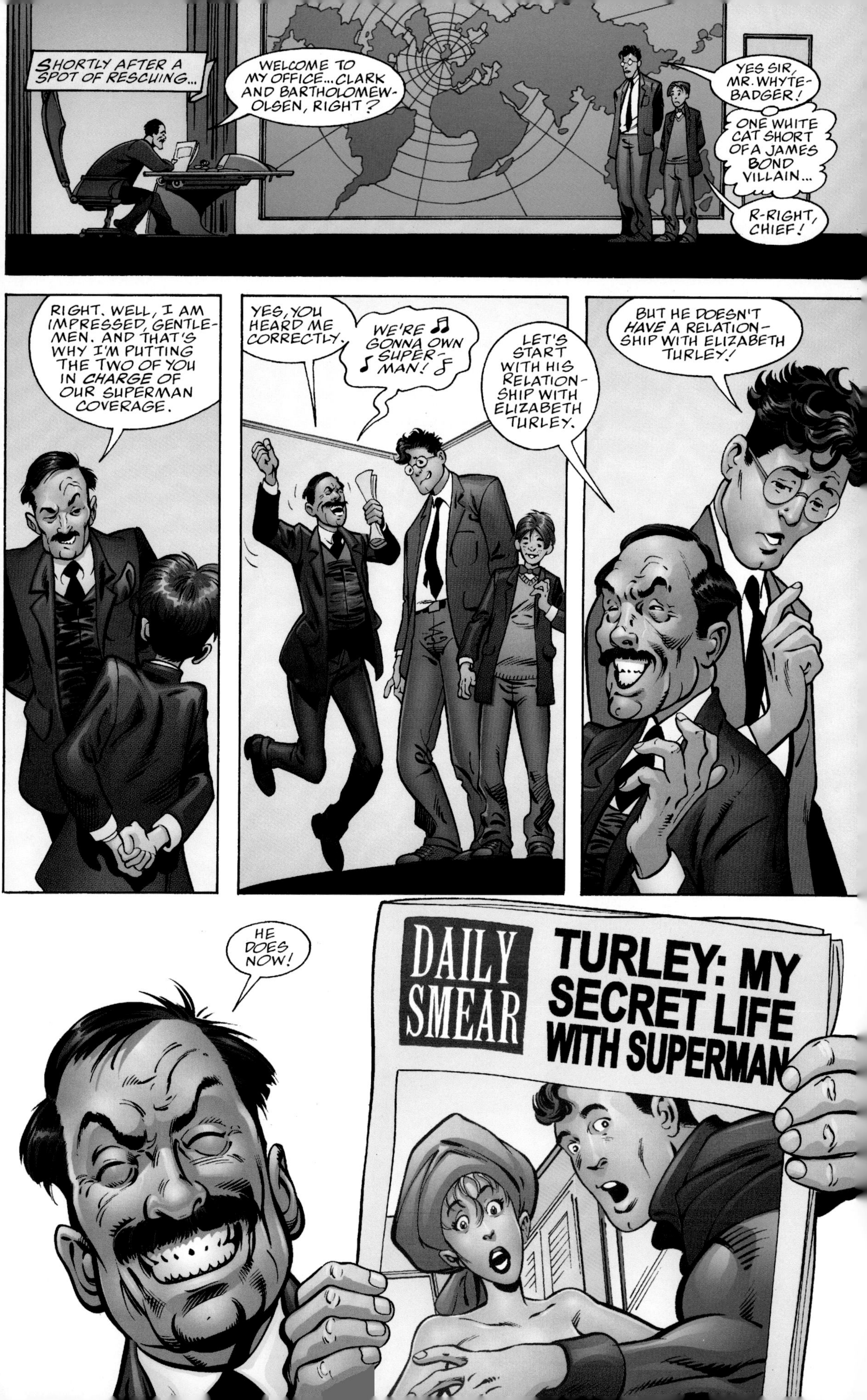
SHORTLY AFTER A SPOT OF RESCUING...
WELCOME TO MY OFFICE...CLARK AND BARTHOLOMEW-OLSEN, RIGHT?
YES SIR, MR. WHYTE-BADGER!
ONE WHITE CAT SHORT OF A JAMES BOND VILLAIN...
R-RIGHT, CHIEF!
RIGHT. WELL, I AM IMPRESSED, GENTLEMEN. AND THAT'S WHY I'M PUTTING THE TWO OF YOU IN CHARGE OF OUR SUPERMAN COVERAGE.
YES, YOU HEARD ME CORRECTLY.
WE'RE GONNA OWN SUPERMAN!
LET'S START WITH HIS RELATIONSHIP WITH ELIZABETH TURLEY.
BUT HE DOESN'T HAVE A RELATIONSHIP WITH ELIZABETH TURLEY!
HE DOES NOW!
DAILY SMEAR
TURLEY: MY SECRET LIFE WITH SUPERMAN

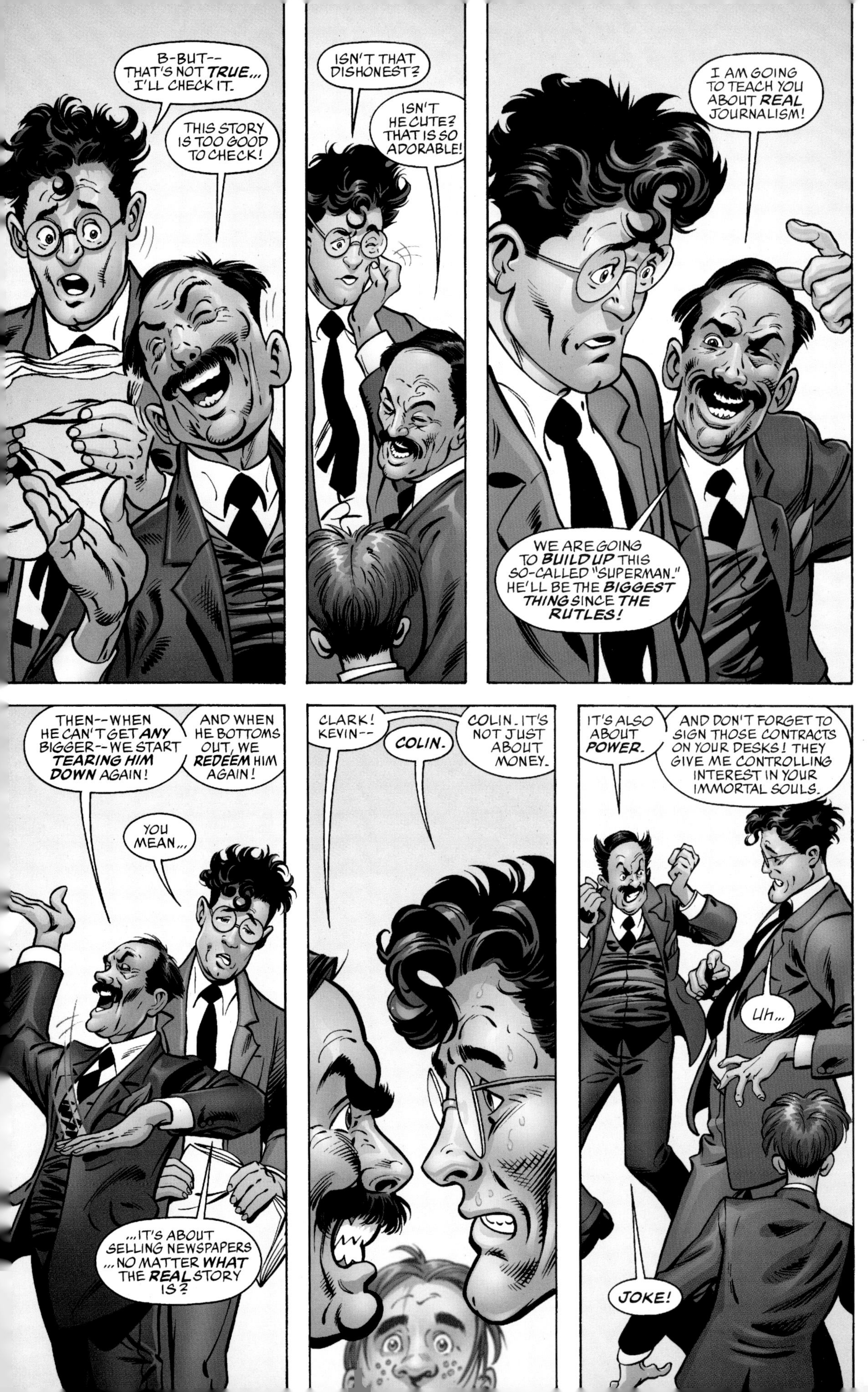
B-BUT-- THAT'S NOT TRUE... I'LL CHECK IT.
THIS STORY IS TOO GOOD TO CHECK!
ISN'T THAT DISHONEST?
ISN'T HE CUTE? THAT IS SO ADORABLE!
I AM GOING TO TEACH YOU ABOUT REAL JOURNALISM!
WE ARE GOING TO BUILD UP THIS SO-CALLED "SUPERMAN." HE'LL BE THE BIGGEST THING SINCE THE RUTLES!
THEN--WHEN HE CAN'T GET ANY BIGGER--WE START TEARING HIM DOWN AGAIN!
AND WHEN HE BOTTOMS OUT, WE REDEEM HIM AGAIN!
YOU MEAN...
...IT'S ABOUT SELLING NEWSPAPERS ...NO MATTER WHAT THE REAL STORY IS?
CLARK! KEVIN--
COLIN.
COLIN. IT'S NOT JUST ABOUT MONEY.
IT'S ALSO ABOUT POWER.
AND DON'T FORGET TO SIGN THOSE CONTRACTS ON YOUR DESKS! THEY GIVE ME CONTROLLING INTEREST IN YOUR IMMORTAL SOULS.
UH...
JOKE!

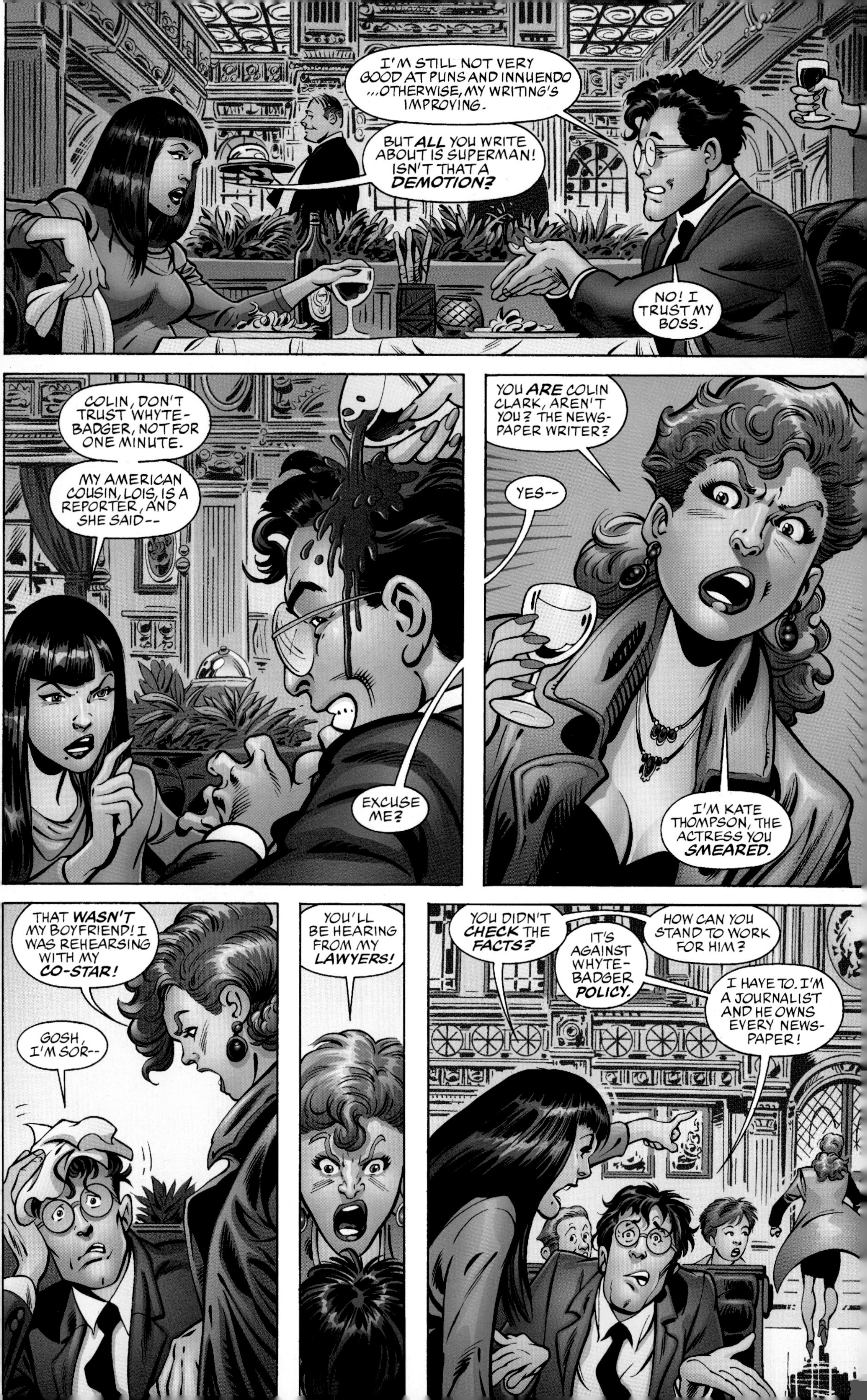
I'M STILL NOT VERY GOOD AT PUNS AND INNUENDO ...OTHERWISE, MY WRITING'S IMPROVING.
BUT **ALL** YOU WRITE ABOUT IS SUPERMAN! ISN'T THAT A ***DEMOTION?***
NO! I TRUST MY BOSS.
COLIN, DON'T TRUST WHYTE-BADGER, NOT FOR ONE MINUTE.
MY AMERICAN COUSIN, LOIS, IS A REPORTER, AND SHE SAID--
EXCUSE ME?
YOU **ARE** COLIN CLARK, AREN'T YOU? THE NEWSPAPER WRITER?
YES--
I'M KATE THOMPSON, THE ACTRESS YOU ***SMEARED.***
THAT **WASN'T** MY BOYFRIEND! I WAS REHEARSING WITH MY ***CO-STAR!***
GOSH, I'M SOR--
YOU'LL BE HEARING FROM MY ***LAWYERS!***
YOU DIDN'T **CHECK** THE ***FACTS?***
IT'S AGAINST WHYTE-BADGER ***POLICY.***
HOW CAN YOU STAND TO WORK FOR HIM?
I HAVE TO. I'M A JOURNALIST AND HE OWNS EVERY NEWSPAPER!

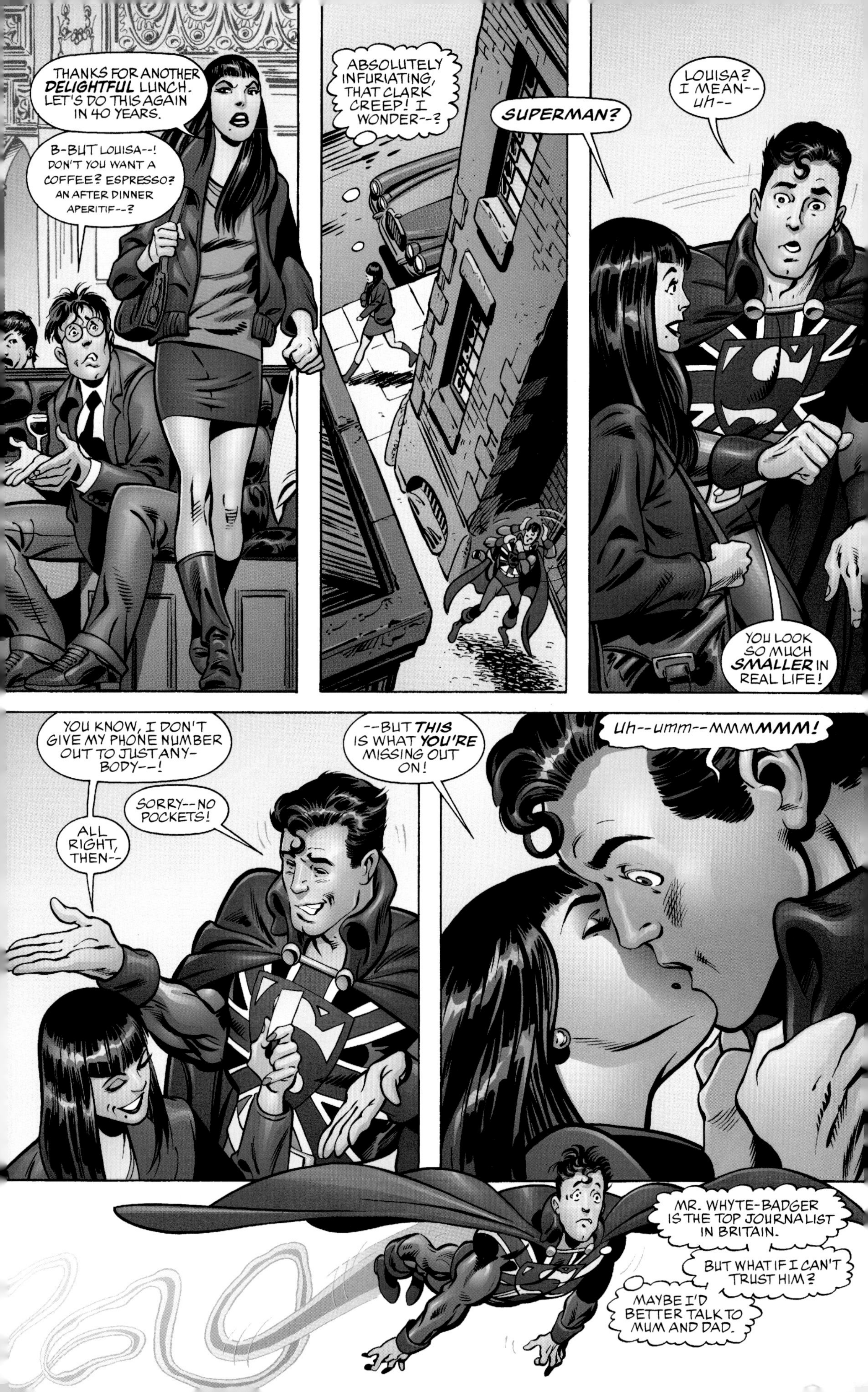
THANKS FOR ANOTHER DELIGHTFUL LUNCH. LET'S DO THIS AGAIN IN 40 YEARS.
B-BUT LOUISA--! DON'T YOU WANT A COFFEE? ESPRESSO? AN AFTER DINNER APERITIF--?
ABSOLUTELY INFURIATING, THAT CLARK CREEP! I WONDER--?
SUPERMAN?
LOUISA? I MEAN-- UH--
YOU LOOK SO MUCH SMALLER IN REAL LIFE!
YOU KNOW, I DON'T GIVE MY PHONE NUMBER OUT TO JUST ANY-BODY--!
ALL RIGHT, THEN--
SORRY--NO POCKETS!
--BUT THIS IS WHAT YOU'RE MISSING OUT ON!
UH--UMM--MMMMMM!
MR. WHYTE-BADGER IS THE TOP JOURNALIST IN BRITAIN.
BUT WHAT IF I CAN'T TRUST HIM?
MAYBE I'D BETTER TALK TO MUM AND DAD.

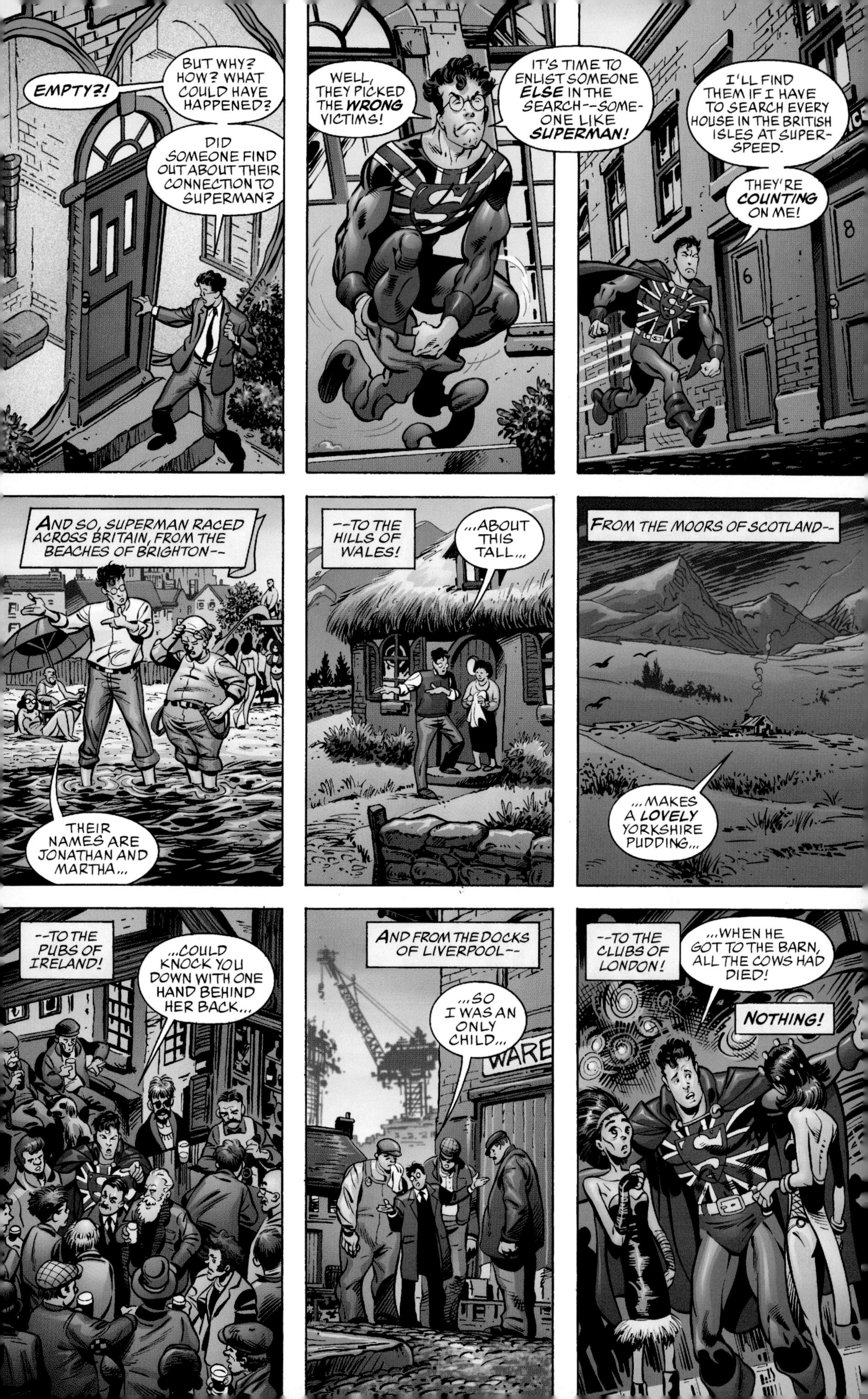
EMPTY?!
BUT WHY? HOW? WHAT COULD HAVE HAPPENED?
DID SOMEONE FIND OUT ABOUT THEIR CONNECTION TO SUPERMAN?
WELL, THEY PICKED THE WRONG VICTIMS!
IT'S TIME TO ENLIST SOMEONE ELSE IN THE SEARCH--SOMEONE LIKE SUPERMAN!
I'LL FIND THEM IF I HAVE TO SEARCH EVERY HOUSE IN THE BRITISH ISLES AT SUPER-SPEED.
THEY'RE COUNTING ON ME!
6
8
AND SO, SUPERMAN RACED ACROSS BRITAIN, FROM THE BEACHES OF BRIGHTON--
THEIR NAMES ARE JONATHAN AND MARTHA...
--TO THE HILLS OF WALES!
...ABOUT THIS TALL...
FROM THE MOORS OF SCOTLAND--
...MAKES A LOVELY YORKSHIRE PUDDING...
--TO THE PUBS OF IRELAND!
...COULD KNOCK YOU DOWN WITH ONE HAND BEHIND HER BACK...
AND FROM THE DOCKS OF LIVERPOOL--
...SO I WAS AN ONLY CHILD...
WARE
--TO THE CLUBS OF LONDON!
...WHEN HE GOT TO THE BARN, ALL THE COWS HAD DIED!
NOTHING!

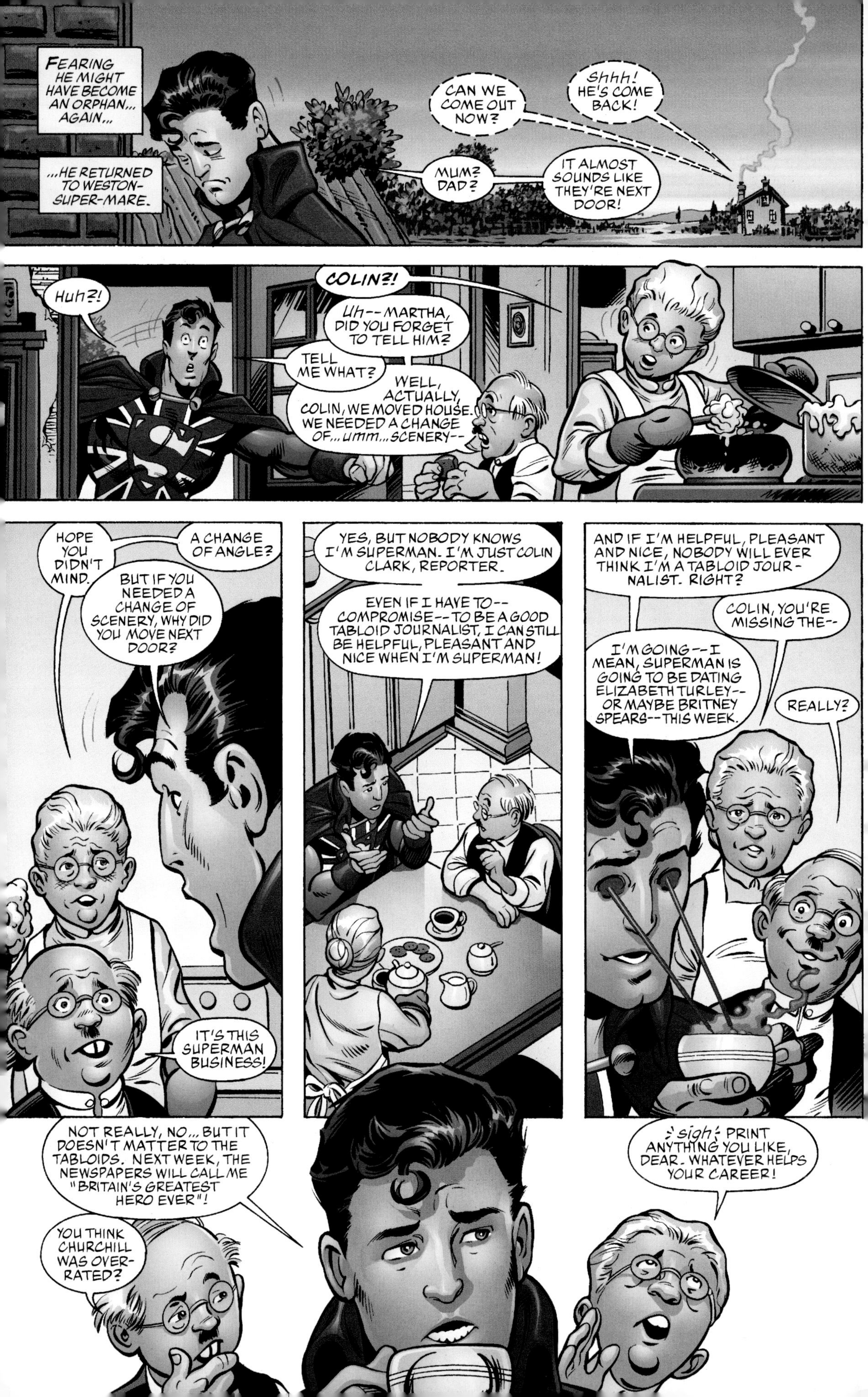
FEARING HE MIGHT HAVE BECOME AN ORPHAN... AGAIN...
...HE RETURNED TO WESTON-SUPER-MARE.
MUM? DAD?
CAN WE COME OUT NOW?
SHHH! HE'S COME BACK!
IT ALMOST SOUNDS LIKE THEY'RE NEXT DOOR!
HUH?!
COLIN?!
UH-- MARTHA, DID YOU FORGET TO TELL HIM?
TELL ME WHAT?
WELL, ACTUALLY, COLIN, WE MOVED HOUSE. WE NEEDED A CHANGE OF... UMM... SCENERY--
A CHANGE OF ANGLE?
HOPE YOU DIDN'T MIND.
BUT IF YOU NEEDED A CHANGE OF SCENERY, WHY DID YOU MOVE NEXT DOOR?
IT'S THIS SUPERMAN BUSINESS!
YES, BUT NOBODY KNOWS I'M SUPERMAN. I'M JUST COLIN CLARK, REPORTER.
EVEN IF I HAVE TO-- COMPROMISE-- TO BE A GOOD TABLOID JOURNALIST, I CAN STILL BE HELPFUL, PLEASANT AND NICE WHEN I'M SUPERMAN!
AND IF I'M HELPFUL, PLEASANT AND NICE, NOBODY WILL EVER THINK I'M A TABLOID JOURNALIST. RIGHT?
COLIN, YOU'RE MISSING THE--
I'M GOING-- I MEAN, SUPERMAN IS GOING TO BE DATING ELIZABETH TURLEY-- OR MAYBE BRITNEY SPEARS-- THIS WEEK.
REALLY?
NOT REALLY, NO... BUT IT DOESN'T MATTER TO THE TABLOIDS. NEXT WEEK, THE NEWSPAPERS WILL CALL ME "BRITAIN'S GREATEST HERO EVER"!
YOU THINK CHURCHILL WAS OVER-RATED?
-SIGH- PRINT ANYTHING YOU LIKE, DEAR. WHATEVER HELPS YOUR CAREER!

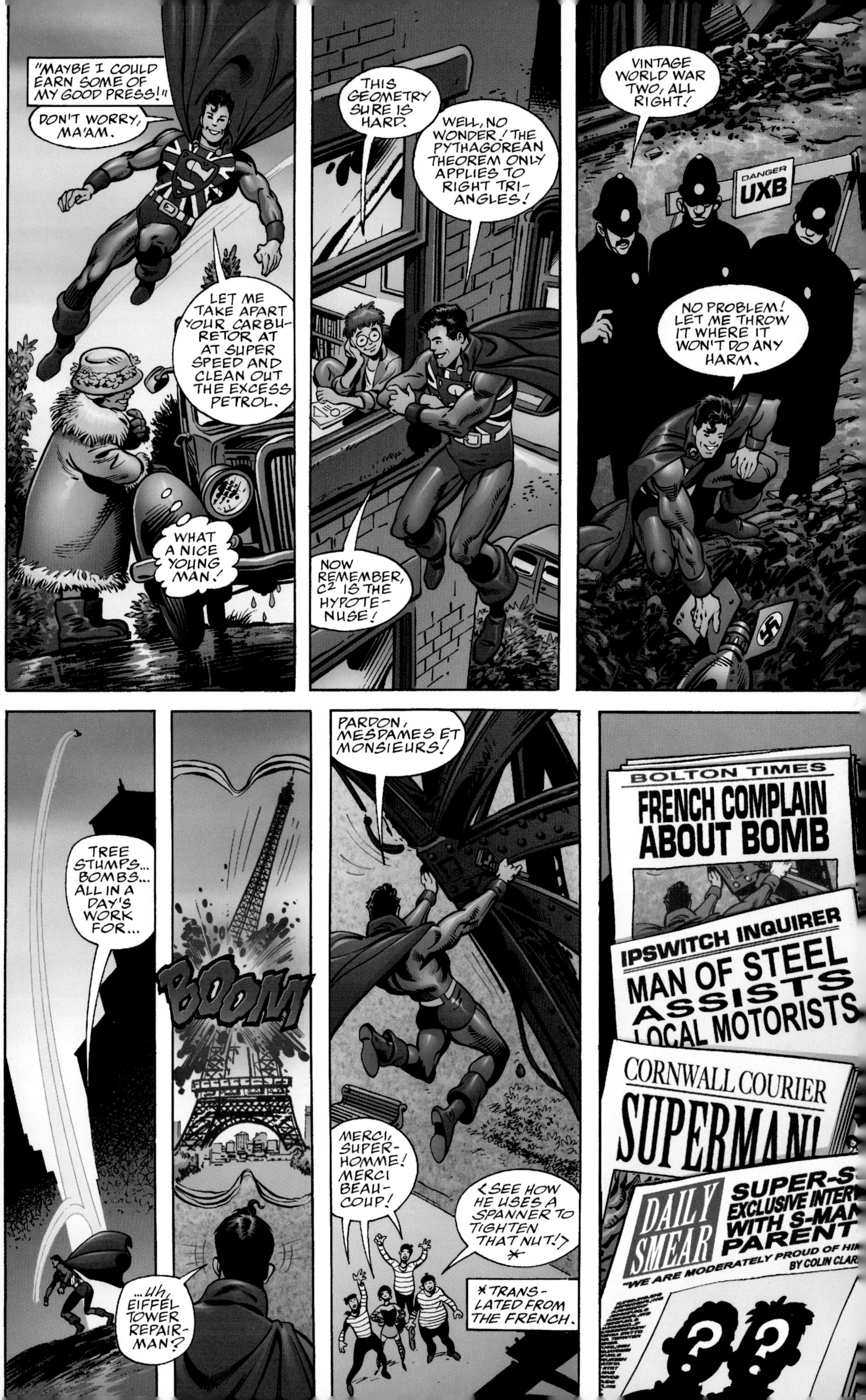
"MAYBE I COULD EARN SOME OF MY GOOD PRESS!"
DON'T WORRY, MA'AM.
LET ME TAKE APART YOUR CARBURETOR AT AT SUPER SPEED AND CLEAN OUT THE EXCESS PETROL.
WHAT A NICE YOUNG MAN!
THIS GEOMETRY SURE IS HARD.
WELL, NO WONDER! THE PYTHAGOREAN THEOREM ONLY APPLIES TO RIGHT TRIANGLES!
NOW REMEMBER, C^2 IS THE HYPOTENUSE!
VINTAGE WORLD WAR TWO, ALL RIGHT!
DANGER UXB
NO PROBLEM! LET ME THROW IT WHERE IT WON'T DO ANY HARM.
TREE STUMPS... BOMBS... ALL IN A DAY'S WORK FOR...
BOOM
...UH, EIFFEL TOWER REPAIRMAN?
PARDON, MESDAMES ET MONSIEURS!
MERCI, SUPER-HOMME! MERCI BEAUCOUP!
<SEE HOW HE USES A SPANNER TO TIGHTEN THAT NUT!> *
*TRANSLATED FROM THE FRENCH.
BOLTON TIMES
FRENCH COMPLAIN ABOUT BOMB
IPSWITCH INQUIRER
MAN OF STEEL ASSISTS LOCAL MOTORISTS
CORNWALL COURIER
SUPERMAN!
DAILY SMEAR
"WE ARE MODERATELY PROUD OF HI
BY COLIN CLAR
??

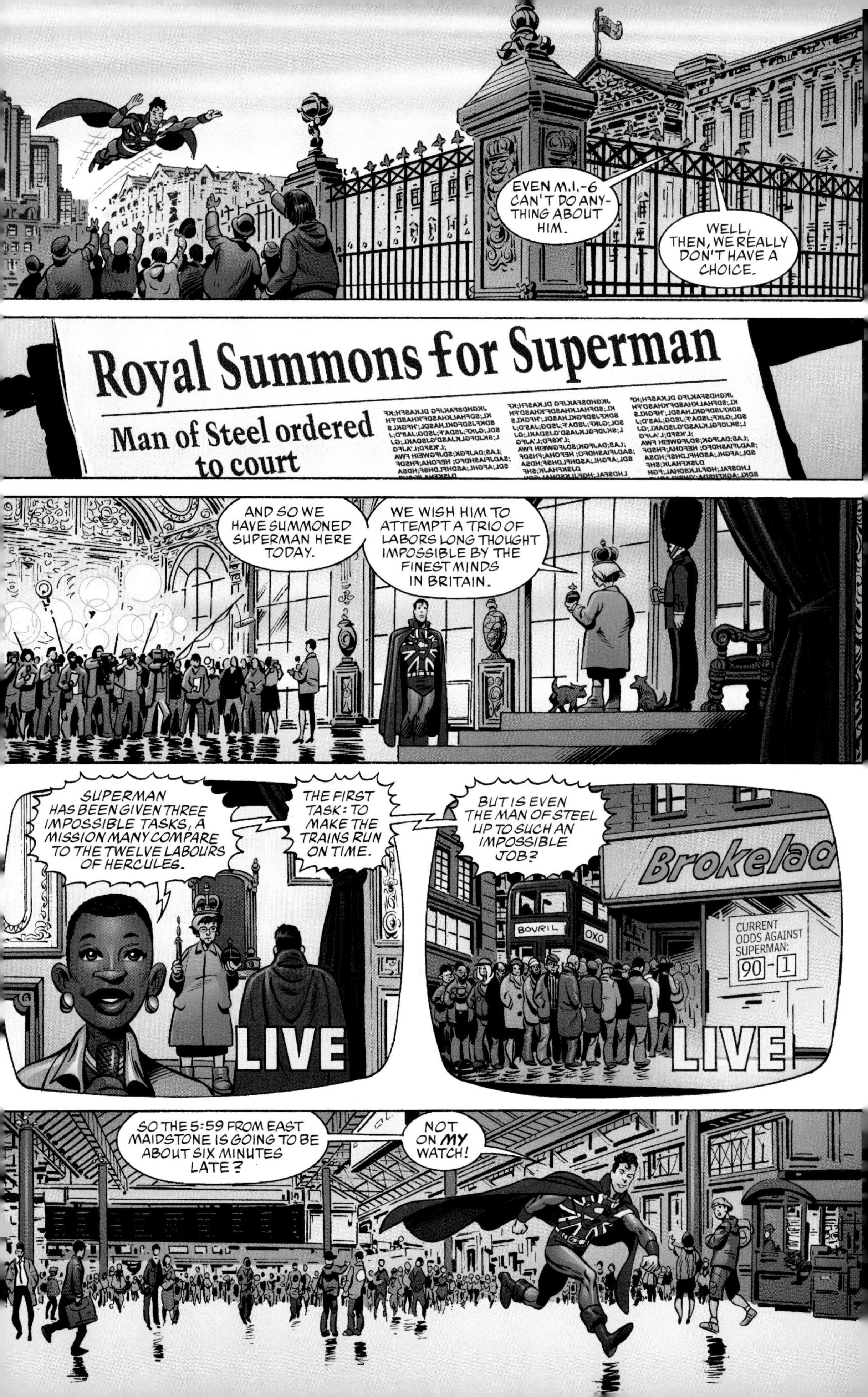
EVEN M.I.-6 CAN'T DO ANYTHING ABOUT HIM.
WELL, THEN, WE REALLY DON'T HAVE A CHOICE.
Royal Summons for Superman
Man of Steel ordered to court
AND SO WE HAVE SUMMONED SUPERMAN HERE TODAY.
WE WISH HIM TO ATTEMPT A TRIO OF LABORS LONG THOUGHT IMPOSSIBLE BY THE FINEST MINDS IN BRITAIN.
SUPERMAN HAS BEEN GIVEN THREE IMPOSSIBLE TASKS, A MISSION MANY COMPARE TO THE TWELVE LABOURS OF HERCULES.
THE FIRST TASK: TO MAKE THE TRAINS RUN ON TIME.
LIVE
BUT IS EVEN THE MAN OF STEEL UP TO SUCH AN IMPOSSIBLE JOB?
Brokelad
BOVRIL
OXO
CURRENT ODDS AGAINST SUPERMAN:
90-1
LIVE
SO THE 5:59 FROM EAST MAIDSTONE IS GOING TO BE ABOUT SIX MINUTES LATE?
NOT ON *MY* WATCH!

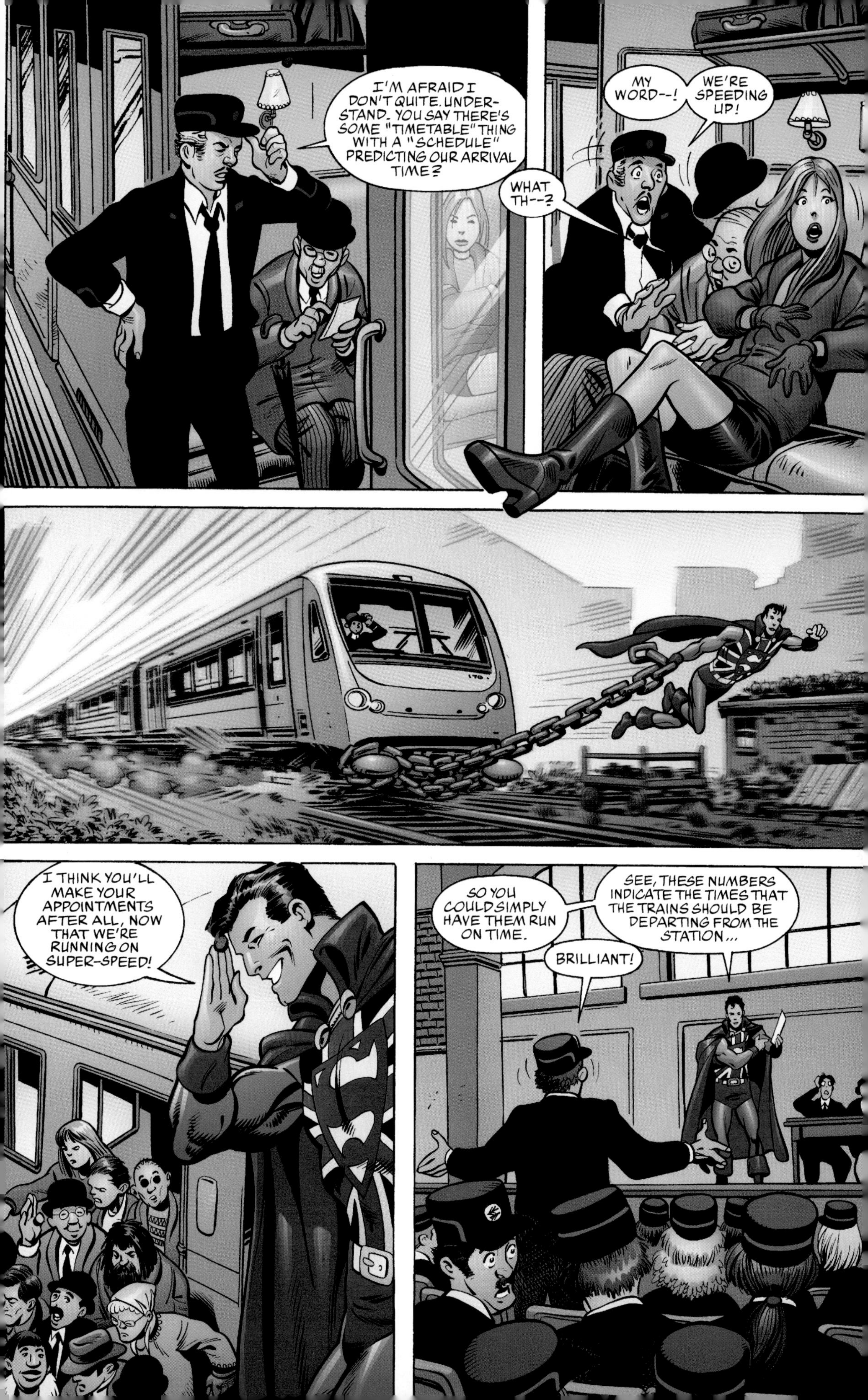
I'M AFRAID I DON'T QUITE. UNDERSTAND. YOU SAY THERE'S SOME "TIMETABLE" THING WITH A "SCHEDULE" PREDICTING OUR ARRIVAL TIME?
MY WORD--!
WE'RE SPEEDING UP!
WHAT TH--?
I THINK YOU'LL MAKE YOUR APPOINTMENTS AFTER ALL, NOW THAT WE'RE RUNNING ON SUPER-SPEED!
SEE, THESE NUMBERS INDICATE THE TIMES THAT THE TRAINS SHOULD BE DEPARTING FROM THE STATION...
SO YOU COULD SIMPLY HAVE THEM RUN ON TIME.
BRILLIANT!

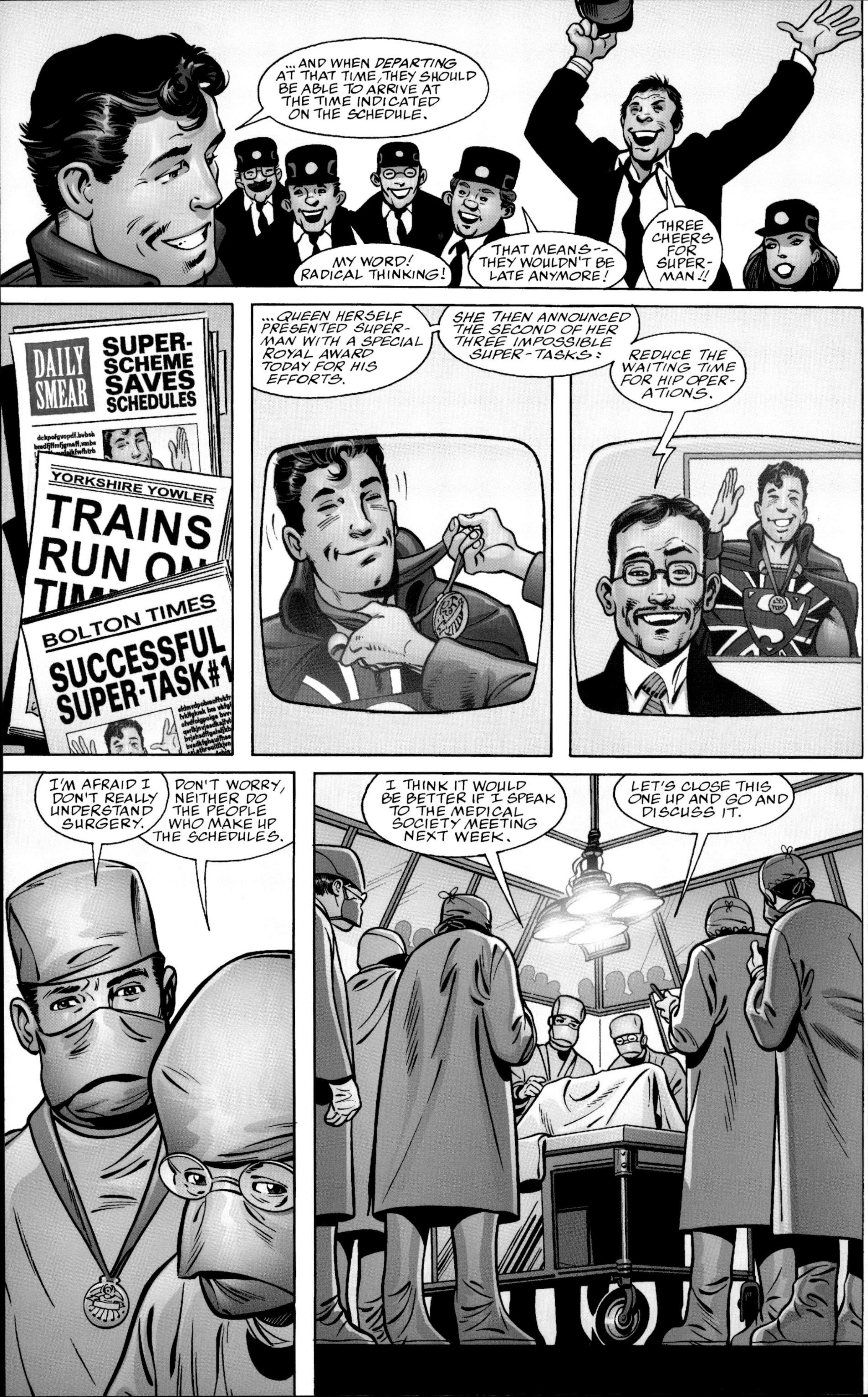
...AND WHEN DEPARTING AT THAT TIME, THEY SHOULD BE ABLE TO ARRIVE AT THE TIME INDICATED ON THE SCHEDULE.
MY WORD! RADICAL THINKING!
THAT MEANS-- THEY WOULDN'T BE LATE ANYMORE!
THREE CHEERS FOR SUPER-MAN!!
DAILY SMEAR
SUPER-SCHEME SAVES SCHEDULES
YORKSHIRE YOWLER
TRAINS RUN ON
BOLTON TIMES
SUCCESSFUL SUPER-TASK#1
...QUEEN HERSELF PRESENTED SUPER-MAN WITH A SPECIAL ROYAL AWARD TODAY FOR HIS EFFORTS.
SHE THEN ANNOUNCED THE SECOND OF HER THREE IMPOSSIBLE SUPER-TASKS:
REDUCE THE WAITING TIME FOR HIP OPER-ATIONS.
I'M AFRAID I DON'T REALLY UNDERSTAND SURGERY.
DON'T WORRY, NEITHER DO THE PEOPLE WHO MAKE UP THE SCHEDULES.
I THINK IT WOULD BE BETTER IF I SPEAK TO THE MEDICAL SOCIETY MEETING NEXT WEEK.
LET'S CLOSE THIS ONE UP AND GO AND DISCUSS IT.

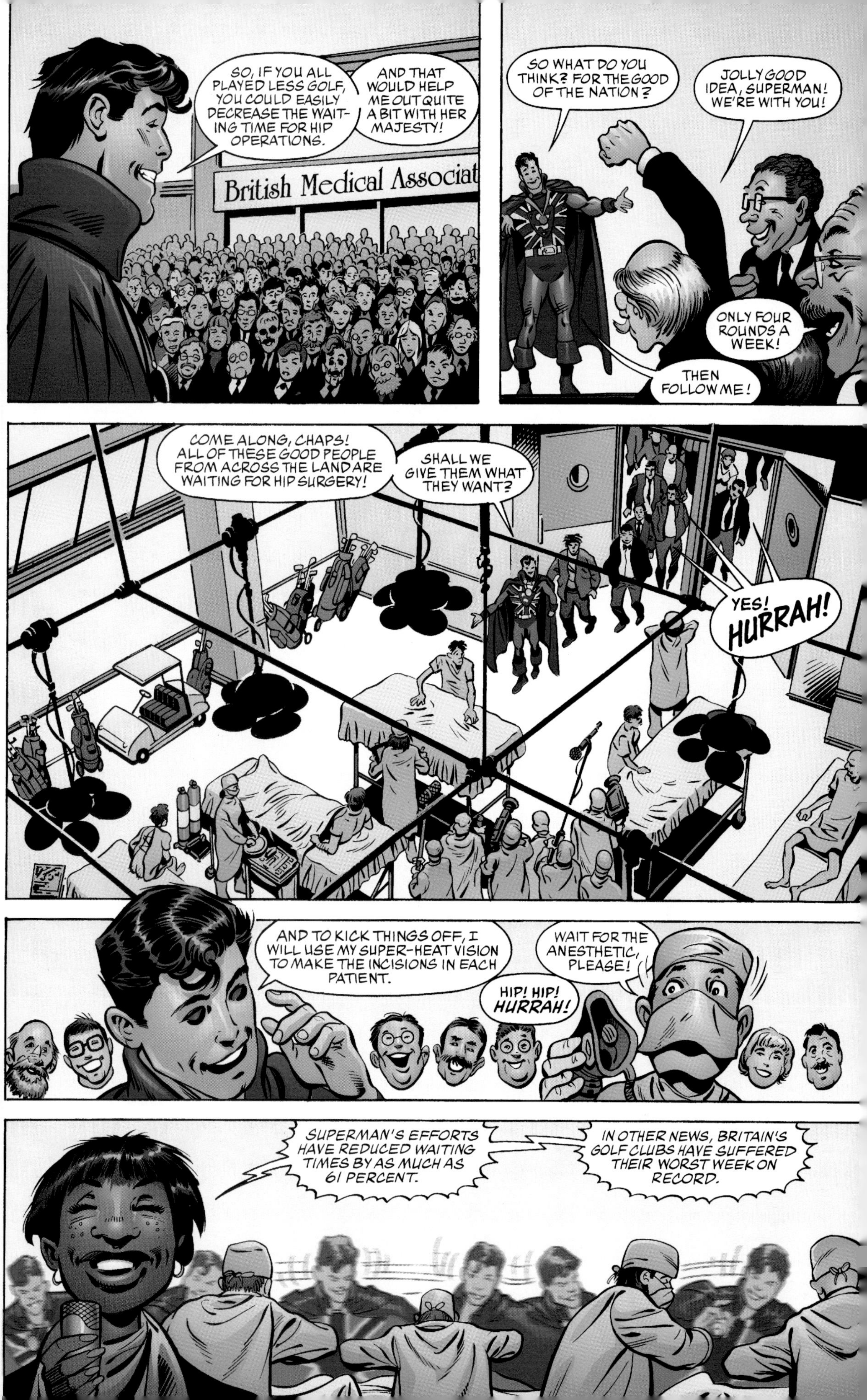
SO, IF YOU ALL PLAYED LESS GOLF, YOU COULD EASILY DECREASE THE WAITING TIME FOR HIP OPERATIONS.
AND THAT WOULD HELP ME OUT QUITE A BIT WITH HER MAJESTY!
British Medical Associat
SO WHAT DO YOU THINK? FOR THE GOOD OF THE NATION?
JOLLY GOOD IDEA, SUPERMAN! WE'RE WITH YOU!
ONLY FOUR ROUNDS A WEEK!
THEN FOLLOW ME!
COME ALONG, CHAPS! ALL OF THESE GOOD PEOPLE FROM ACROSS THE LAND ARE WAITING FOR HIP SURGERY!
SHALL WE GIVE THEM WHAT THEY WANT?
YES! HURRAH!
AND TO KICK THINGS OFF, I WILL USE MY SUPER-HEAT VISION TO MAKE THE INCISIONS IN EACH PATIENT.
WAIT FOR THE ANESTHETIC, PLEASE!
HIP! HIP! HURRAH!
SUPERMAN'S EFFORTS HAVE REDUCED WAITING TIMES BY AS MUCH AS 61 PERCENT.
IN OTHER NEWS, BRITAIN'S GOLF CLUBS HAVE SUFFERED THEIR WORST WEEK ON RECORD.

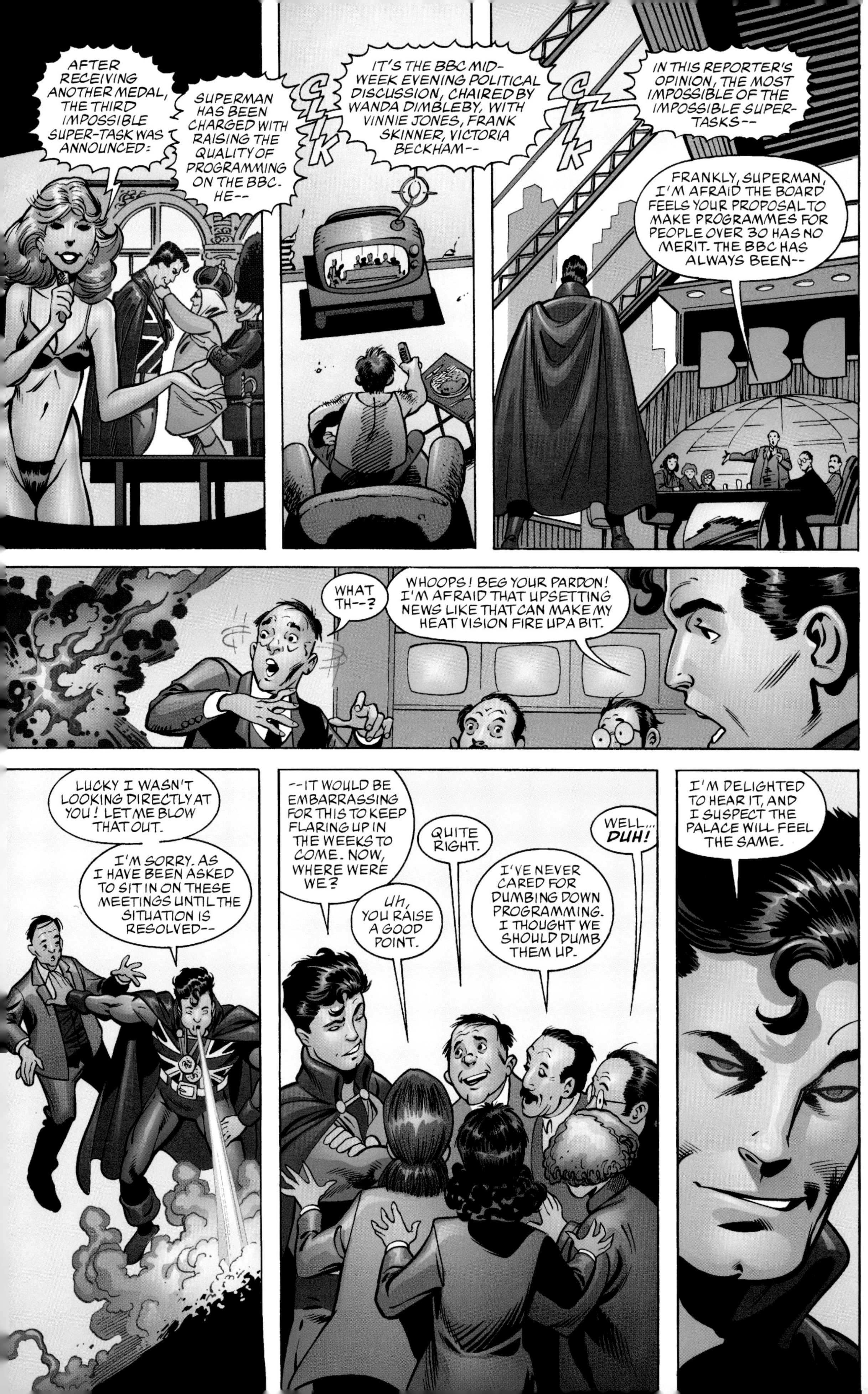
AFTER RECEIVING ANOTHER MEDAL, THE THIRD IMPOSSIBLE SUPER-TASK WAS ANNOUNCED:
SUPERMAN HAS BEEN CHARGED WITH RAISING THE QUALITY OF PROGRAMMING ON THE BBC. HE--
CLIK
IT'S THE BBC MID-WEEK EVENING POLITICAL DISCUSSION, CHAIRED BY WANDA DIMBLEBY, WITH VINNIE JONES, FRANK SKINNER, VICTORIA BECKHAM--
CLIK
IN THIS REPORTER'S OPINION, THE MOST IMPOSSIBLE OF THE IMPOSSIBLE SUPER-TASKS--
FRANKLY, SUPERMAN, I'M AFRAID THE BOARD FEELS YOUR PROPOSAL TO MAKE PROGRAMMES FOR PEOPLE OVER 30 HAS NO MERIT. THE BBC HAS ALWAYS BEEN--
BBC
WHAT TH--?
WHOOPS! BEG YOUR PARDON! I'M AFRAID THAT UPSETTING NEWS LIKE THAT CAN MAKE MY HEAT VISION FIRE UP A BIT.
LUCKY I WASN'T LOOKING DIRECTLY AT YOU! LET ME BLOW THAT OUT.
I'M SORRY. AS I HAVE BEEN ASKED TO SIT IN ON THESE MEETINGS UNTIL THE SITUATION IS RESOLVED--
--IT WOULD BE EMBARRASSING FOR THIS TO KEEP FLARING UP IN THE WEEKS TO COME. NOW, WHERE WERE WE?
UH, YOU RAISE A GOOD POINT.
QUITE RIGHT.
I'VE NEVER CARED FOR DUMBING DOWN PROGRAMMING. I THOUGHT WE SHOULD DUMB THEM UP.
WELL... DUH!
I'M DELIGHTED TO HEAR IT, AND I SUSPECT THE PALACE WILL FEEL THE SAME.

GOOD PICTURE, JIMMY!

WE'RE A GOOD TEAM, COLIN. AS LONG AS SUPERMAN STAYS THIS POPULAR, THE SKY'S THE LIMIT FOR US!

SUPERMAN TRIUMPHANT
MAN OF STEEL IS THREE FOR THREE

WELL DONE, LADS! LOVE THE SUPERMAN PIECES, LOVE 'EM! WHAT'S NEXT FOR MY FAVOURITE CIRCULATION-BUILDER?

WELL, SIR, HE'S CUTTING A COUPLE OF RIBBONS THIS WEEK, BY REQUEST OF THE PALACE--

AND HE MAY ACCOMPANY HER MAJESTY TO CHRISTEN A SHIP. GREAT PHOTO-OP!

OH, DEAR. NOTHING INTERESTING, EH?

THERE'S TALK OF AN M.B.E.

CAN'T GET MUCH DULLER THAN THAT!

LET'S HAVE ANOTHER EXCLUSIVE INTERVEIW, THEN. MAYBE CONFESS TO SOMETHING.?

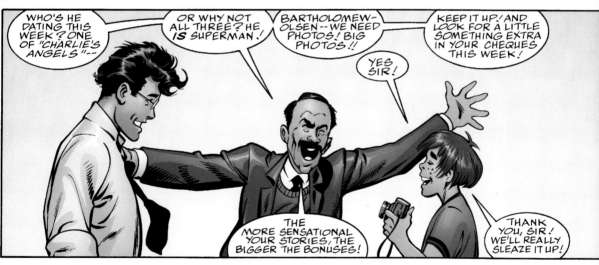

WHO'S HE DATING THIS WEEK? ONE OF "CHARLIE'S ANGELS"--

OR WHY NOT ALL THREE? HE IS SUPERMAN!

BARTHOLOMEW-OLSEN-- WE NEED PHOTOS! BIG PHOTOS!!

KEEP IT UP! AND LOOK FOR A LITTLE SOMETHING EXTRA IN YOUR CHEQUES THIS WEEK!

YES SIR!

THE MORE SENSATIONAL YOUR STORIES, THE BIGGER THE BONUSES!

THANK YOU, SIR! WE'LL REALLY SLEAZE IT UP!

SLEAZE IT UP?

COLIN! WHYTE-BADGER LIKES US! IT CAN'T GET MUCH BETTER THAN THIS!

THAT SOUNDS LIKE A WARNING.

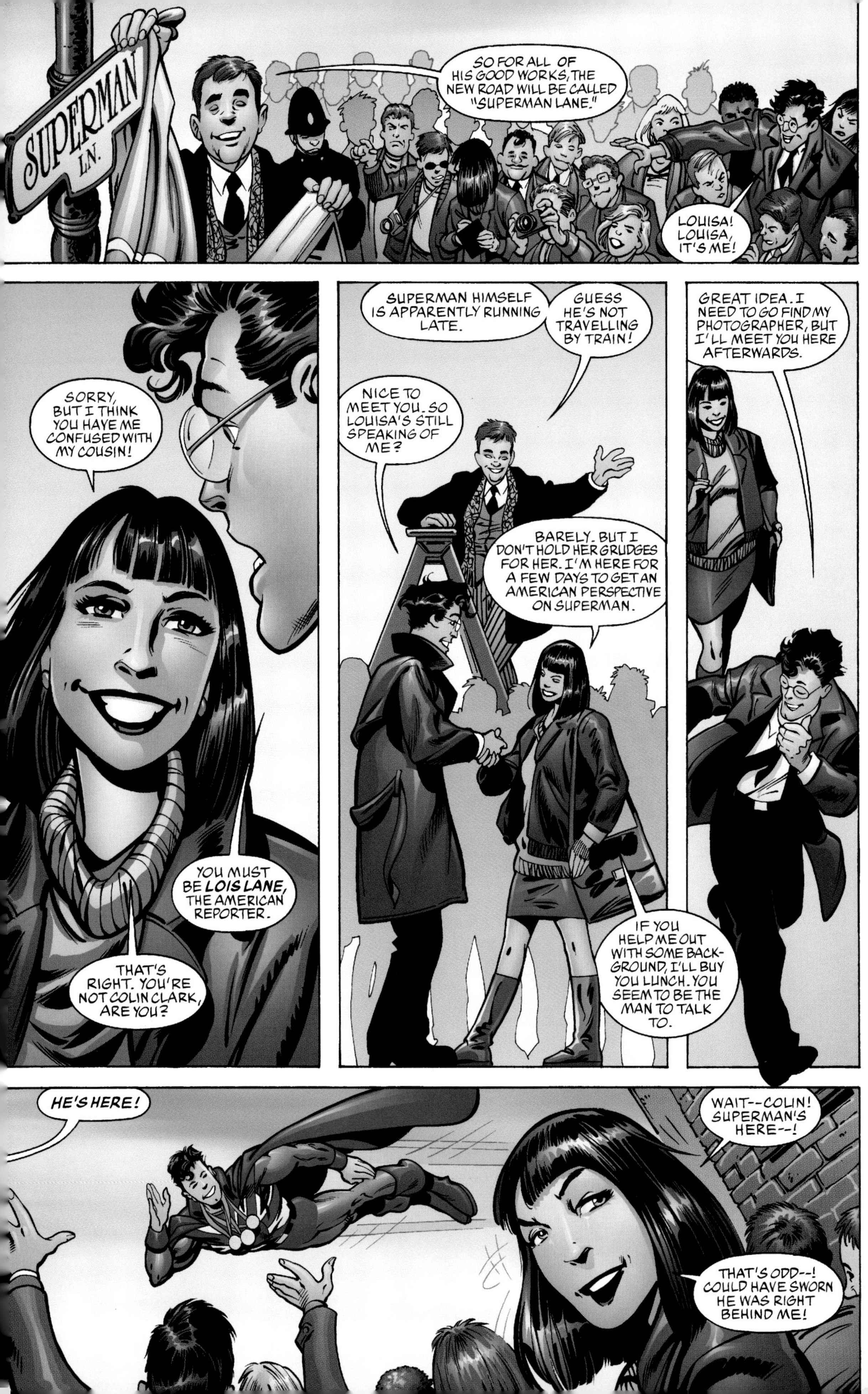
SUPERMAN LN.
SO FOR ALL OF HIS GOOD WORKS, THE NEW ROAD WILL BE CALLED "SUPERMAN LANE."
LOUISA! LOUISA, IT'S ME!
SORRY, BUT I THINK YOU HAVE ME CONFUSED WITH MY COUSIN!
YOU MUST BE LOIS LANE, THE AMERICAN REPORTER.
THAT'S RIGHT. YOU'RE NOT COLIN CLARK, ARE YOU?
SUPERMAN HIMSELF IS APPARENTLY RUNNING LATE.
GUESS HE'S NOT TRAVELLING BY TRAIN!
NICE TO MEET YOU. SO LOUISA'S STILL SPEAKING OF ME?
BARELY. BUT I DON'T HOLD HER GRUDGES FOR HER. I'M HERE FOR A FEW DAYS TO GET AN AMERICAN PERSPECTIVE ON SUPERMAN.
IF YOU HELP ME OUT WITH SOME BACK-GROUND, I'LL BUY YOU LUNCH. YOU SEEM TO BE THE MAN TO TALK TO.
GREAT IDEA. I NEED TO GO FIND MY PHOTOGRAPHER, BUT I'LL MEET YOU HERE AFTERWARDS.
HE'S HERE!
WAIT--COLIN! SUPERMAN'S HERE--!
THAT'S ODD--! COULD HAVE SWORN HE WAS RIGHT BEHIND ME!

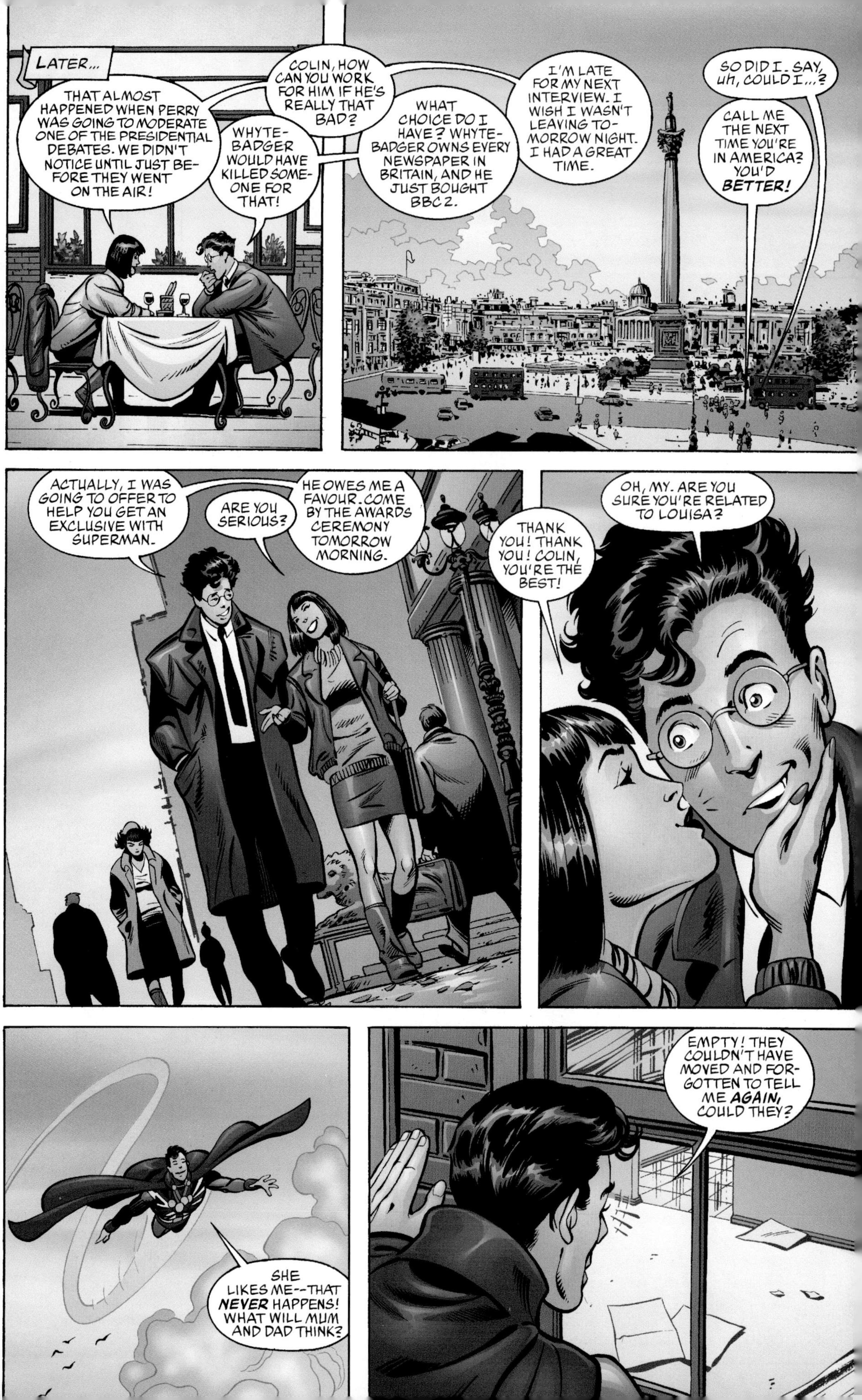
LATER...
THAT ALMOST HAPPENED WHEN PERRY WAS GOING TO MODERATE ONE OF THE PRESIDENTIAL DEBATES. WE DIDN'T NOTICE UNTIL JUST BEFORE THEY WENT ON THE AIR!
WHYTE-BADGER WOULD HAVE KILLED SOMEONE FOR THAT!
COLIN, HOW CAN YOU WORK FOR HIM IF HE'S REALLY THAT BAD?
WHAT CHOICE DO I HAVE? WHYTE-BADGER OWNS EVERY NEWSPAPER IN BRITAIN, AND HE JUST BOUGHT BBC 2.
I'M LATE FOR MY NEXT INTERVIEW. I WISH I WASN'T LEAVING TOMORROW NIGHT. I HAD A GREAT TIME.
SO DID I. SAY, uh, COULD I...?
CALL ME THE NEXT TIME YOU'RE IN AMERICA? YOU'D BETTER!
ACTUALLY, I WAS GOING TO OFFER TO HELP YOU GET AN EXCLUSIVE WITH SUPERMAN.
ARE YOU SERIOUS?
HE OWES ME A FAVOUR. COME BY THE AWARDS CEREMONY TOMORROW MORNING.
THANK YOU! THANK YOU! COLIN, YOU'RE THE BEST!
OH, MY. ARE YOU SURE YOU'RE RELATED TO LOUISA?
SHE LIKES ME--THAT NEVER HAPPENS! WHAT WILL MUM AND DAD THINK?
EMPTY! THEY COULDN'T HAVE MOVED AND FORGOTTEN TO TELL ME AGAIN, COULD THEY?

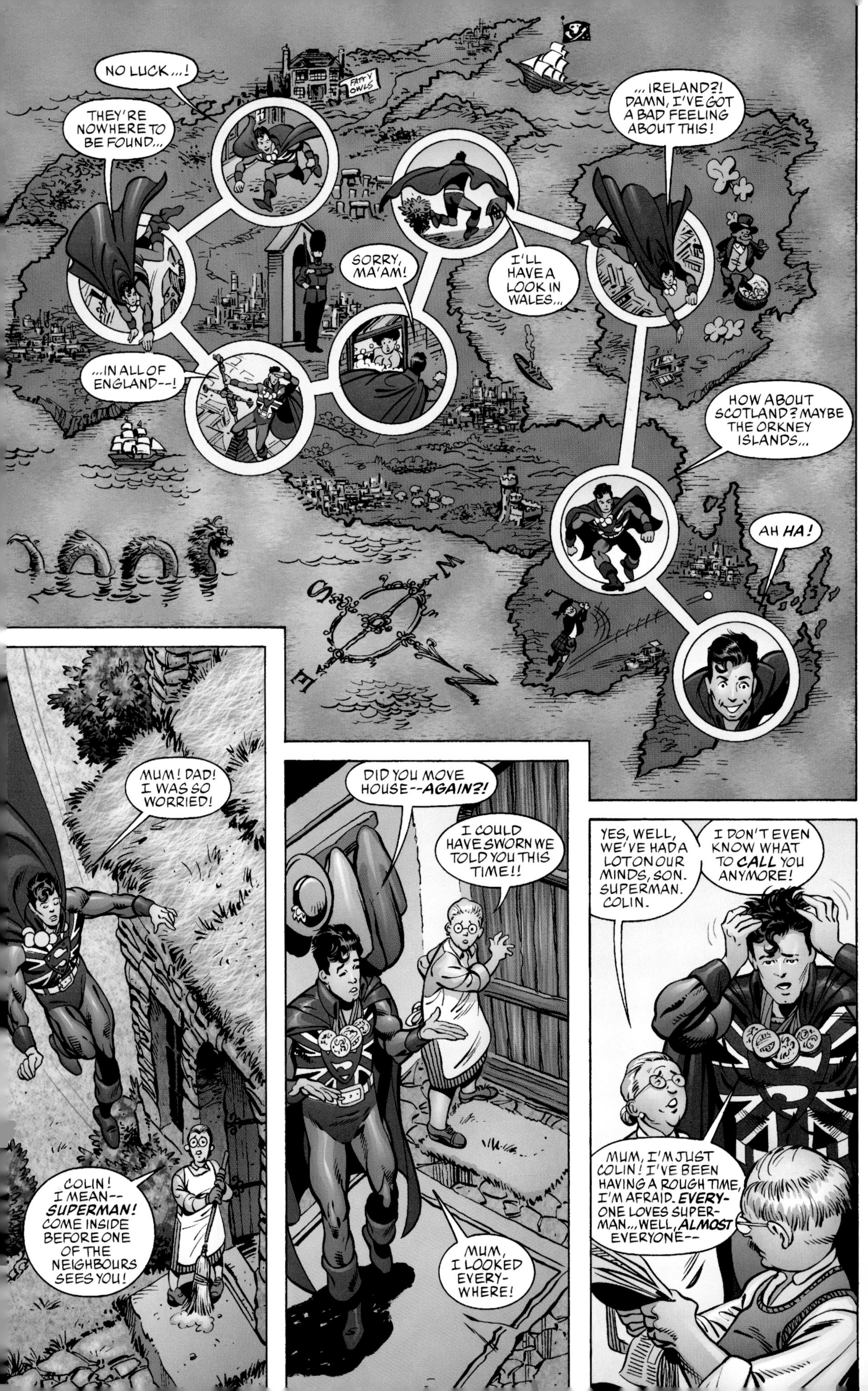

NO LUCK...!
THEY'RE NOWHERE TO BE FOUND...
...IN ALL OF ENGLAND--!
SORRY, MA'AM!
I'LL HAVE A LOOK IN WALES...
...IRELAND?! DAMN, I'VE GOT A BAD FEELING ABOUT THIS!
HOW ABOUT SCOTLAND? MAYBE THE ORKNEY ISLANDS...
AH HA!
FATTY OWLS
MUM! DAD! I WAS SO WORRIED!
COLIN! I MEAN-- SUPERMAN! COME INSIDE BEFORE ONE OF THE NEIGHBOURS SEES YOU!
DID YOU MOVE HOUSE--AGAIN?!
I COULD HAVE SWORN WE TOLD YOU THIS TIME!!
MUM, I LOOKED EVERY-WHERE!
YES, WELL, WE'VE HAD A LOT ON OUR MINDS, SON. SUPERMAN. COLIN.
I DON'T EVEN KNOW WHAT TO CALL YOU ANYMORE!
MUM, I'M JUST COLIN! I'VE BEEN HAVING A ROUGH TIME, I'M AFRAID. EVERY-ONE LOVES SUPER-MAN... WELL, ALMOST EVERYONE--

AND MR. WHYTE BADGER IS VERY HAPPY WITH ME, BUT I HAVE TO WRITE THESE DREADFUL STORIES.

IF I DON'T MAKE THEM LURID ENOUGH, THEY'RE REWRITTEN UNTIL THEY'RE *REALLY* SLEAZY.

I THOUGHT JOURNALISM WAS ABOUT REPORTING, BUT THEY'VE LOST INTEREST IN ANY KIND OF REALITY--

SON, DO YOU *HAVE* TO WEAR THAT GETUP IN THE HOUSE?

WHAT?

OH, SORRY DAD... TURN YOUR HEAD PLEASE, MUM.

THE QUEEN IS HAPPY WITH SUPERMAN, BUT I STILL FEEL GUILTY.

NEVER MIND, DEAR.

I MET THIS GREAT GIRL YESTERDAY, BUT SHE HAS TO GO BACK TO AMERICA.

WHY DON'T YOU JUST COME BACK HERE AND GET A PART-TIME JOB WITH THE WESTON-SUPER-MARE MERCURY?

BUT-- I MEAN, MUM, WHAT DO YOU THINK?

BEST LISTEN TO YOUR FATHER, DEAR. GIVE UP THIS SILLY SUPERMAN BUSINESS OR IT'LL END IN TEARS.

AND SO...

WHAT IF THEY'RE *RIGHT*? MAYBE I *SHOULD* QUIT!

IT *IS* A BIT OF A SILLY COSTUME. EMBARRASSING TIGHTS, SILLY CAPE--

HERE HE COMES!

DAILY SMEAR

CONGRATULATIONS, SUPERMAN

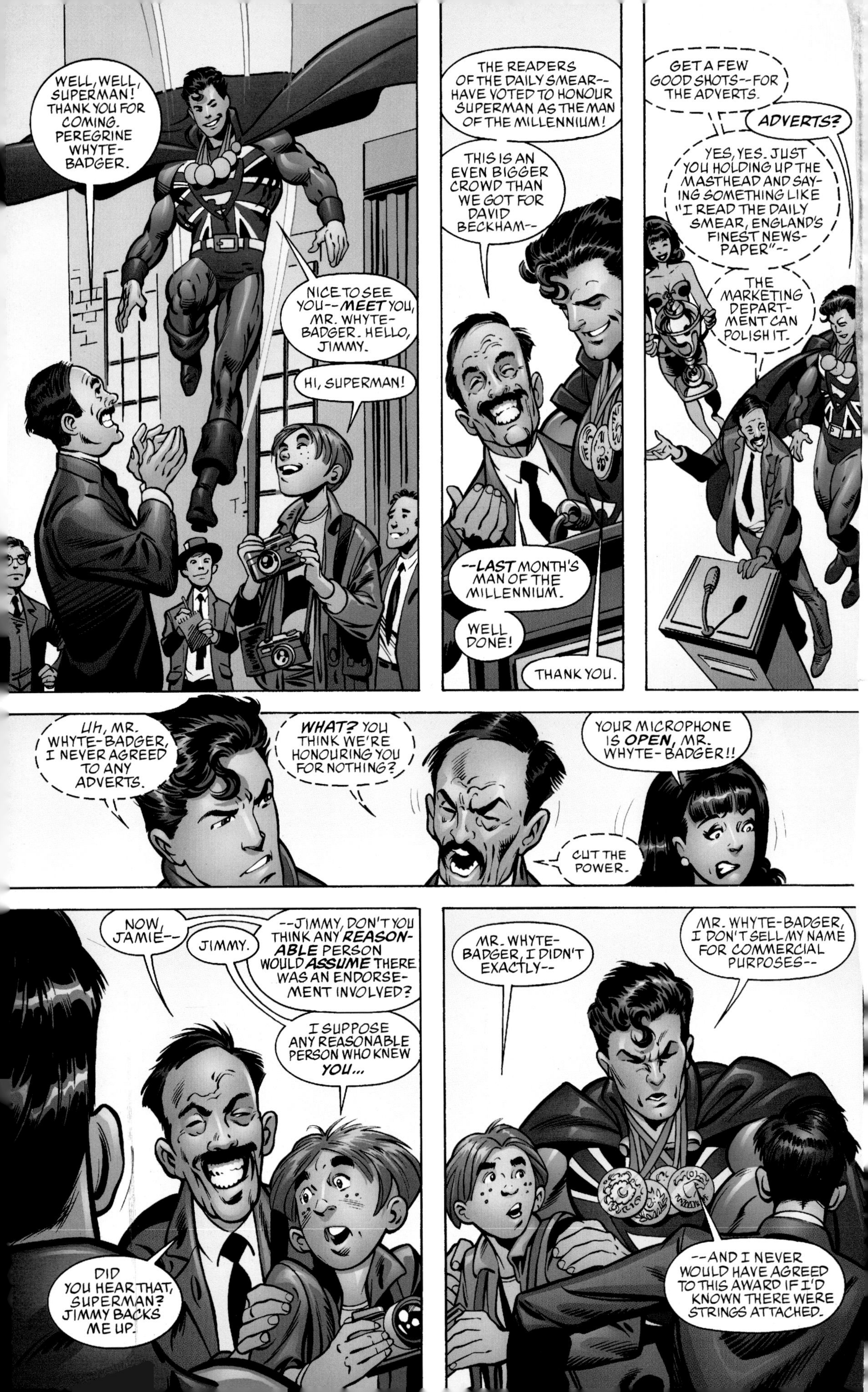
WELL, WELL, SUPERMAN! THANK YOU FOR COMING. PEREGRINE WHYTE-BADGER.
NICE TO SEE YOU--MEET YOU, MR. WHYTE-BADGER. HELLO, JIMMY.
HI, SUPERMAN!
THE READERS OF THE DAILY SMEAR--HAVE VOTED TO HONOUR SUPERMAN AS THE MAN OF THE MILLENNIUM!
THIS IS AN EVEN BIGGER CROWD THAN WE GOT FOR DAVID BECKHAM--
--LAST MONTH'S MAN OF THE MILLENNIUM.
WELL DONE!
THANK YOU.
GET A FEW GOOD SHOTS--FOR THE ADVERTS.
ADVERTS?
YES, YES. JUST YOU HOLDING UP THE MASTHEAD AND SAYING SOMETHING LIKE "I READ THE DAILY SMEAR, ENGLAND'S FINEST NEWSPAPER"--
THE MARKETING DEPARTMENT CAN POLISH IT.
UH, MR. WHYTE-BADGER, I NEVER AGREED TO ANY ADVERTS.
WHAT? YOU THINK WE'RE HONOURING YOU FOR NOTHING?
YOUR MICROPHONE IS OPEN, MR. WHYTE-BADGER!!
CUT THE POWER.
NOW, JAMIE--
JIMMY.
--JIMMY, DON'T YOU THINK ANY REASONABLE PERSON WOULD ASSUME THERE WAS AN ENDORSEMENT INVOLVED?
I SUPPOSE ANY REASONABLE PERSON WHO KNEW YOU...
DID YOU HEAR THAT, SUPERMAN? JIMMY BACKS ME UP.
MR. WHYTE-BADGER, I DIDN'T EXACTLY--
MR. WHYTE-BADGER, I DON'T SELL MY NAME FOR COMMERCIAL PURPOSES--
--AND I NEVER WOULD HAVE AGREED TO THIS AWARD IF I'D KNOWN THERE WERE STRINGS ATTACHED.

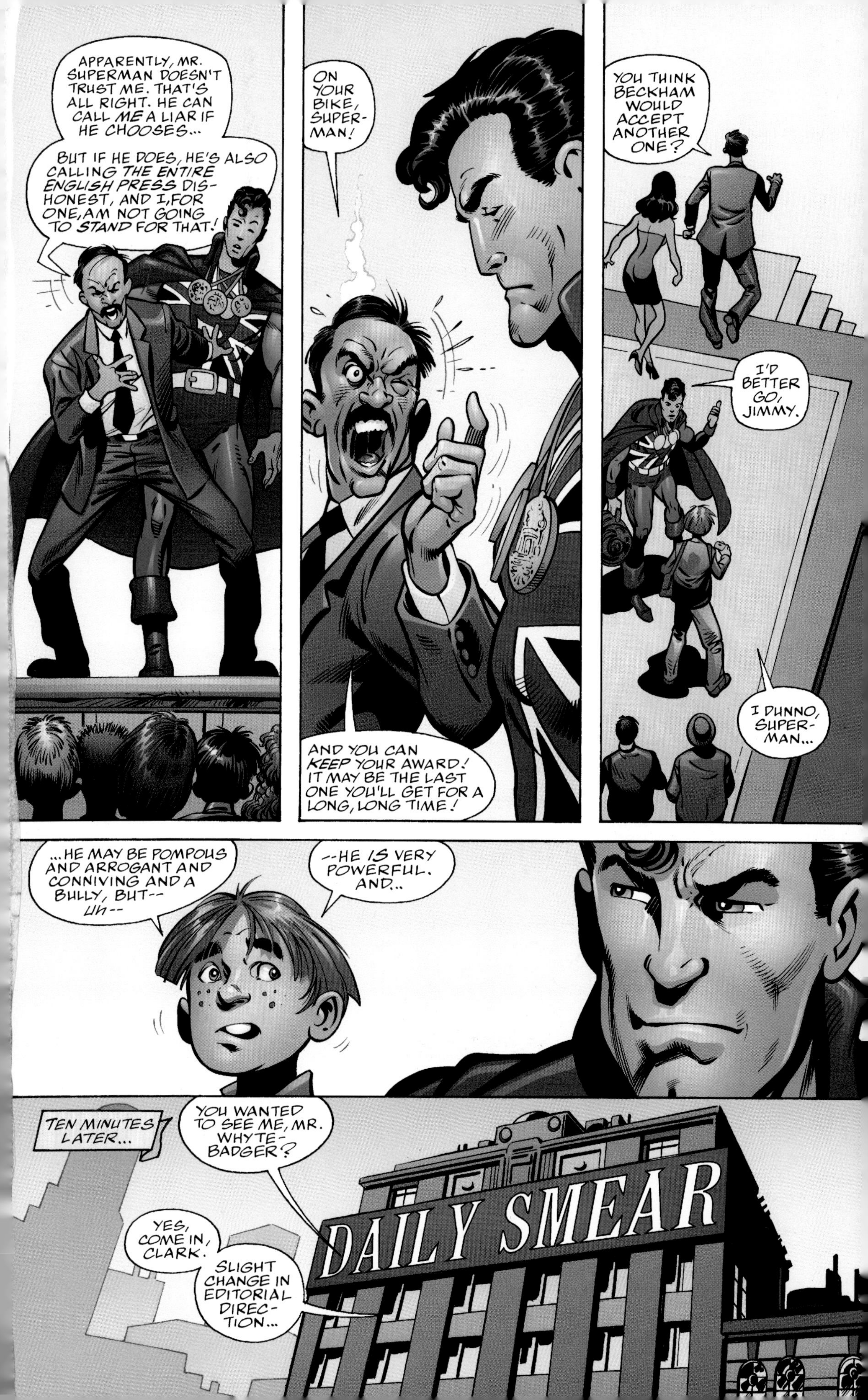
APPARENTLY, MR. SUPERMAN DOESN'T TRUST ME. THAT'S ALL RIGHT. HE CAN CALL *ME* A LIAR IF HE CHOOSES...
BUT IF HE DOES, HE'S ALSO CALLING *THE ENTIRE ENGLISH PRESS* DISHONEST, AND I, FOR ONE, AM NOT GOING TO *STAND* FOR THAT!
ON YOUR BIKE, SUPER-MAN!
AND YOU CAN *KEEP* YOUR AWARD! IT MAY BE THE LAST ONE YOU'LL GET FOR A LONG, LONG TIME!
YOU THINK BECKHAM WOULD ACCEPT ANOTHER ONE?
I'D BETTER GO, JIMMY.
I DUNNO, SUPER-MAN...
...HE MAY BE POMPOUS AND ARROGANT AND CONNIVING AND A BULLY, BUT-- *UH*--
--HE *IS* VERY POWERFUL. AND..
TEN MINUTES LATER...
YOU WANTED TO SEE ME, MR. WHYTE-BADGER?
DAILY SMEAR
YES, COME IN, CLARK.
SLIGHT CHANGE IN EDITORIAL DIRECTION...

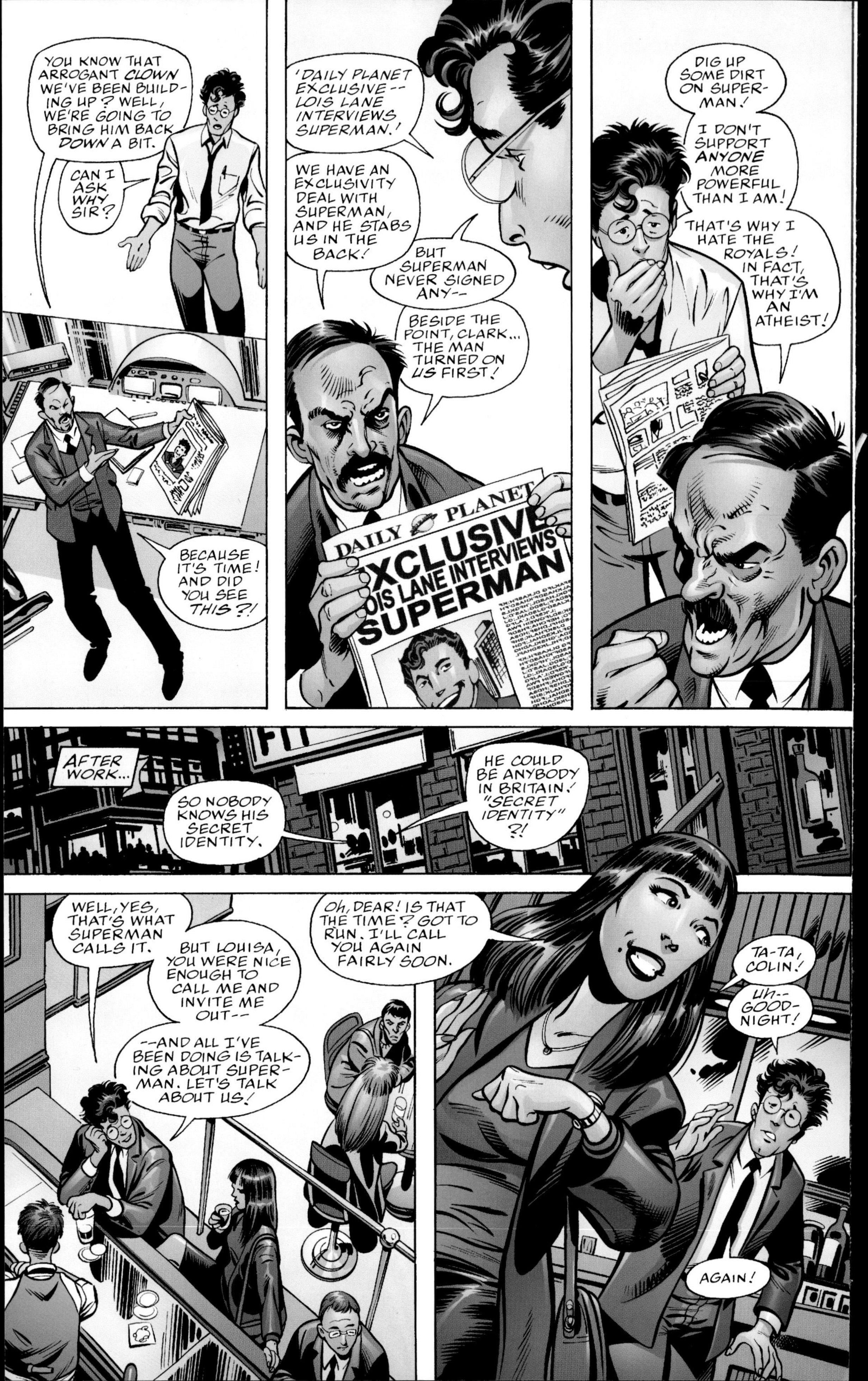

YOU KNOW THAT ARROGANT CLOWN WE'VE BEEN BUILDING UP? WELL, WE'RE GOING TO BRING HIM BACK DOWN A BIT.
CAN I ASK WHY SIR?
BECAUSE IT'S TIME! AND DID YOU SEE THIS?!
'DAILY PLANET EXCLUSIVE -- LOIS LANE INTERVIEWS SUPERMAN.'
WE HAVE AN EXCLUSIVITY DEAL WITH SUPERMAN, AND HE STABS US IN THE BACK!
BUT SUPERMAN NEVER SIGNED ANY--
BESIDE THE POINT, CLARK... THE MAN TURNED ON US FIRST!
DAILY PLANET
EXCLUSIVE
LOIS LANE INTERVIEWS SUPERMAN
DIG UP SOME DIRT ON SUPERMAN!
I DON'T SUPPORT ANYONE MORE POWERFUL THAN I AM!
THAT'S WHY I HATE THE ROYALS! IN FACT, THAT'S WHY I'M AN ATHEIST!
AFTER WORK...
SO NOBODY KNOWS HIS SECRET IDENTITY.
HE COULD BE ANYBODY IN BRITAIN! "SECRET IDENTITY"?!
WELL, YES, THAT'S WHAT SUPERMAN CALLS IT.
BUT LOUISA, YOU WERE NICE ENOUGH TO CALL ME AND INVITE ME OUT--
--AND ALL I'VE BEEN DOING IS TALKING ABOUT SUPERMAN. LET'S TALK ABOUT US!
Oh, DEAR! IS THAT THE TIME? GOT TO RUN. I'LL CALL YOU AGAIN FAIRLY SOON.
TA-TA, COLIN!
UH-- GOOD-NIGHT!
AGAIN!

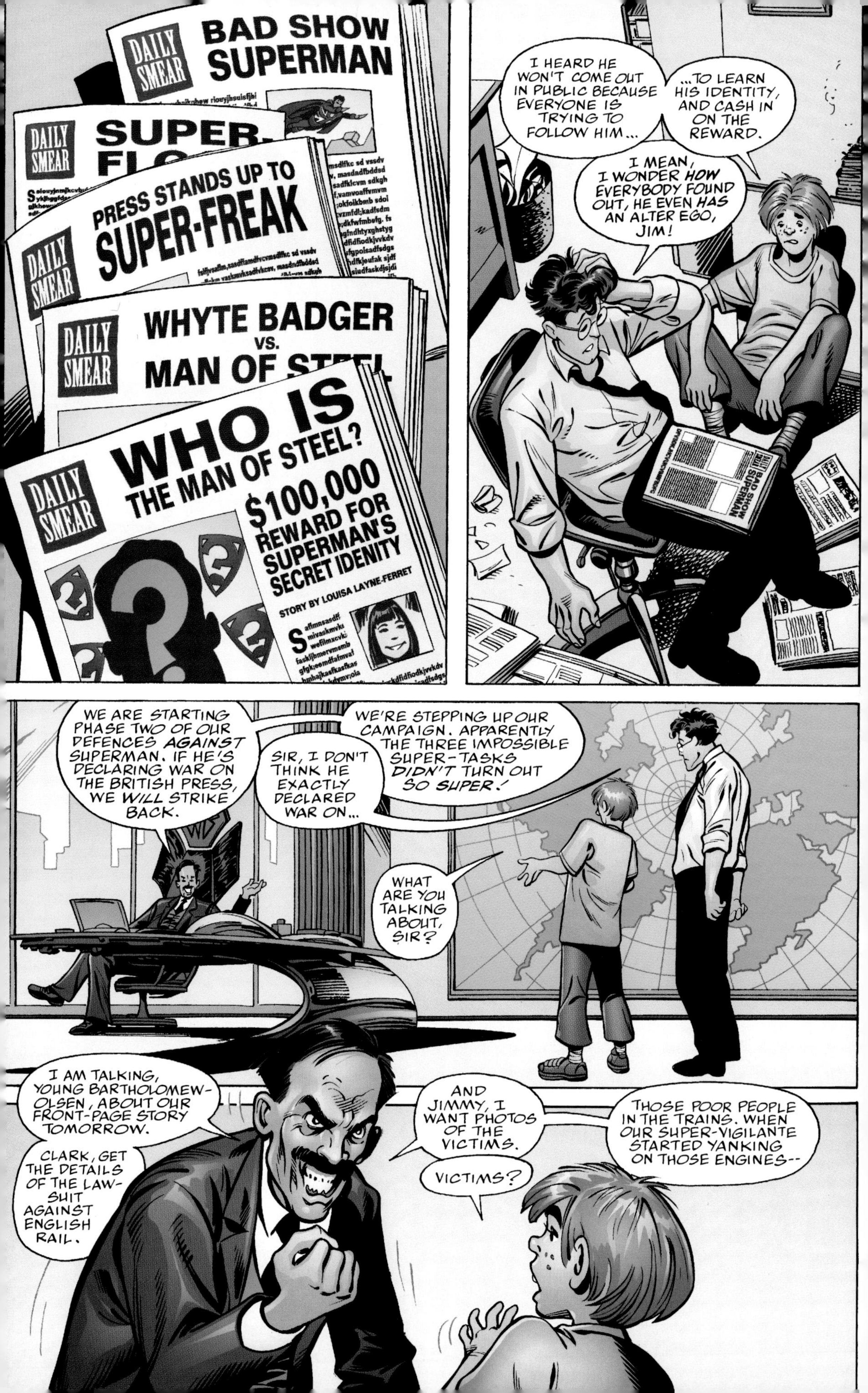
DAILY SMEAR
BAD SHOW SUPERMAN
DAILY SMEAR
SUPER-
DAILY SMEAR
PRESS STANDS UP TO SUPER-FREAK
DAILY SMEAR
WHYTE BADGER VS. MAN OF STEEL
DAILY SMEAR
WHO IS THE MAN OF STEEL?
$100,000 REWARD FOR SUPERMAN'S SECRET IDENITY
STORY BY LOUISA LAYNE-FERRET
I HEARD HE WON'T COME OUT IN PUBLIC BECAUSE EVERYONE IS TRYING TO FOLLOW HIM...
...TO LEARN HIS IDENTITY, AND CASH IN ON THE REWARD.
I MEAN, I WONDER HOW EVERYBODY FOUND OUT, HE EVEN HAS AN ALTER EGO, JIM!
WE ARE STARTING PHASE TWO OF OUR DEFENCES AGAINST SUPERMAN. IF HE'S DECLARING WAR ON THE BRITISH PRESS, WE WILL STRIKE BACK.
SIR, I DON'T THINK HE EXACTLY DECLARED WAR ON...
WE'RE STEPPING UP OUR CAMPAIGN. APPARENTLY THE THREE IMPOSSIBLE SUPER-TASKS DIDN'T TURN OUT SO SUPER.!
WHAT ARE YOU TALKING ABOUT, SIR?
I AM TALKING, YOUNG BARTHOLOMEW-OLSEN, ABOUT OUR FRONT-PAGE STORY TOMORROW.
CLARK, GET THE DETAILS OF THE LAW-SUIT AGAINST ENGLISH RAIL.
AND JIMMY, I WANT PHOTOS OF THE VICTIMS.
VICTIMS?
THOSE POOR PEOPLE IN THE TRAINS. WHEN OUR SUPER-VIGILANTE STARTED YANKING ON THOSE ENGINES--

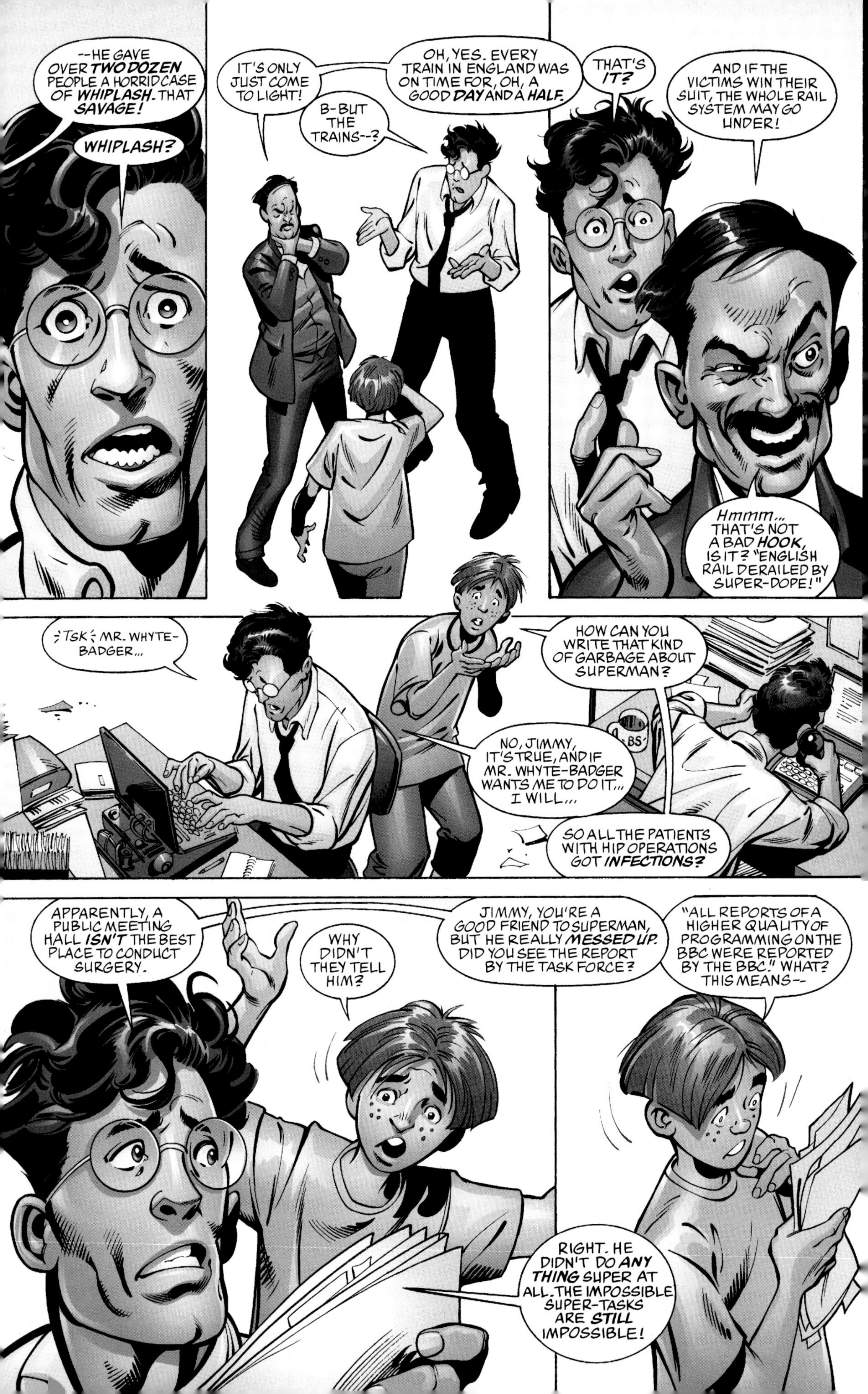
--HE GAVE OVER TWO DOZEN PEOPLE A HORRID CASE OF WHIPLASH- THAT SAVAGE!
WHIPLASH?
IT'S ONLY JUST COME TO LIGHT!
OH, YES. EVERY TRAIN IN ENGLAND WAS ON TIME FOR, OH, A GOOD DAY AND A HALF.
B-BUT THE TRAINS--?
THAT'S IT?
AND IF THE VICTIMS WIN THEIR SUIT, THE WHOLE RAIL SYSTEM MAY GO UNDER!
Hmmm... THAT'S NOT A BAD HOOK, IS IT? "ENGLISH RAIL DERAILED BY SUPER-DOPE!"
TSK MR. WHYTE-BADGER...
HOW CAN YOU WRITE THAT KIND OF GARBAGE ABOUT SUPERMAN?
BS
NO, JIMMY, IT'S TRUE, AND IF MR. WHYTE-BADGER WANTS ME TO DO IT... I WILL...
SO ALL THE PATIENTS WITH HIP OPERATIONS GOT INFECTIONS?
APPARENTLY, A PUBLIC MEETING HALL ISN'T THE BEST PLACE TO CONDUCT SURGERY.
WHY DIDN'T THEY TELL HIM?
JIMMY, YOU'RE A GOOD FRIEND TO SUPERMAN, BUT HE REALLY MESSED UP. DID YOU SEE THE REPORT BY THE TASK FORCE?
"ALL REPORTS OF A HIGHER QUALITY OF PROGRAMMING ON THE BBC WERE REPORTED BY THE BBC." WHAT? THIS MEANS--
RIGHT. HE DIDN'T DO ANY THING SUPER AT ALL. THE IMPOSSIBLE SUPER-TASKS ARE STILL IMPOSSIBLE!

AND SO, SUPERMAN, YOU **OWE** THE NATION A GREAT SERVICE FOR THE **DISSERVICE** YOU HAVE DONE WITH YOUR **SO-CALLED** SUPER-TASKS!

IF YOU WANT TO PAY BACK THE NATION, THEN WE CALL ON YOU TO PAY OFF THE NATIONAL DEBT--

NATIONAL DEBT? YOU PAY ME £178 A WEEK!

MAYBE I COULD DO SOMETHING TO BRING IN A FEW MILLION IF NOT **BILLIONS.**

"NO OFFICE WOULD PAY THAT KIND OF MONEY FOR AN EMPLOYEE... **EVEN** IF HE HAS SUPER-SPEED..."

"...AND NEITHER WOULD THE FOOD SERVICE INDUSTRY.

"NO WORK IN **CONSTRUCTION** FOR ME....

"...OR IN ANY FACTORY...

"...AND THERE IS NOT ENOUGH COAL IN THE WORLD TO MAKE THAT KIND OF--!

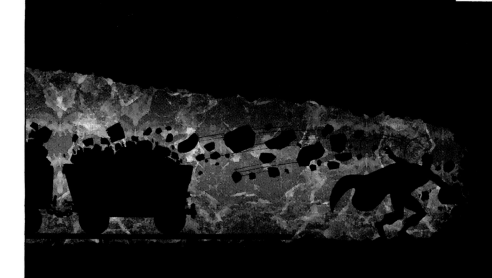

"WAIT A MINUTE! THAT'S IT!"

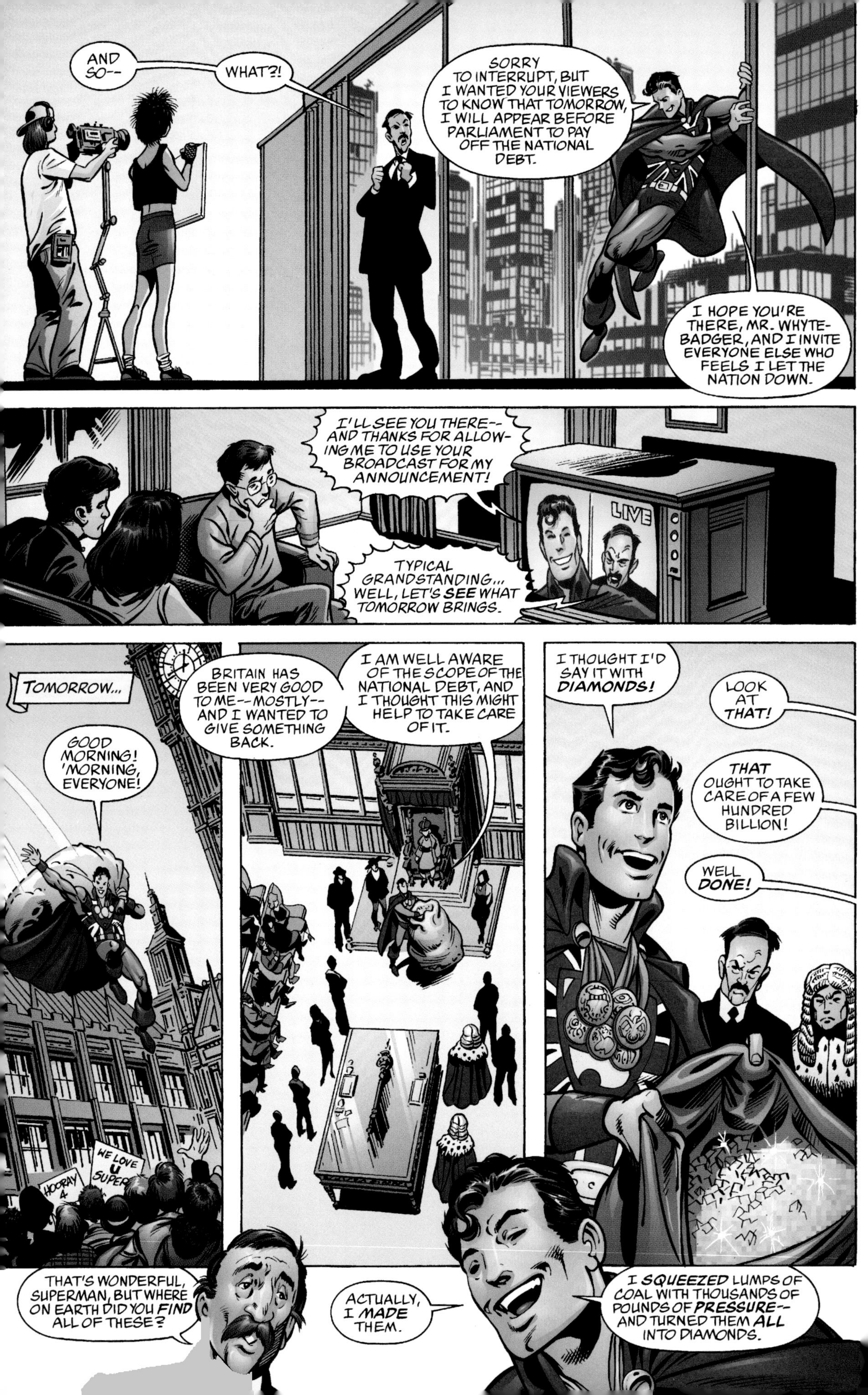
AND SO--
WHAT?!
SORRY TO INTERRUPT, BUT I WANTED YOUR VIEWERS TO KNOW THAT TOMORROW, I WILL APPEAR BEFORE PARLIAMENT TO PAY OFF THE NATIONAL DEBT.
I HOPE YOU'RE THERE, MR. WHYTE-BADGER, AND I INVITE EVERYONE ELSE WHO FEELS I LET THE NATION DOWN.
I'LL SEE YOU THERE-- AND THANKS FOR ALLOWING ME TO USE YOUR BROADCAST FOR MY ANNOUNCEMENT!
LIVE
TYPICAL GRANDSTANDING... WELL, LET'S SEE WHAT TOMORROW BRINGS.
TOMORROW...
GOOD MORNING! 'MORNING, EVERYONE!
WE LOVE U SUPER
HOORAY 4
BRITAIN HAS BEEN VERY GOOD TO ME--MOSTLY-- AND I WANTED TO GIVE SOMETHING BACK.
I AM WELL AWARE OF THE SCOPE OF THE NATIONAL DEBT, AND I THOUGHT THIS MIGHT HELP TO TAKE CARE OF IT.
I THOUGHT I'D SAY IT WITH DIAMONDS!
LOOK AT THAT!
THAT OUGHT TO TAKE CARE OF A FEW HUNDRED BILLION!
WELL DONE!
THAT'S WONDERFUL, SUPERMAN, BUT WHERE ON EARTH DID YOU FIND ALL OF THESE?
ACTUALLY, I MADE THEM.
I SQUEEZED LUMPS OF COAL WITH THOUSANDS OF POUNDS OF PRESSURE-- AND TURNED THEM ALL INTO DIAMONDS.

OF COURSE, MOTHER NATURE TAKES *MILLIONS* OF YEARS. MY WAY JUST TOOK A COUPLE OF *HOURS.*

NOW, IF YOU'LL EXCUSE ME, I'LL DELIVER THESE TO THE TREASURY.

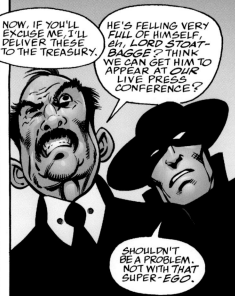

HE'S FELLING VERY *FULL* OF HIMSELF, EH, *LORD STOAT-BAGGE?* THINK WE CAN GET HIM TO APPEAR AT *OUR* LIVE PRESS CONFERENCE?

SHOULDN'T BE A PROBLEM. NOT WITH THAT *SUPER-EGO.*

ONE LIVE PRESS CONFERENCE LATER...

EXCUSE ME, LADIES AND GENTLEMEN, WE'LL BEGIN AS SOON AS *SUPERMAN* ARRIVES.

WHY DON'T YOU GET UP CLOSER TO THE FRONT, *JIMMY?* I'LL STAY BACK A BIT...

GOOD IDEA, COL... I WON'T MISS A *THING!*

WELCOME, SUPER-MAN...

SORRY... I'M RUNNING LATE. IT'S GETTING *HARDER* TO FLY WITH ALL THESE *MEDALS* I'M AFRAID.

MAY I PRESENT TO YOU LORD BARTHOLOMEW STOAT-BAGGE?

I *THINK* I MET HIS LORDSHIP AT THE HOUSE OF COMMONS, WHEN I WIPED OUT THE NATIONAL DEBT. HE *DOES* SEEM FAMILIAR.

YES, SUPER-MAN, THAT WAS A NICE *ATTEMPT,* ANYWAY.

I BEG YOUR PARDON?

YOU SAY YOU *ACTUALLY MADE* ALL OF THOSE DIAMONDS *YOURSELF?*

THAT'S RIGHT. I DUG UP EVERY LUMP OF COAL IN THE BRITISH ISLES TO CON-VERT INTO SHINY DIAMONDS.

JUST A MATTER OF PROCESSING GRAPH-ITE INTO ANOTHER FORM OF CARBON. I ALWAYS HAD A *KNACK* FOR CHEMISTRY.

DID YOU HAVE MUCH GRASP OF *BASIC ECONOMIC THEORY,* THEN?

ECONOMIC THEORY?

LET ME EXPLAIN THIS *VERY* SIMPLY.

DIAMONDS ARE OF GREAT VALUE ONLY BECAUSE OF THEIR *SCARCITY.* DO YOU FOLLOW ME?

UH-OH.

BECAUSE YOU HAVE CREATED LITERALLY *TONS* OF DIAMONDS, THEY HAVE NOW BECOME DEVALUED--

--SO THAT A LUMP OF COAL IS NOW WORTH *MORE* THAN A DIAMOND. OF COURSE, A LUMP OF COAL CAN STILL BE USED FOR FUEL--

--WHICH IS *MORE* THAN A DIAMOND CAN DO!

HMMM--I'M AFRAID I CAN'T UN-SQUEEZE THEM...

"ALL ACROSS BRITAIN, POOR FAMILIES ARE STRUGGLING TO STAY WARM WITH *NO COAL*..."

"...AND THE COAL MINERS ARE OUT OF JOBS -- THEIR FAMILIES... *DESTITUTE!*"

CLOSED FOREVER

HMMM... HERE'S A THOUGHT...

SUPPOSE I FLY OFF INTO OUTER SPACE, AND START LOOKING FOR GOLD ON DISTANT PLANETS.

IF I FOUND EACH POOR FAMILY A HUNDRED POUNDS OF GOLD--

YOU JUST DON'T GET IT, DO YOU, SUPERMAN?

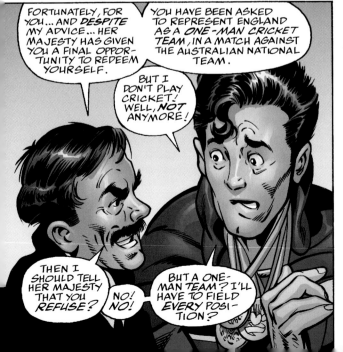

FORTUNATELY, FOR YOU... AND *DESPITE* MY ADVICE... HER MAJESTY HAS GIVEN YOU A FINAL OPPORTUNITY TO REDEEM YOURSELF.

YOU HAVE BEEN ASKED TO REPRESENT ENGLAND AS A *ONE-MAN CRICKET TEAM*, IN A MATCH AGAINST THE AUSTRALIAN NATIONAL TEAM.

BUT I DON'T PLAY CRICKET! WELL, *NOT* ANYMORE!

THEN I SHOULD TELL HER MAJESTY THAT YOU *REFUSE?*

NO! NO!

BUT A ONE-MAN TEAM? I'LL HAVE TO FIELD *EVERY* POSI-TION?

HER MAJESTY FELT YOU COULD EMPLOY WHAT YOU REFER TO AS YOUR , QUOTE-UNQUOTE , *SUPER-SPEED.*

YES...YES OF COURSE...

TELL HER MAJESTY I'LL BE... UM ...ER... DE-LIGHTED.

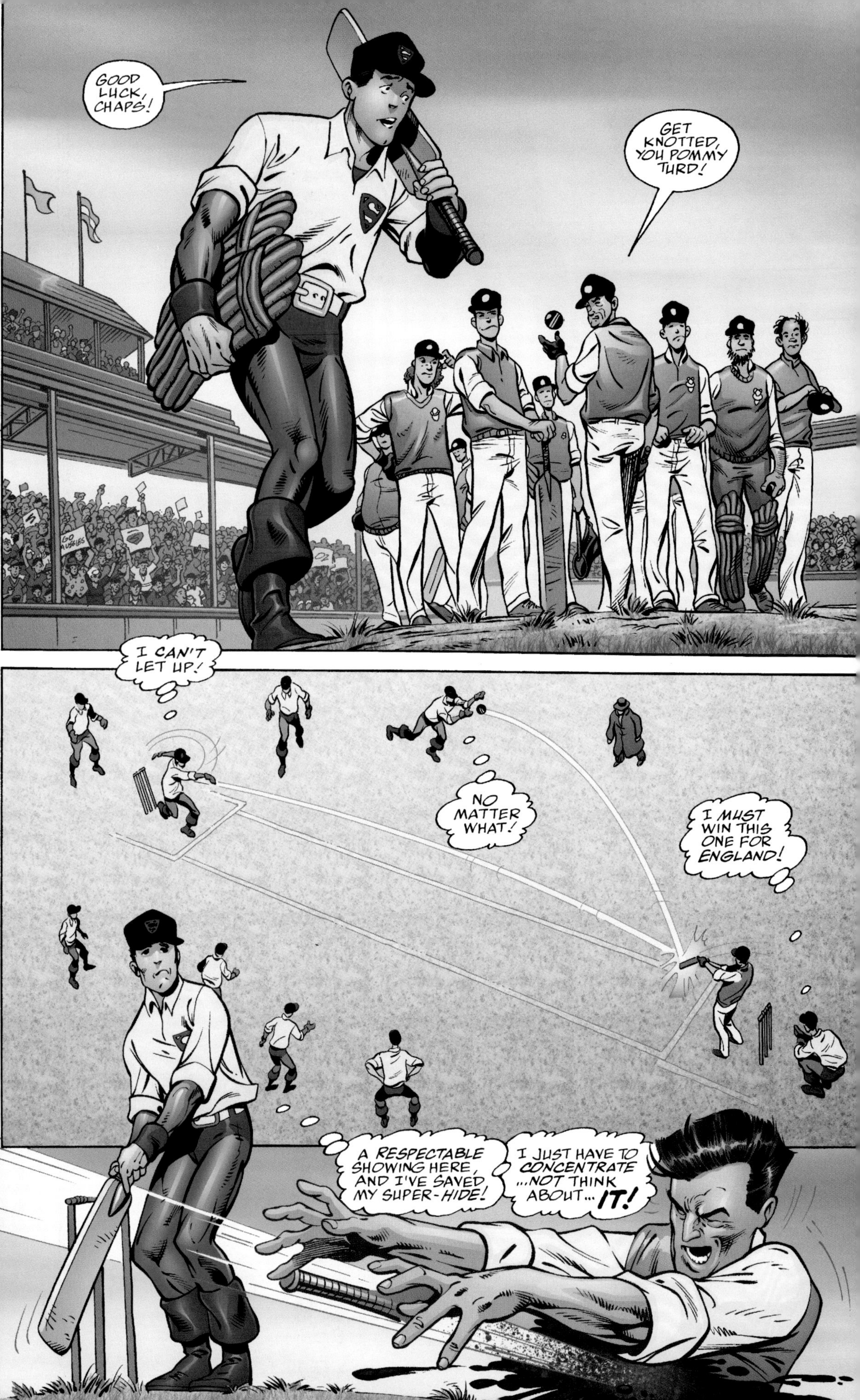
GOOD LUCK, CHAPS!
GET KNOTTED, YOU POMMY TURD!
I CAN'T LET UP!
NO MATTER WHAT!
I MUST WIN THIS ONE FOR ENGLAND!
A RESPECTABLE SHOWING HERE, AND I'VE SAVED MY SUPER-HIDE!
I JUST HAVE TO CONCENTRATE ...NOT THINK ABOUT... IT!

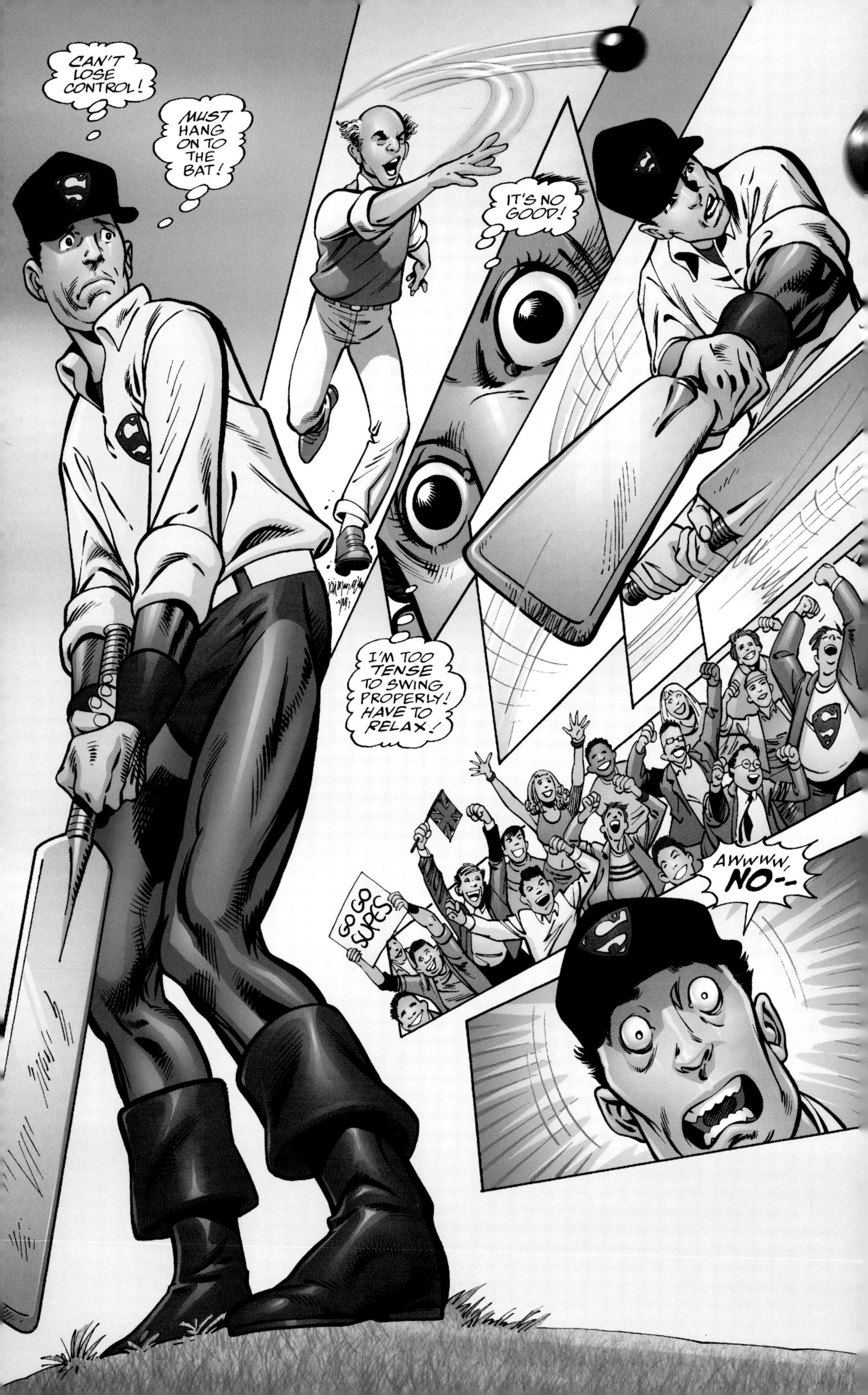
CAN'T LOSE CONTROL!
MUST HANG ON TO THE BAT!
IT'S NO GOOD!
I'M TOO TENSE TO SWING PROPERLY! HAVE TO RELAX!
GO GO SUPES
AWWWW, NO--

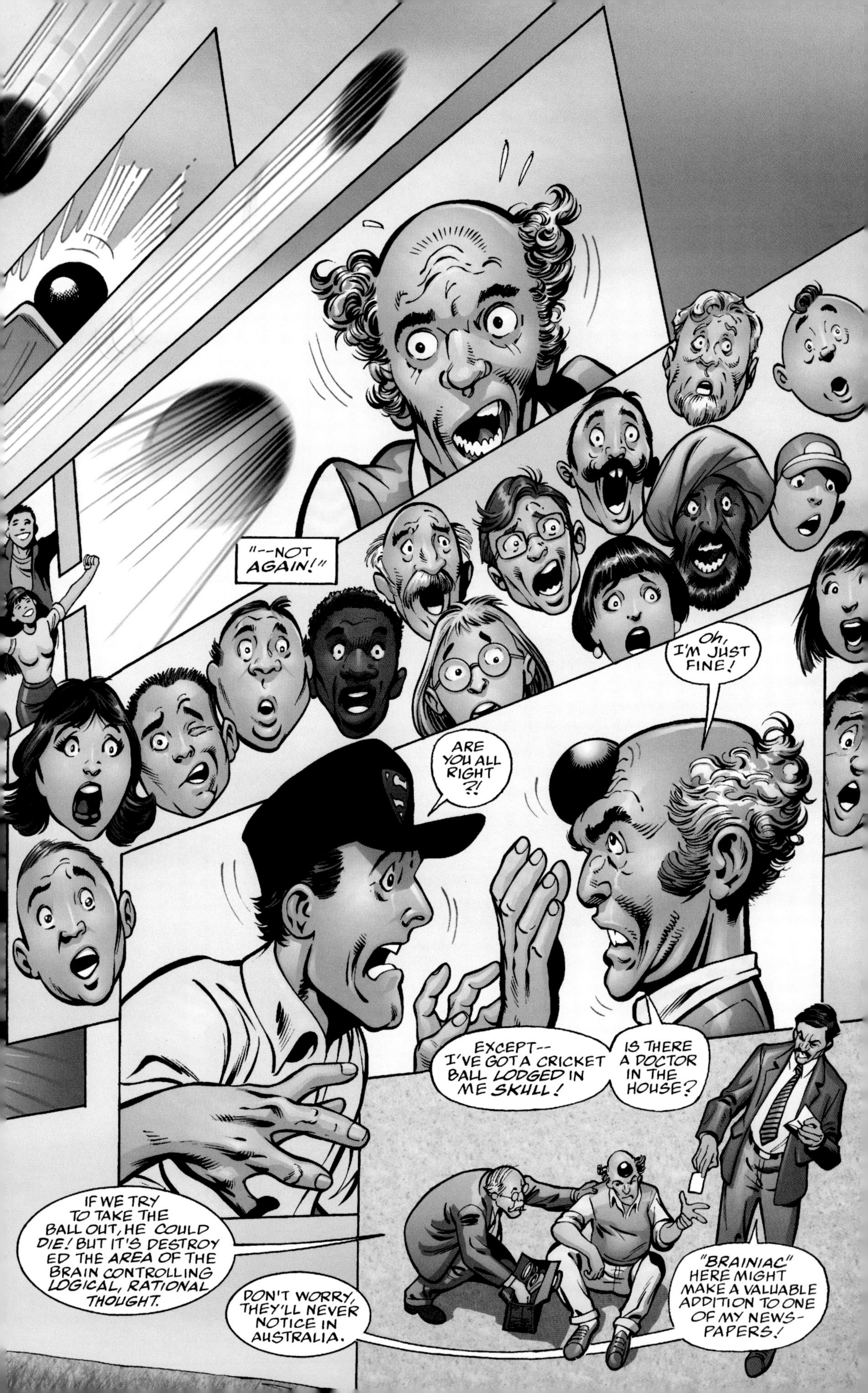
"--NOT AGAIN!"
ARE YOU ALL RIGHT ?!
Oh, I'M JUST FINE!
EXCEPT-- I'VE GOT A CRICKET BALL LODGED IN ME SKULL!
IS THERE A DOCTOR IN THE HOUSE?
IF WE TRY TO TAKE THE BALL OUT, HE COULD DIE! BUT IT'S DESTROYED THE AREA OF THE BRAIN CONTROLLING LOGICAL, RATIONAL THOUGHT.
DON'T WORRY, THEY'LL NEVER NOTICE IN AUSTRALIA.
"BRAINIAC" HERE MIGHT MAKE A VALUABLE ADDITION TO ONE OF MY NEWS-PAPERS!

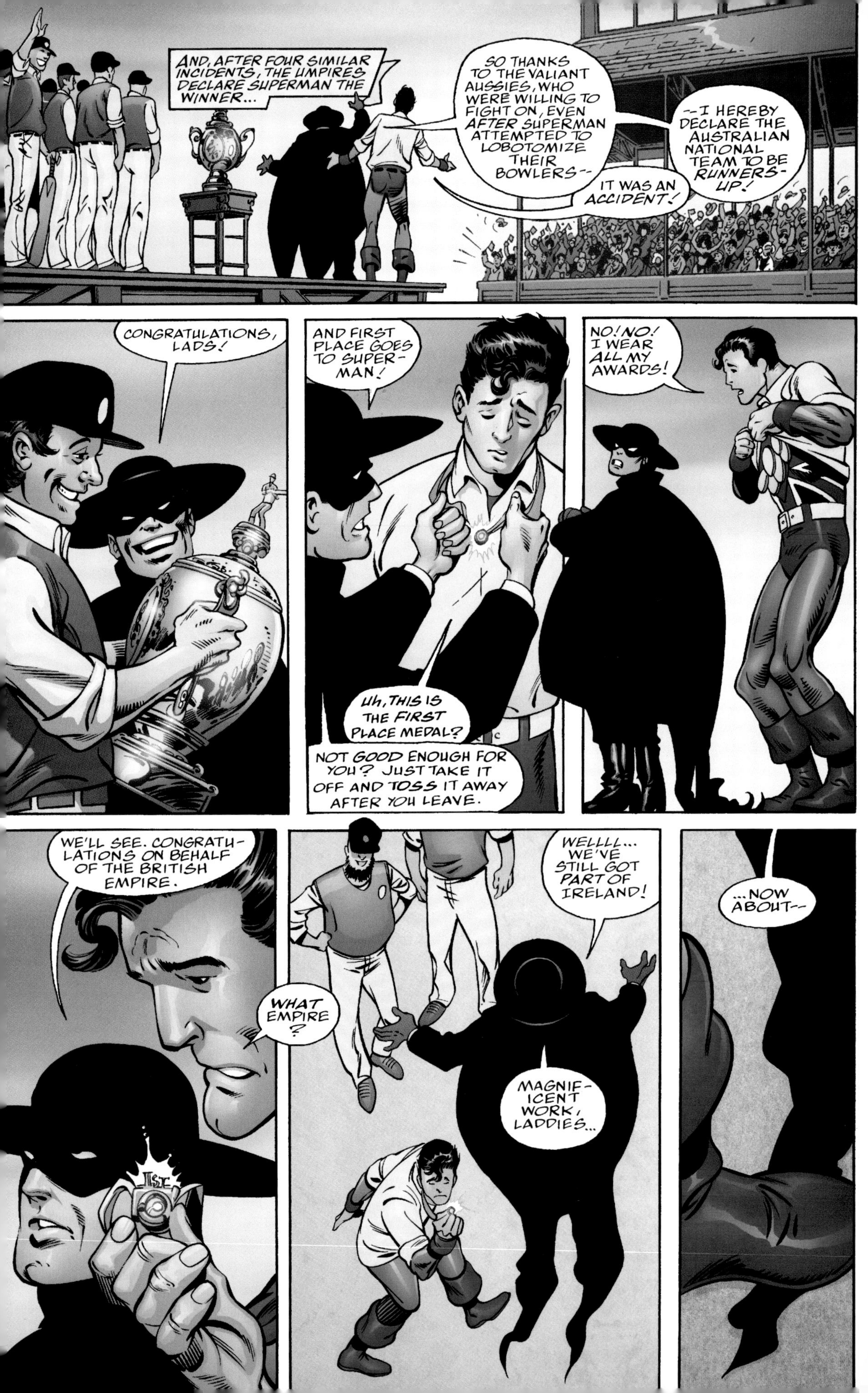
AND, AFTER FOUR SIMILAR INCIDENTS, THE UMPIRES DECLARE SUPERMAN THE WINNER...
SO THANKS TO THE VALIANT AUSSIES, WHO WERE WILLING TO FIGHT ON, EVEN AFTER SUPERMAN ATTEMPTED TO LOBOTOMIZE THEIR BOWLERS--
--I HEREBY DECLARE THE AUSTRALIAN NATIONAL TEAM TO BE RUNNERS-UP!
IT WAS AN ACCIDENT!
CONGRATULATIONS, LADS!
AND FIRST PLACE GOES TO SUPER-MAN!
UH, THIS IS THE FIRST PLACE MEDAL?
NOT GOOD ENOUGH FOR YOU? JUST TAKE IT OFF AND TOSS IT AWAY AFTER YOU LEAVE.
NO! NO! I WEAR ALL MY AWARDS!
WE'LL SEE. CONGRATU-LATIONS ON BEHALF OF THE BRITISH EMPIRE.
1ST
WHAT EMPIRE?
WELLLL... WE'VE STILL GOT PART OF IRELAND!
MAGNIF-ICENT WORK, LADDIES...
...NOW ABOUT--

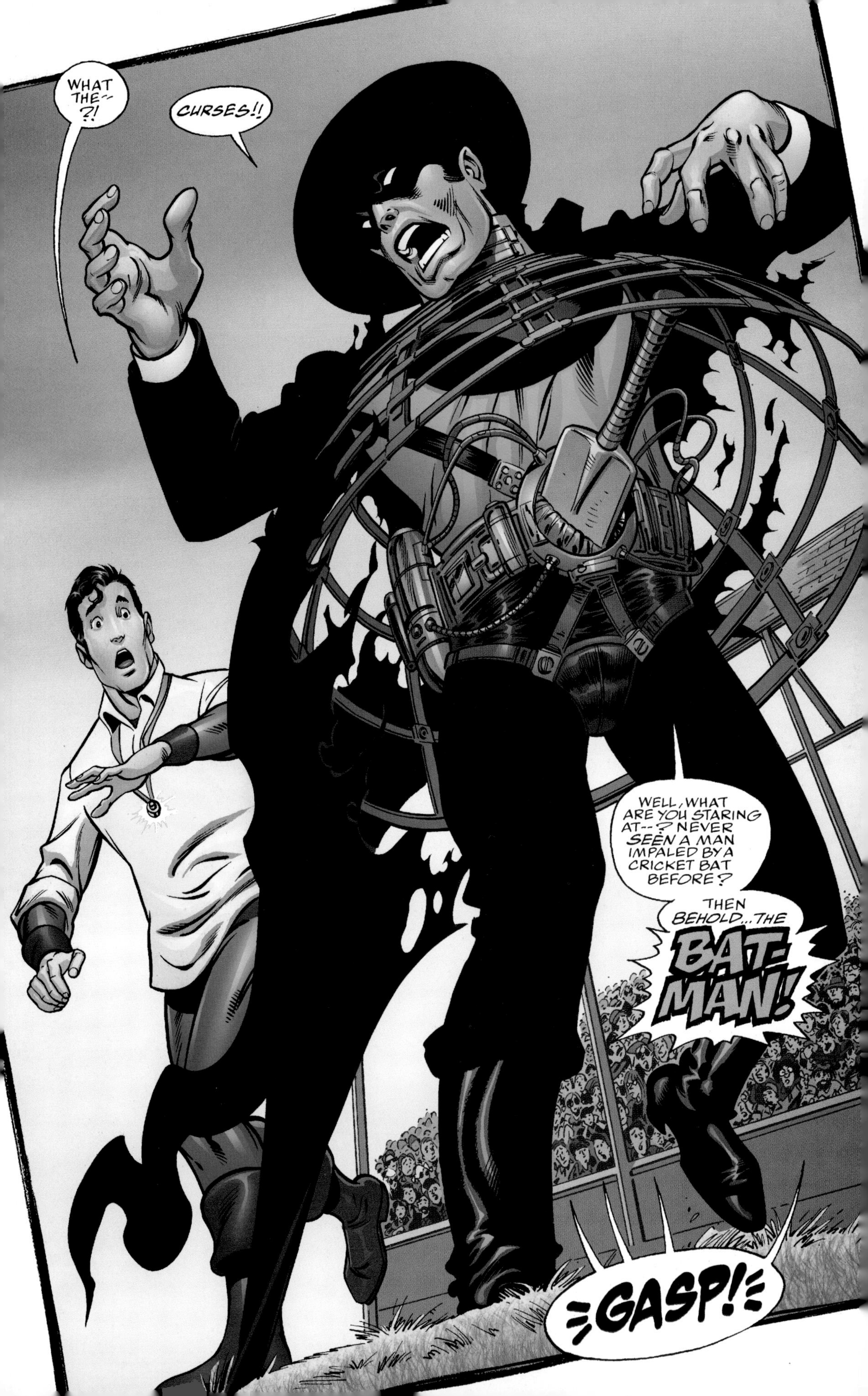
WHAT THE--?!
CURSES!!
WELL, WHAT ARE YOU STARING AT--? NEVER SEEN A MAN IMPALED BY A CRICKET BAT BEFORE?
THEN BEHOLD... THE
BAT-MAN!
GASP!

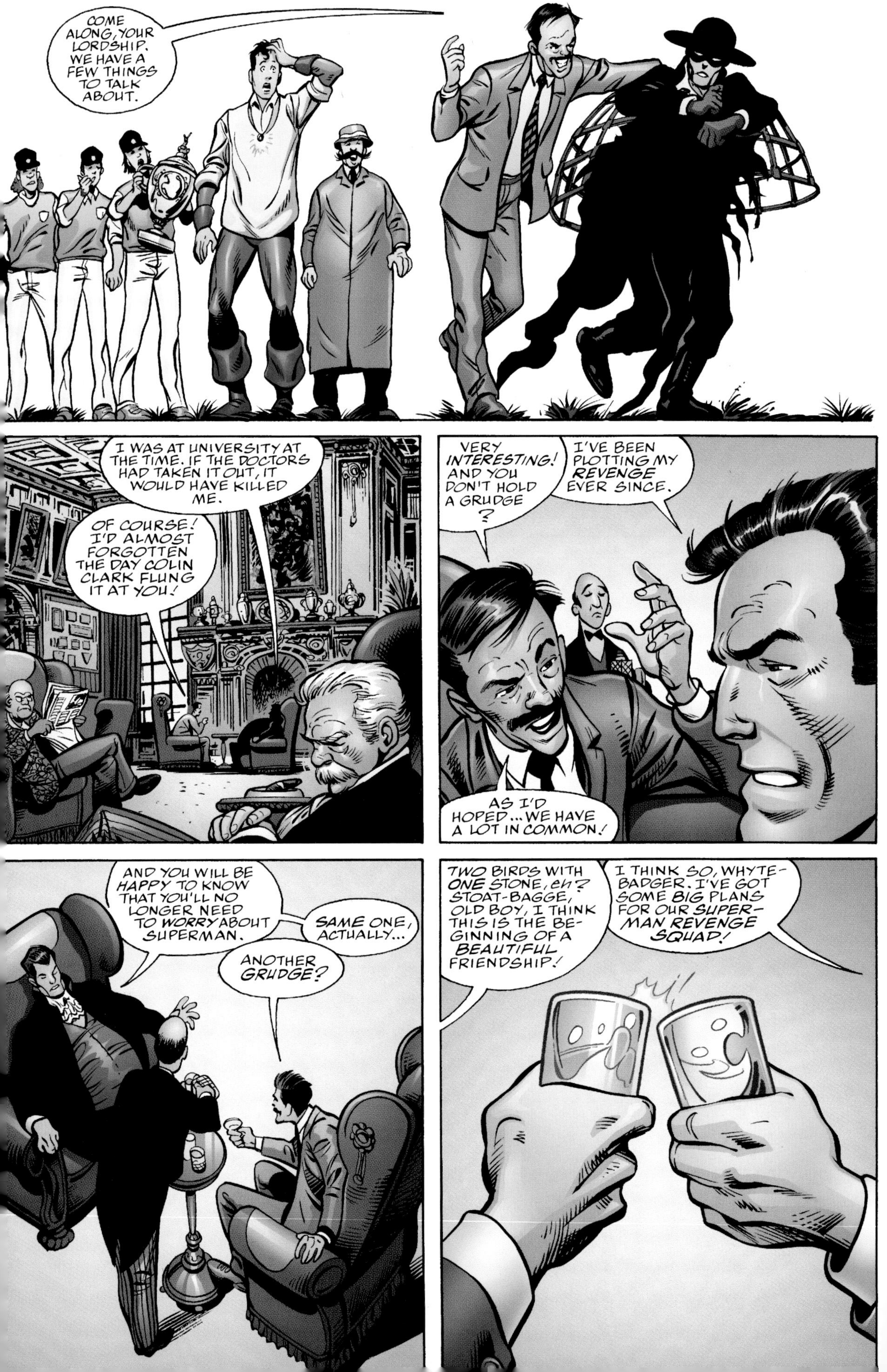
COME ALONG, YOUR LORDSHIP. WE HAVE A FEW THINGS TO TALK ABOUT.
I WAS AT UNIVERSITY AT THE TIME. IF THE DOCTORS HAD TAKEN IT OUT, IT WOULD HAVE KILLED ME.
OF COURSE! I'D ALMOST FORGOTTEN THE DAY COLIN CLARK FLUNG IT AT YOU!
VERY INTERESTING! AND YOU DON'T HOLD A GRUDGE ?
I'VE BEEN PLOTTING MY REVENGE EVER SINCE.
AS I'D HOPED... WE HAVE A LOT IN COMMON!
AND YOU WILL BE HAPPY TO KNOW THAT YOU'LL NO LONGER NEED TO WORRY ABOUT SUPERMAN.
ANOTHER GRUDGE?
SAME ONE, ACTUALLY...
TWO BIRDS WITH ONE STONE, eh? STOAT-BAGGE, OLD BOY, I THINK THIS IS THE BEGINNING OF A BEAUTIFUL FRIENDSHIP!
I THINK SO, WHYTE-BADGER. I'VE GOT SOME BIG PLANS FOR OUR SUPERMAN REVENGE SQUAD!

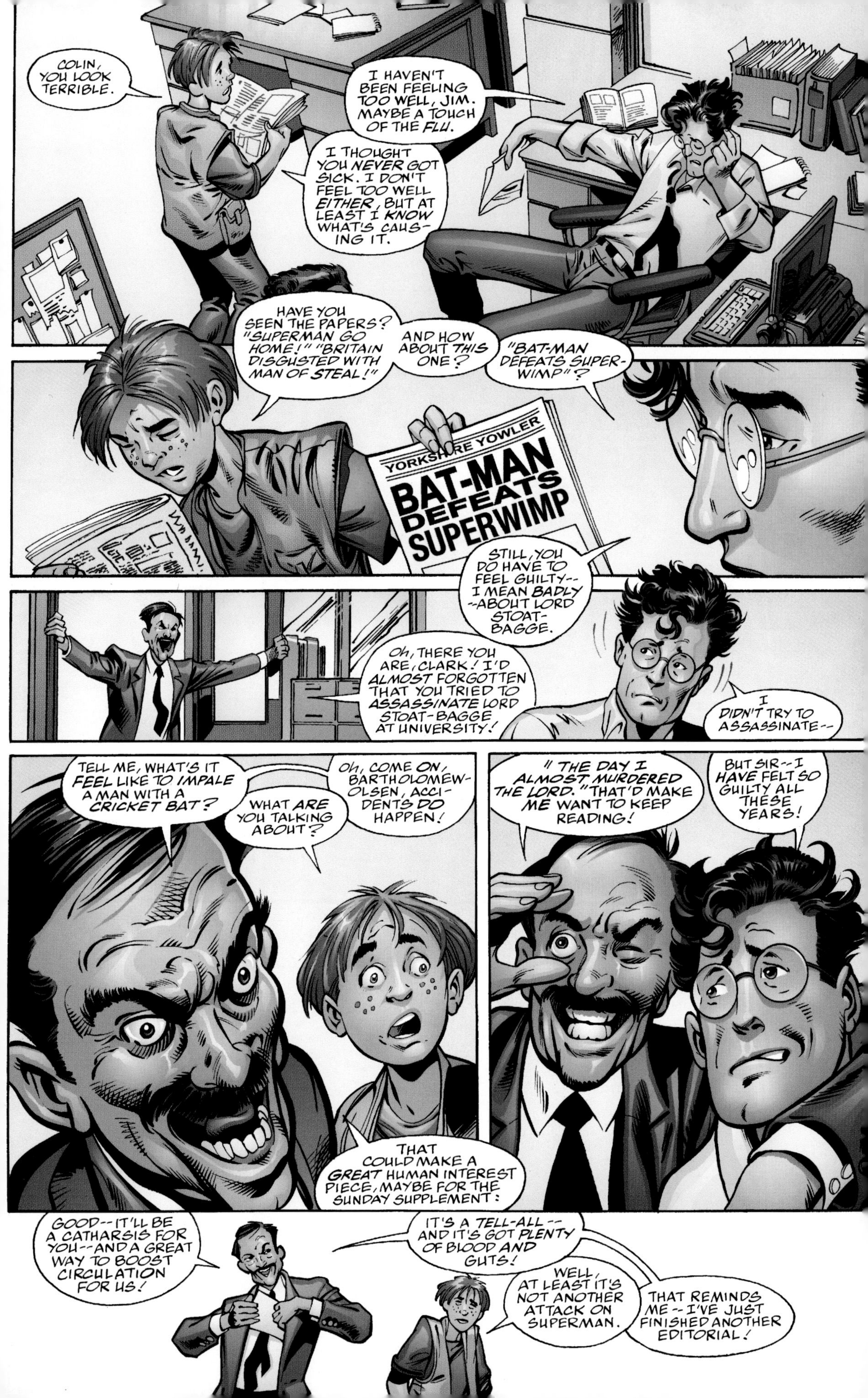
COLIN, YOU LOOK TERRIBLE.
I HAVEN'T BEEN FEELING TOO WELL, JIM. MAYBE A TOUCH OF THE FLU.
I THOUGHT YOU NEVER GOT SICK. I DON'T FEEL TOO WELL EITHER, BUT AT LEAST I KNOW WHAT'S CAUSING IT.
HAVE YOU SEEN THE PAPERS? "SUPERMAN GO HOME!" "BRITAIN DISGUSTED WITH MAN OF STEAL!"
AND HOW ABOUT THIS ONE?
"BAT-MAN DEFEATS SUPER-WIMP"?
YORKSHIRE YOWLER
BAT-MAN DEFEATS SUPERWIMP
STILL, YOU DO HAVE TO FEEL GUILTY-- I MEAN BADLY --ABOUT LORD STOAT-BAGGE.
Oh, THERE YOU ARE, CLARK! I'D ALMOST FORGOTTEN THAT YOU TRIED TO ASSASSINATE LORD STOAT-BAGGE AT UNIVERSITY!
I DIDN'T TRY TO ASSASSINATE--
TELL ME, WHAT'S IT FEEL LIKE TO IMPALE A MAN WITH A CRICKET BAT?
WHAT ARE YOU TALKING ABOUT?
Oh, COME ON, BARTHOLOMEW-OLSEN, ACCIDENTS DO HAPPEN!
THAT COULD MAKE A GREAT HUMAN INTEREST PIECE, MAYBE FOR THE SUNDAY SUPPLEMENT:
" THE DAY I ALMOST MURDERED THE LORD." THAT'D MAKE ME WANT TO KEEP READING!
BUT SIR-- I HAVE FELT SO GUILTY ALL THESE YEARS!
GOOD--IT'LL BE A CATHARSIS FOR YOU--AND A GREAT WAY TO BOOST CIRCULATION FOR US!
IT'S A TELL-ALL-- AND IT'S GOT PLENTY OF BLOOD AND GUTS!
WELL, AT LEAST IT'S NOT ANOTHER ATTACK ON SUPERMAN.
THAT REMINDS ME-- I'VE JUST FINISHED ANOTHER EDITORIAL!

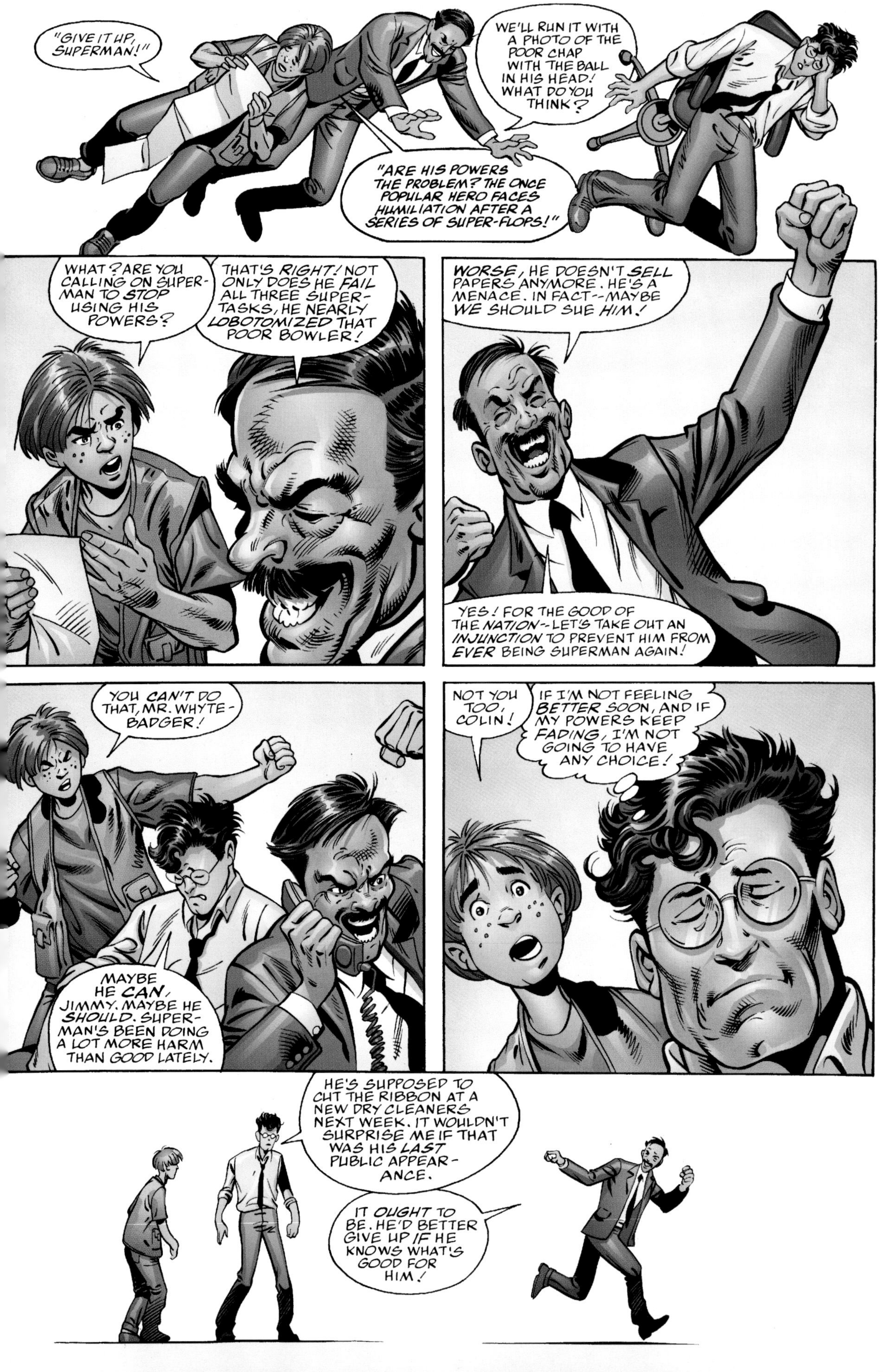
"GIVE IT UP, SUPERMAN!"
WE'LL RUN IT WITH A PHOTO OF THE POOR CHAP WITH THE BALL IN HIS HEAD! WHAT DO YOU THINK?
"ARE HIS POWERS THE PROBLEM? THE ONCE POPULAR HERO FACES HUMILIATION AFTER A SERIES OF SUPER-FLOPS!"
WHAT? ARE YOU CALLING ON SUPERMAN TO STOP USING HIS POWERS?
THAT'S RIGHT! NOT ONLY DOES HE FAIL ALL THREE SUPER-TASKS, HE NEARLY LOBOTOMIZED THAT POOR BOWLER!
WORSE, HE DOESN'T SELL PAPERS ANYMORE. HE'S A MENACE. IN FACT--MAYBE WE SHOULD SUE HIM!
YES! FOR THE GOOD OF THE NATION--LET'S TAKE OUT AN INJUNCTION TO PREVENT HIM FROM EVER BEING SUPERMAN AGAIN!
YOU CAN'T DO THAT, MR. WHYTE-BADGER!
MAYBE HE CAN, JIMMY. MAYBE HE SHOULD. SUPERMAN'S BEEN DOING A LOT MORE HARM THAN GOOD LATELY.
NOT YOU TOO, COLIN!
IF I'M NOT FEELING BETTER SOON, AND IF MY POWERS KEEP FADING, I'M NOT GOING TO HAVE ANY CHOICE!
HE'S SUPPOSED TO CUT THE RIBBON AT A NEW DRY CLEANERS NEXT WEEK. IT WOULDN'T SURPRISE ME IF THAT WAS HIS LAST PUBLIC APPEARANCE.
IT OUGHT TO BE. HE'D BETTER GIVE UP IF HE KNOWS WHAT'S GOOD FOR HIM!

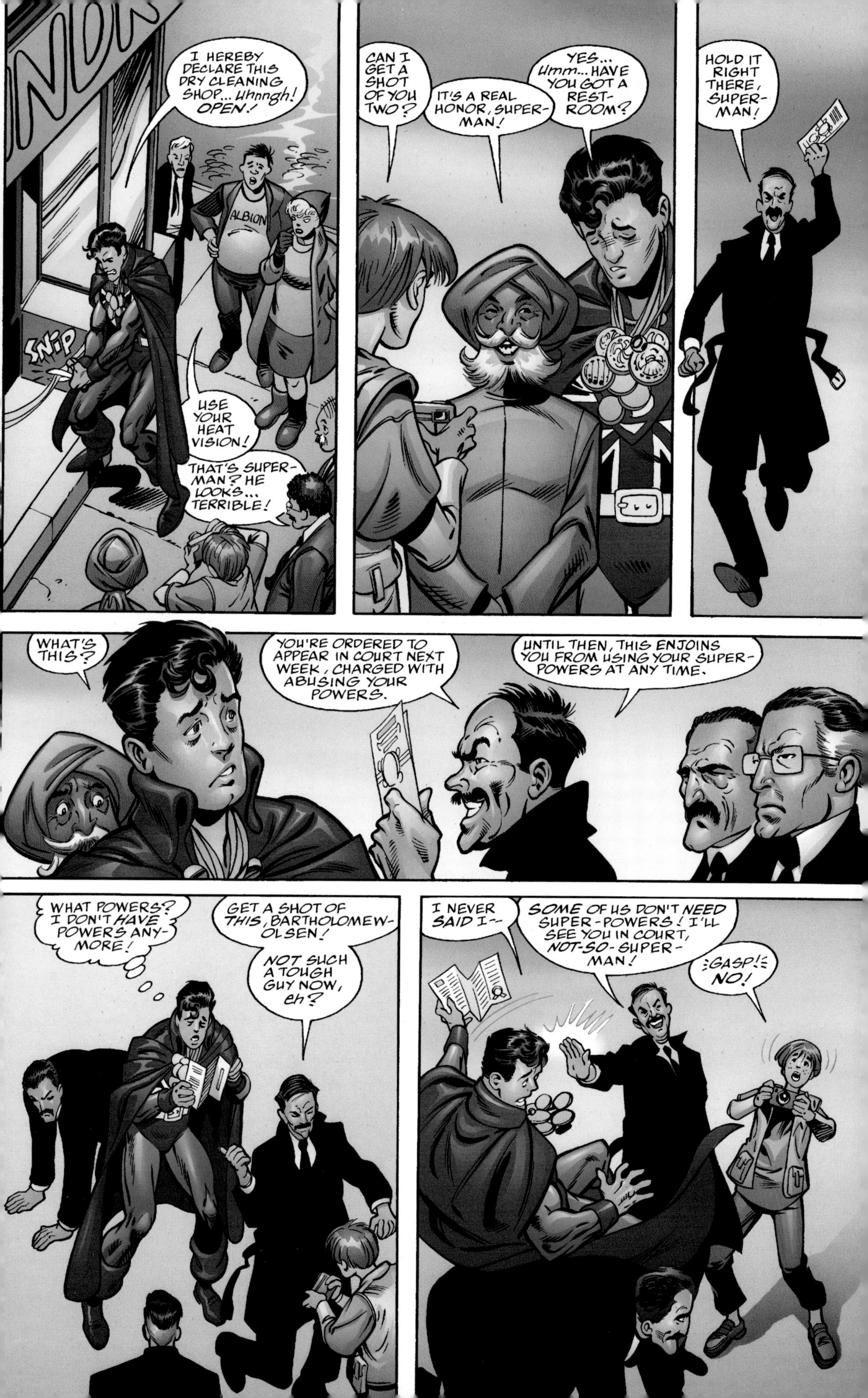

I HEREBY DECLARE THIS DRY CLEANING SHOP... Uhnngh! OPEN!
ALBION
SNIP
USE YOUR HEAT VISION!
THAT'S SUPERMAN? HE LOOKS... TERRIBLE!
CAN I GET A SHOT OF YOU TWO?
IT'S A REAL HONOR, SUPERMAN!
YES... Umm... HAVE YOU GOT A RESTROOM?
HOLD IT RIGHT THERE, SUPERMAN!
WHAT'S THIS?
YOU'RE ORDERED TO APPEAR IN COURT NEXT WEEK, CHARGED WITH ABUSING YOUR POWERS.
UNTIL THEN, THIS ENJOINS YOU FROM USING YOUR SUPERPOWERS AT ANY TIME.
WHAT POWERS? I DON'T HAVE POWERS ANYMORE!
GET A SHOT OF THIS, BARTHOLOMEW OLSEN!
NOT SUCH A TOUGH GUY NOW, eh?
I NEVER SAID I--
SOME OF US DON'T NEED SUPER-POWERS! I'LL SEE YOU IN COURT, NOT-SO-SUPERMAN!
GASP! NO!

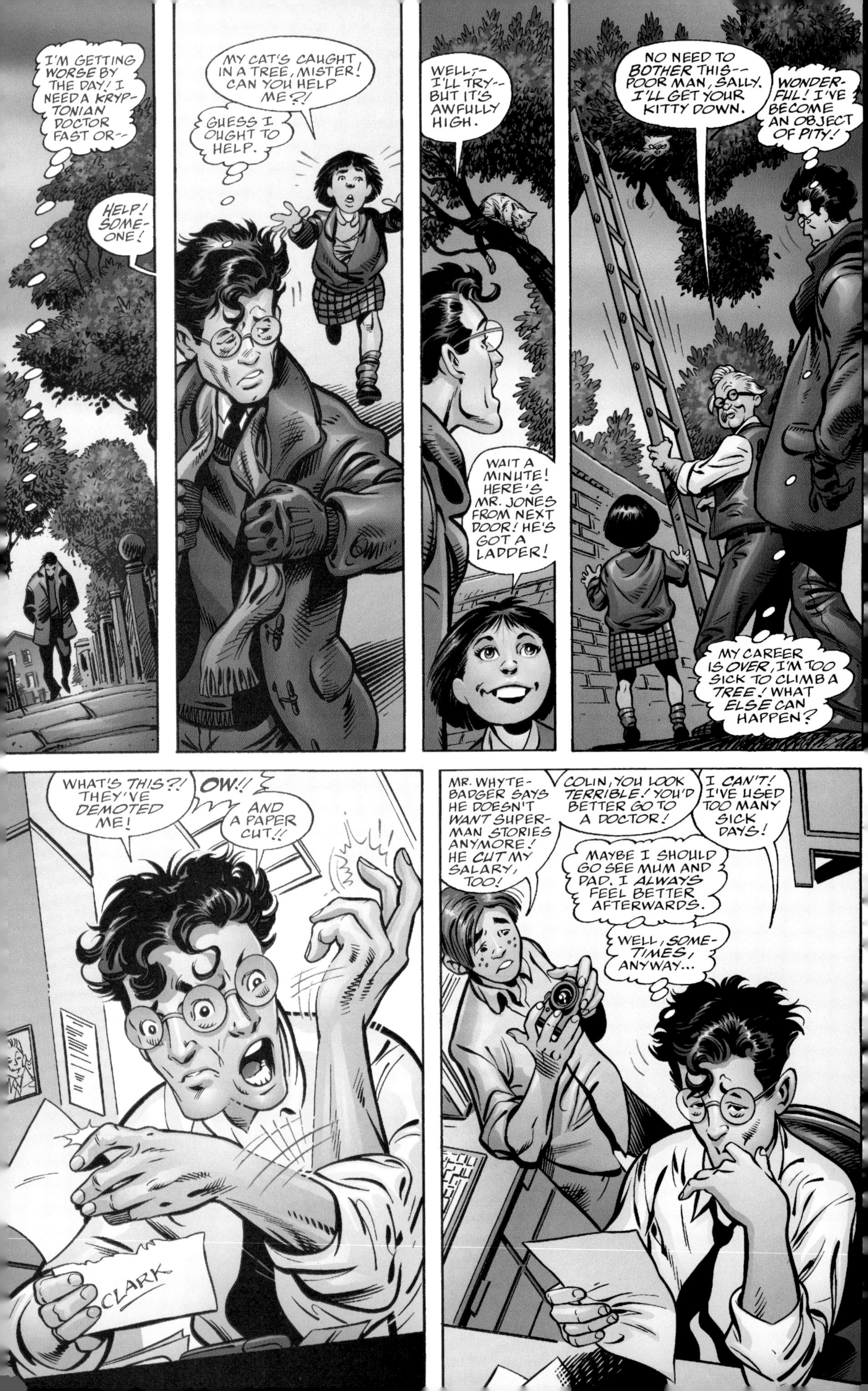

I'M GETTING WORSE BY THE DAY! I NEED A KRYPTONIAN DOCTOR FAST OR--
HELP! SOMEONE!
MY CAT'S CAUGHT IN A TREE, MISTER! CAN YOU HELP ME?!
GUESS I OUGHT TO HELP.
WELL,-- I'LL TRY-- BUT IT'S AWFULLY HIGH.
WAIT A MINUTE! HERE'S MR. JONES FROM NEXT DOOR! HE'S GOT A LADDER!
NO NEED TO BOTHER THIS-- POOR MAN, SALLY. I'LL GET YOUR KITTY DOWN.
WONDERFUL! I'VE BECOME AN OBJECT OF PITY!
MY CAREER IS OVER, I'M TOO SICK TO CLIMB A TREE! WHAT ELSE CAN HAPPEN?
WHAT'S THIS?! THEY'VE DEMOTED ME!
OW!!
AND A PAPER CUT!!
CLARK
MR. WHYTE-BADGER SAYS HE DOESN'T WANT SUPERMAN STORIES ANYMORE! HE CUT MY SALARY, TOO!
COLIN, YOU LOOK TERRIBLE! YOU'D BETTER GO TO A DOCTOR!
I CAN'T! I'VE USED TOO MANY SICK DAYS!
MAYBE I SHOULD GO SEE MUM AND DAD. I ALWAYS FEEL BETTER AFTERWARDS.
WELL, SOMETIMES, ANYWAY...

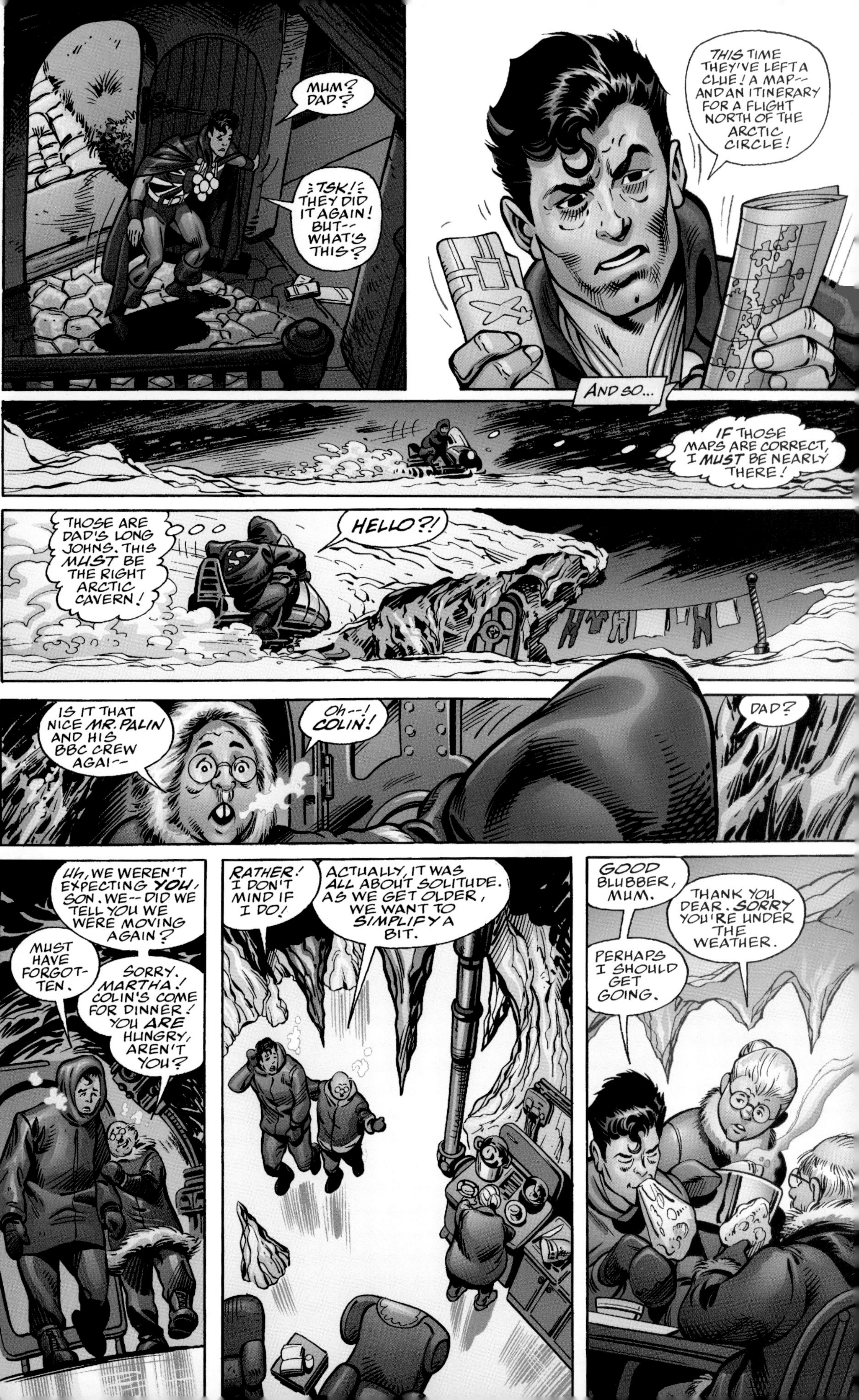
MUM? DAD?
TSK! THEY DID IT AGAIN! BUT-- WHAT'S THIS?
THIS TIME THEY'VE LEFT A CLUE! A MAP-- AND AN ITINERARY FOR A FLIGHT NORTH OF THE ARCTIC CIRCLE!
AND SO...
IF THOSE MAPS ARE CORRECT, I MUST BE NEARLY THERE!
THOSE ARE DAD'S LONG JOHNS. THIS MUST BE THE RIGHT ARCTIC CAVERN!
HELLO?!
IS IT THAT NICE MR. PALIN AND HIS BBC CREW AGAI--
Oh--! COLIN!
DAD?
Uh, WE WEREN'T EXPECTING YOU, SON. WE-- DID WE TELL YOU WE WERE MOVING AGAIN?
MUST HAVE FORGOT-TEN.
SORRY. MARTHA! COLIN'S COME FOR DINNER! YOU ARE HUNGRY, AREN'T YOU?
RATHER! I DON'T MIND IF I DO!
ACTUALLY, IT WAS ALL ABOUT SOLITUDE. AS WE GET OLDER, WE WANT TO SIMPLIFY A BIT.
GOOD BLUBBER, MUM.
THANK YOU DEAR. SORRY YOU'RE UNDER THE WEATHER.
PERHAPS I SHOULD GET GOING.

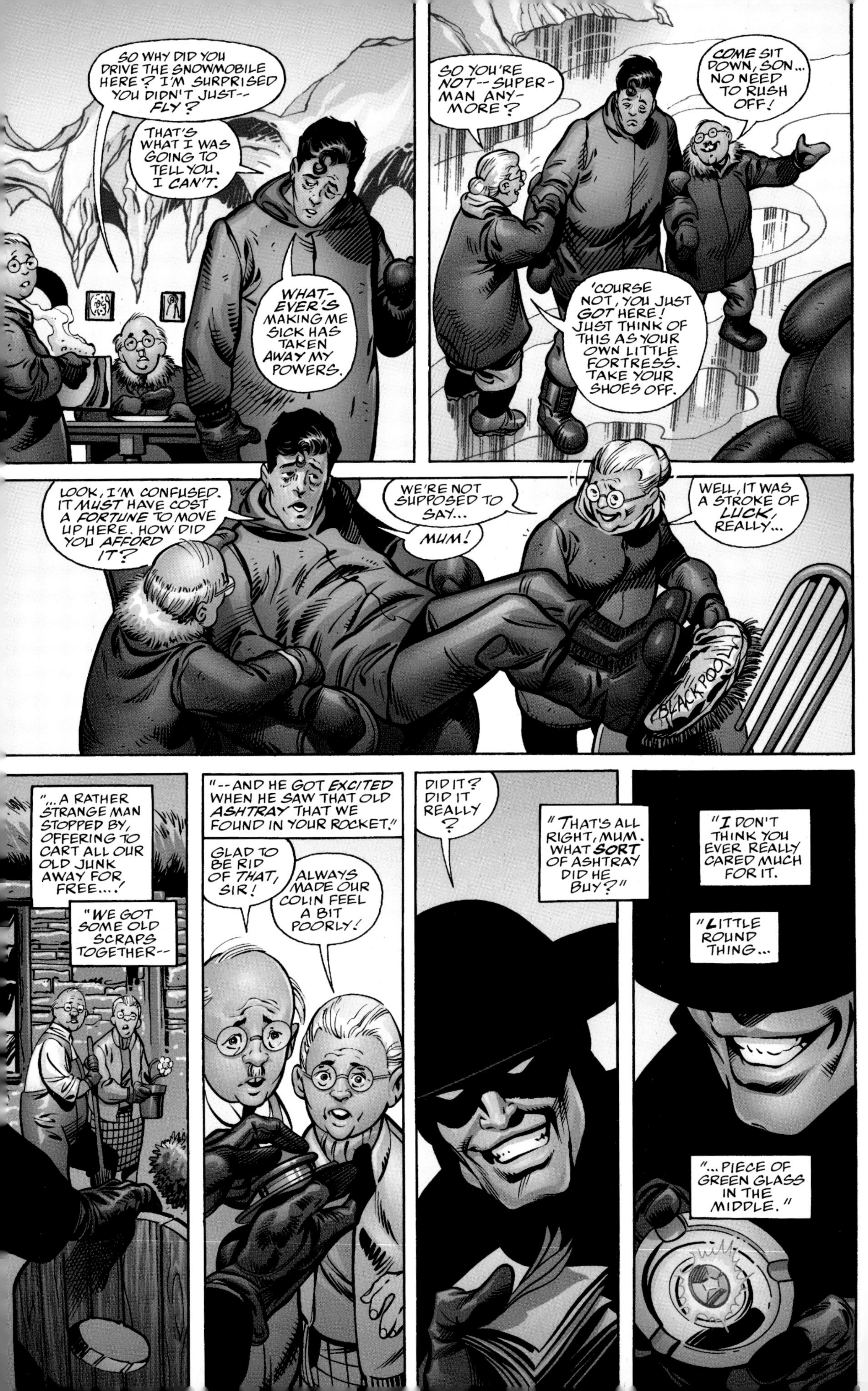

SO WHY DID YOU DRIVE THE SNOWMOBILE HERE? I'M SURPRISED YOU DIDN'T JUST--FLY?
THAT'S WHAT I WAS GOING TO TELL YOU. I CAN'T.
WHAT-EVER'S MAKING ME SICK HAS TAKEN AWAY MY POWERS.
SO YOU'RE NOT--SUPER-MAN ANY-MORE?
COME SIT DOWN, SON... NO NEED TO RUSH OFF!
'COURSE NOT, YOU JUST GOT HERE! JUST THINK OF THIS AS YOUR OWN LITTLE FORTRESS. TAKE YOUR SHOES OFF.
LOOK, I'M CONFUSED. IT MUST HAVE COST A FORTUNE TO MOVE UP HERE. HOW DID YOU AFFORD IT?
WE'RE NOT SUPPOSED TO SAY...
MUM!
WELL, IT WAS A STROKE OF LUCK, REALLY...
BLACKPOOL
"...A RATHER STRANGE MAN STOPPED BY, OFFERING TO CART ALL OUR OLD JUNK AWAY FOR FREE....'
"WE GOT SOME OLD SCRAPS TOGETHER--
"--AND HE GOT EXCITED WHEN HE SAW THAT OLD ASHTRAY THAT WE FOUND IN YOUR ROCKET."
GLAD TO BE RID OF THAT, SIR!
ALWAYS MADE OUR COLIN FEEL A BIT POORLY!
DID IT? DID IT REALLY?
"THAT'S ALL RIGHT, MUM. WHAT SORT OF ASHTRAY DID HE BUY?"
"I DON'T THINK YOU EVER REALLY CARED MUCH FOR IT.
"LITTLE ROUND THING...
"...PIECE OF GREEN GLASS IN THE MIDDLE."

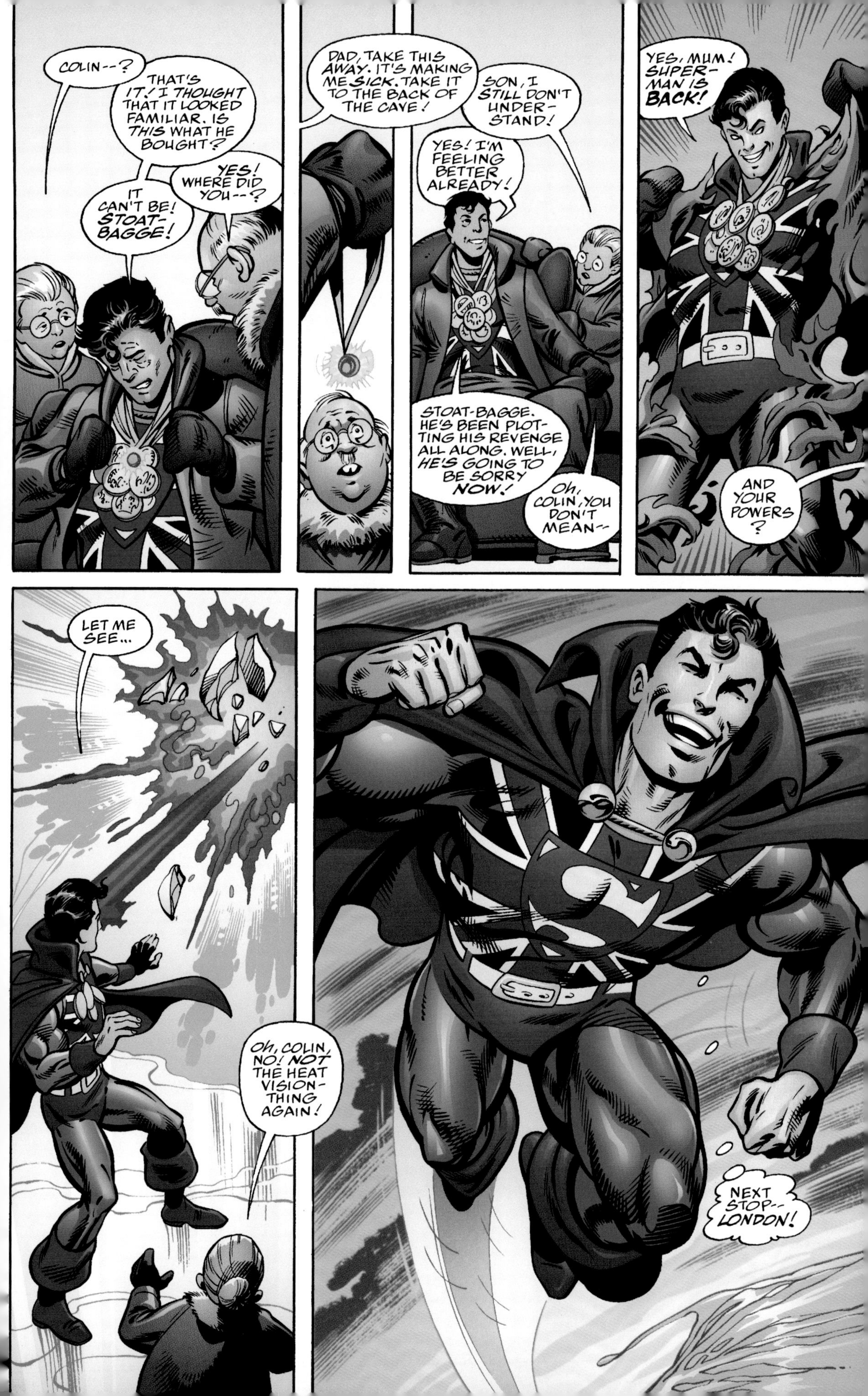
COLIN--?
THAT'S IT! I THOUGHT THAT IT LOOKED FAMILIAR. IS THIS WHAT HE BOUGHT?
YES! WHERE DID YOU--?
IT CAN'T BE! STOAT-BAGGE!
DAD, TAKE THIS AWAY. IT'S MAKING ME SICK. TAKE IT TO THE BACK OF THE CAVE!
SON, I STILL DON'T UNDER-STAND!
YES! I'M FEELING BETTER ALREADY!
STOAT-BAGGE. HE'S BEEN PLOTTING HIS REVENGE ALL ALONG. WELL, HE'S GOING TO BE SORRY NOW!
OH, COLIN, YOU DON'T MEAN--
YES, MUM! SUPER-MAN IS BACK!
AND YOUR POWERS?
LET ME SEE...
OH, COLIN, NO! NOT THE HEAT VISION-THING AGAIN!
NEXT STOP-- LONDON!

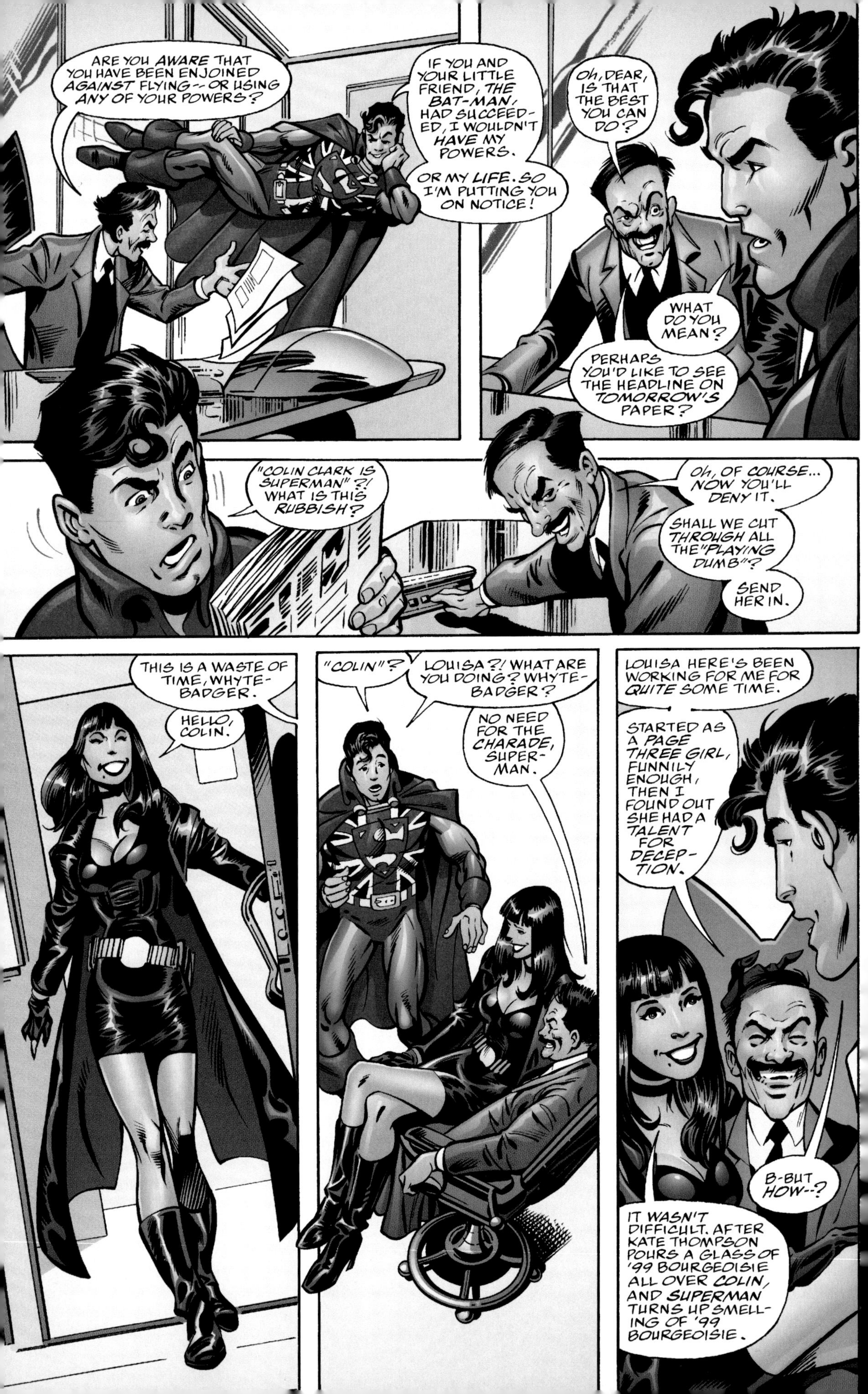

ARE YOU AWARE THAT YOU HAVE BEEN ENJOINED AGAINST FLYING--OR USING ANY OF YOUR POWERS?
IF YOU AND YOUR LITTLE FRIEND, THE BAT-MAN, HAD SUCCEEDED, I WOULDN'T HAVE MY POWERS.
OR MY LIFE. SO I'M PUTTING YOU ON NOTICE!
Oh, DEAR, IS THAT THE BEST YOU CAN DO?
WHAT DO YOU MEAN?
PERHAPS YOU'D LIKE TO SEE THE HEADLINE ON TOMORROW'S PAPER?
"COLIN CLARK IS SUPERMAN"?! WHAT IS THIS RUBBISH?
Oh, OF COURSE... NOW YOU'LL DENY IT.
SHALL WE CUT THROUGH ALL THE "PLAYING DUMB"?
SEND HER IN.
THIS IS A WASTE OF TIME, WHYTE-BADGER.
HELLO, COLIN.
"COLIN"?
LOUISA?! WHAT ARE YOU DOING? WHYTE-BADGER?
NO NEED FOR THE CHARADE, SUPERMAN.
LOUISA HERE'S BEEN WORKING FOR ME FOR QUITE SOME TIME.
STARTED AS A PAGE THREE GIRL, FUNNILY ENOUGH, THEN I FOUND OUT SHE HAD A TALENT FOR DECEPTION.
B-BUT HOW--?
IT WASN'T DIFFICULT. AFTER KATE THOMPSON POURS A GLASS OF '99 BOURGEOISIE ALL OVER COLIN, AND SUPERMAN TURNS UP SMELLING OF '99 BOURGEOISIE.

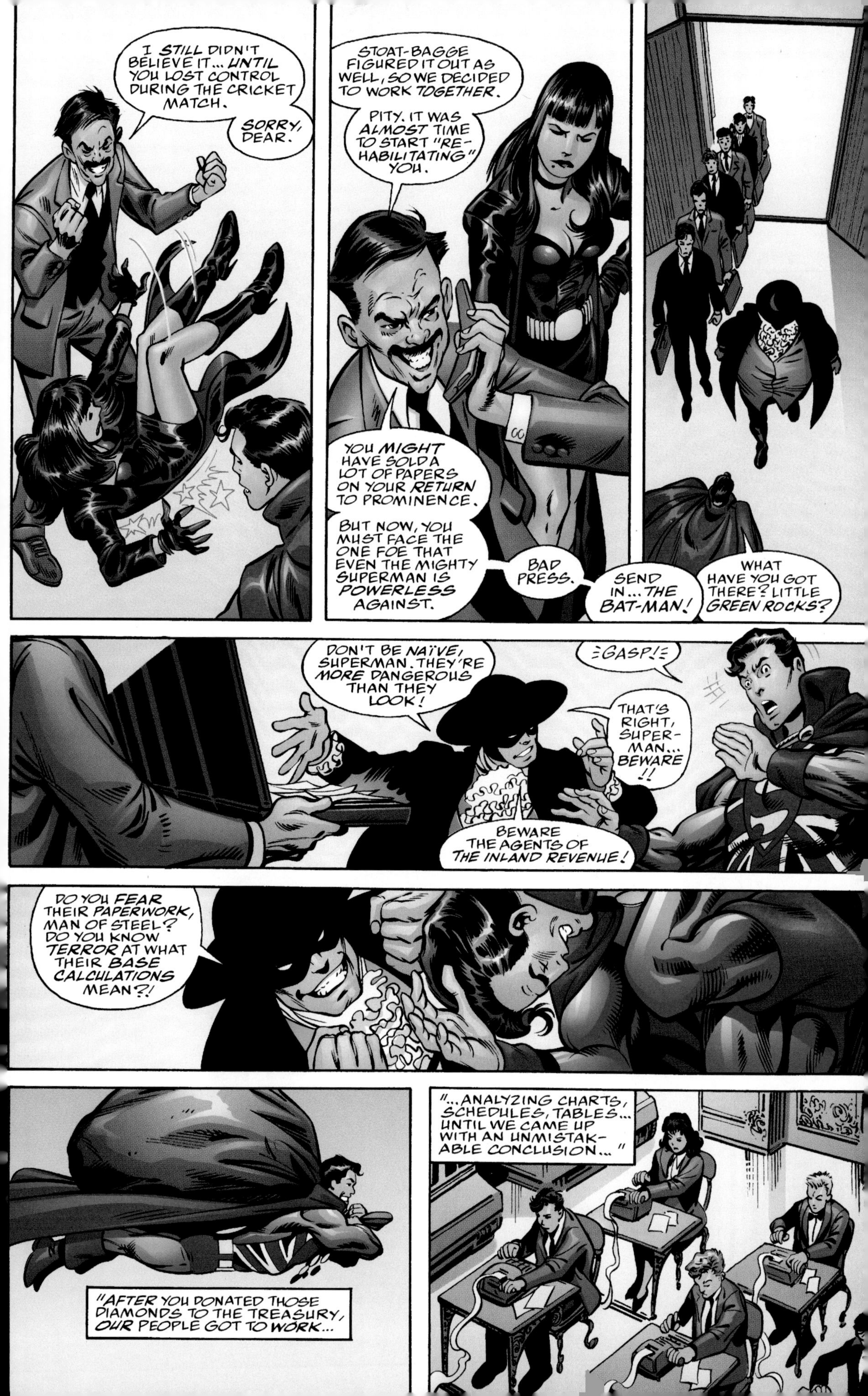

I STILL DIDN'T BELIEVE IT... UNTIL YOU LOST CONTROL DURING THE CRICKET MATCH.
SORRY, DEAR.
STOAT-BAGGE FIGURED IT OUT AS WELL, SO WE DECIDED TO WORK TOGETHER.
PITY. IT WAS ALMOST TIME TO START "RE-HABILITATING" YOU.
YOU MIGHT HAVE SOLD A LOT OF PAPERS ON YOUR RETURN TO PROMINENCE.
BUT NOW, YOU MUST FACE THE ONE FOE THAT EVEN THE MIGHTY SUPERMAN IS POWERLESS AGAINST.
BAD PRESS.
SEND IN... THE BAT-MAN!
WHAT HAVE YOU GOT THERE? LITTLE GREEN ROCKS?
DON'T BE NAÏVE, SUPERMAN. THEY'RE MORE DANGEROUS THAN THEY LOOK!
GASP!
THAT'S RIGHT, SUPER-MAN... BEWARE!!
BEWARE THE AGENTS OF THE INLAND REVENUE!
DO YOU FEAR THEIR PAPERWORK, MAN OF STEEL? DO YOU KNOW TERROR AT WHAT THEIR BASE CALCULATIONS MEAN?!
"AFTER YOU DONATED THOSE DIAMONDS TO THE TREASURY, OUR PEOPLE GOT TO WORK...
"...ANALYZING CHARTS, SCHEDULES, TABLES... UNTIL WE CAME UP WITH AN UNMISTAK-ABLE CONCLUSION..."

...YOU MUST PAY TAXES ON THE TOTAL VALUE OF THE DIAMONDS THAT YOU LATER DONATED TO THE GOVERNMENT!

MWOOOOHAHAHA!

THAT'S RIGHT! YOU OWE BILLIONS!

BUT I DON'T HAVE THAT KIND OF MONEY!

HOW SAD.

BUT WEREN'T DIAMONDS DEVALUED!? NOT WHEN THEY CAME INTO YOUR POSSESSION. SECTION 784 PARAGRAPH 767! HA!!

AND IF YOU TRY TO DIG UP GOLD ON THE MOON, OR JEWELS ON JUPITER--

--WE'LL KNOW YOU VIOLATED A COURT ORDER!

TOUGH LUCK, SUPERMAN. LET YOURSELF OUT--THROUGH THE DOOR, PLEASE, NOT THE WINDOW!

SUPERMAN-- COLIN-- I HEARD ABOUT EVERYTHING. WHAT WILL YOU DO?

SORRY, JIMMY. I WISH I COULD HAVE TOLD YOU MYSELF. I'M AFRAID I'M CONTEMPLATING ...

...BANKRUPTCY!

=GASP= SUPERMAN! NO!!

I HAVE NO CHOICE. I CAN'T POSSIBLY COME UP WITH THE MONEY FOR MY TAX BILL.

THE TABLOIDS ARE CALLING FOR ME TO LEAVE BRITAIN FOREVER!

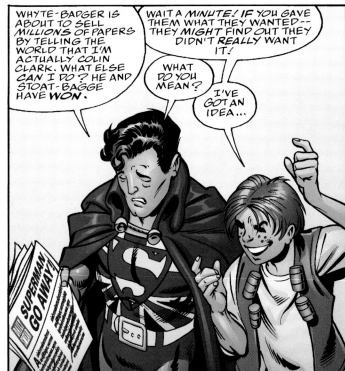

WHYTE-BADGER IS ABOUT TO SELL MILLIONS OF PAPERS BY TELLING THE WORLD THAT I'M ACTUALLY COLIN CLARK. WHAT ELSE CAN I DO? HE AND STOAT-BAGGE HAVE WON.

WAIT A MINUTE! IF YOU GAVE THEM WHAT THEY WANTED-- THEY MIGHT FIND OUT THEY DIDN'T REALLY WANT IT!

WHAT DO YOU MEAN?

I'VE GOT AN IDEA...

SUPERMAN GO AWAY!

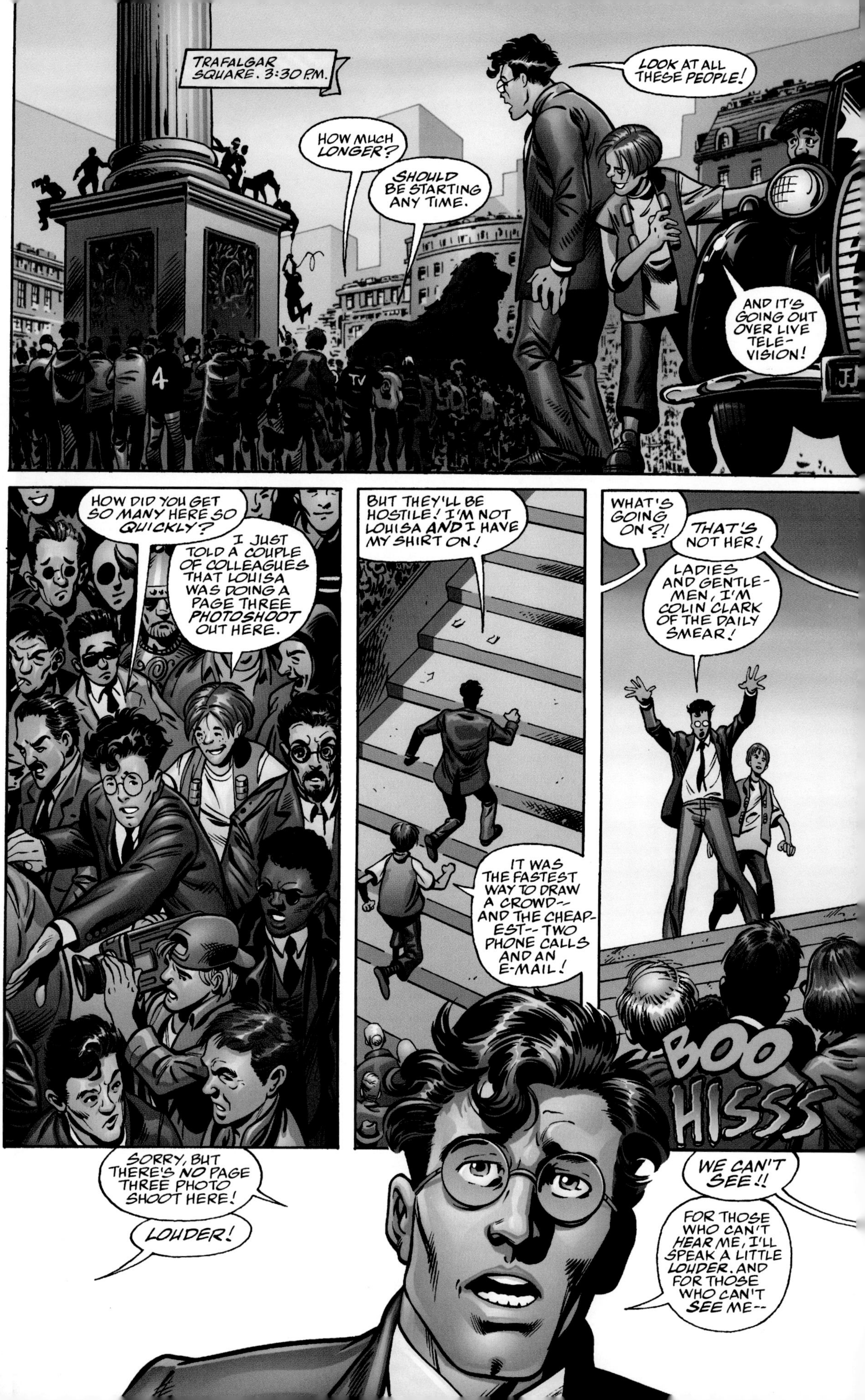
TRAFALGAR SQUARE. 3:30 P.M.
LOOK AT ALL THESE PEOPLE!
HOW MUCH LONGER?
SHOULD BE STARTING ANY TIME.
AND IT'S GOING OUT OVER LIVE TELE-VISION!
4
TV
HOW DID YOU GET SO MANY HERE SO QUICKLY?
I JUST TOLD A COUPLE OF COLLEAGUES THAT LOUISA WAS DOING A PAGE THREE PHOTOSHOOT OUT HERE.
BUT THEY'LL BE HOSTILE! I'M NOT LOUISA AND I HAVE MY SHIRT ON!
IT WAS THE FASTEST WAY TO DRAW A CROWD-- AND THE CHEAP-EST-- TWO PHONE CALLS AND AN E-MAIL!
WHAT'S GOING ON?!
THAT'S NOT HER!
LADIES AND GENTLE-MEN, I'M COLIN CLARK OF THE DAILY SMEAR!
BOO
HISSS
SORRY, BUT THERE'S NO PAGE THREE PHOTO SHOOT HERE!
LOUDER!
WE CAN'T SEE!!
FOR THOSE WHO CAN'T HEAR ME, I'LL SPEAK A LITTLE LOUDER. AND FOR THOSE WHO CAN'T SEE ME--

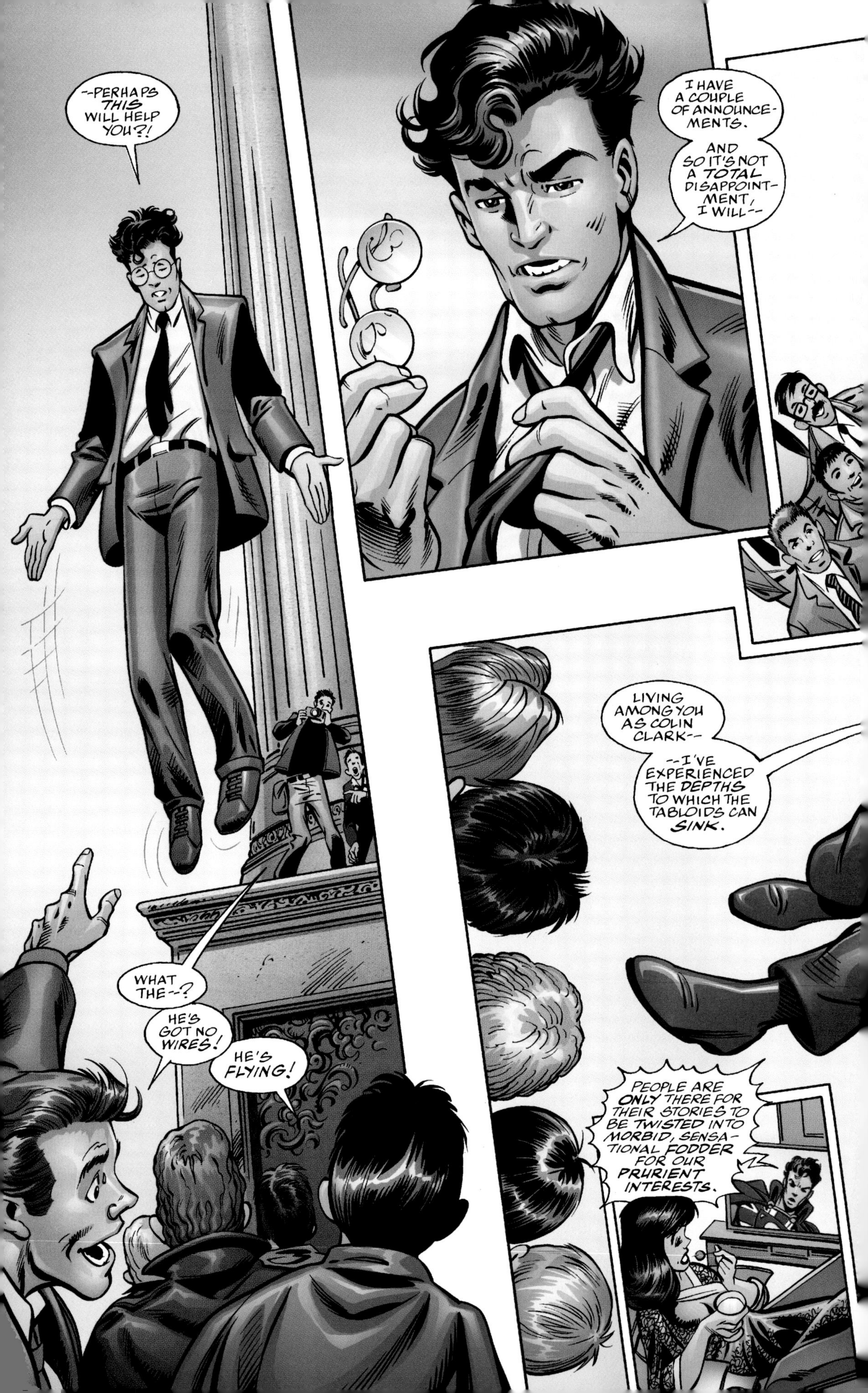
--PERHAPS THIS WILL HELP YOU?!
WHAT THE--?
HE'S GOT NO WIRES!
HE'S FLYING!
I HAVE A COUPLE OF ANNOUNCE-MENTS.
AND SO IT'S NOT A TOTAL DISAPPOINT-MENT, I WILL--
LIVING AMONG YOU AS COLIN CLARK--
--I'VE EXPERIENCED THE DEPTHS TO WHICH THE TABLOIDS CAN SINK.
PEOPLE ARE ONLY THERE FOR THEIR STORIES TO BE TWISTED INTO MORBID, SENSA-TIONAL FODDER FOR OUR PRURIENT INTERESTS.

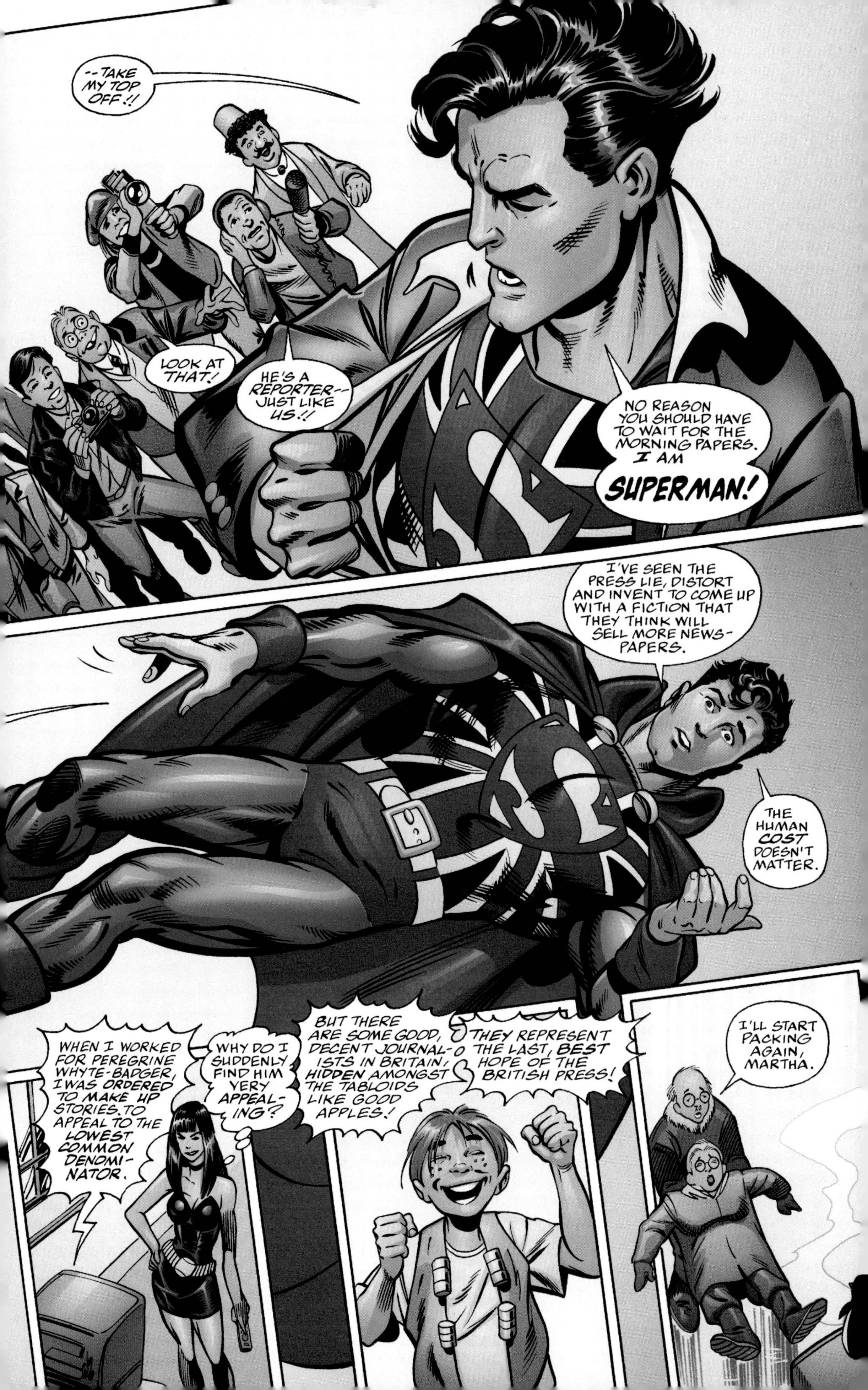
--TAKE MY TOP OFF!!
LOOK AT THAT!
HE'S A REPORTER-- JUST LIKE US!!
NO REASON YOU SHOULD HAVE TO WAIT FOR THE MORNING PAPERS. I AM SUPERMAN!
I'VE SEEN THE PRESS LIE, DISTORT AND INVENT TO COME UP WITH A FICTION THAT THEY THINK WILL SELL MORE NEWS-PAPERS.
THE HUMAN COST DOESN'T MATTER.
WHEN I WORKED FOR PEREGRINE WHYTE-BADGER, I WAS ORDERED TO MAKE UP STORIES. TO APPEAL TO THE LOWEST COMMON DENOMI-NATOR.
WHY DO I SUDDENLY FIND HIM VERY APPEAL-ING?
BUT THERE ARE SOME GOOD, DECENT JOURNAL-ISTS IN BRITAIN, HIDDEN AMONGST THE TABLOIDS LIKE GOOD APPLES!
THEY REPRESENT THE LAST, BEST HOPE OF THE BRITISH PRESS!
I'LL START PACKING AGAIN, MARTHA.

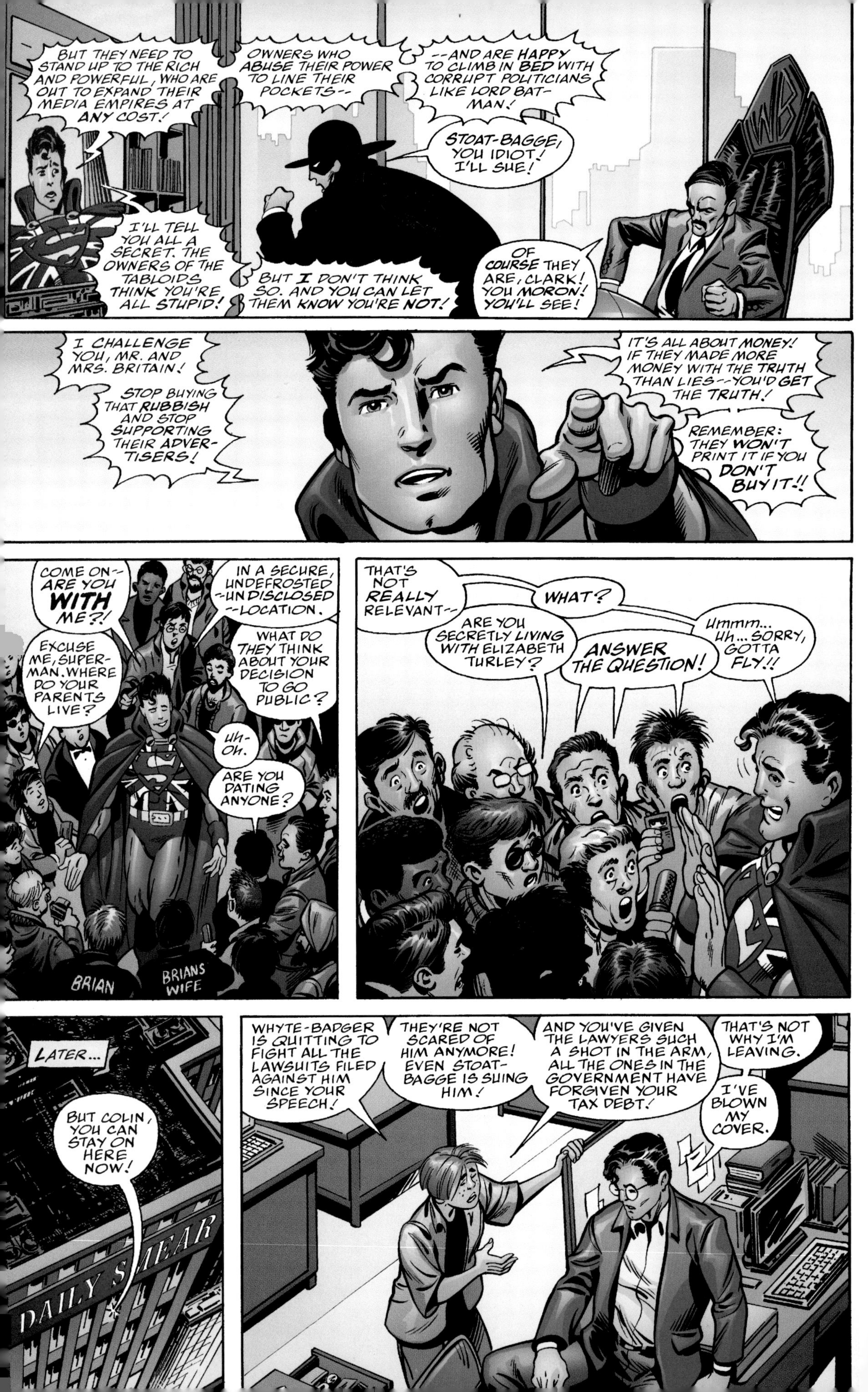
BUT THEY NEED TO STAND UP TO THE RICH AND POWERFUL, WHO ARE OUT TO EXPAND THEIR MEDIA EMPIRES AT ANY COST!
I'LL TELL YOU ALL A SECRET. THE OWNERS OF THE TABLOIDS THINK YOU'RE ALL STUPID!
OWNERS WHO ABUSE THEIR POWER TO LINE THEIR POCKETS--
--AND ARE HAPPY TO CLIMB IN BED WITH CORRUPT POLITICIANS LIKE LORD BATMAN!
STOAT-BAGGE, YOU IDIOT! I'LL SUE!
BUT I DON'T THINK SO. AND YOU CAN LET THEM KNOW YOU'RE NOT!
OF COURSE THEY ARE, CLARK! YOU MORON! YOU'LL SEE!
I CHALLENGE YOU, MR. AND MRS. BRITAIN!
STOP BUYING THAT RUBBISH AND STOP SUPPORTING THEIR ADVERTISERS!
IT'S ALL ABOUT MONEY! IF THEY MADE MORE MONEY WITH THE TRUTH THAN LIES--YOU'D GET THE TRUTH!
REMEMBER: THEY WON'T PRINT IT IF YOU DON'T BUY IT!!
COME ON--ARE YOU WITH ME?!
IN A SECURE, UNDEFROSTED--UNDISCLOSED--LOCATION.
EXCUSE ME, SUPERMAN. WHERE DO YOUR PARENTS LIVE?
WHAT DO THEY THINK ABOUT YOUR DECISION TO GO PUBLIC?
UH-OH.
ARE YOU DATING ANYONE?
BRIAN
BRIANS WIFE
THAT'S NOT REALLY RELEVANT--
WHAT?
ARE YOU SECRETLY LIVING WITH ELIZABETH TURLEY?
ANSWER THE QUESTION!
UMMM... UH... SORRY, GOTTA FLY!!
LATER...
BUT COLIN, YOU CAN STAY ON HERE NOW!
DAILY SMEAR
WHYTE-BADGER IS QUITTING TO FIGHT ALL THE LAWSUITS FILED AGAINST HIM SINCE YOUR SPEECH!
THEY'RE NOT SCARED OF HIM ANYMORE! EVEN STOAT-BAGGE IS SUING HIM!
AND YOU'VE GIVEN THE LAWYERS SUCH A SHOT IN THE ARM, ALL THE ONES IN THE GOVERNMENT HAVE FORGIVEN YOUR TAX DEBT!
THAT'S NOT WHY I'M LEAVING.
I'VE BLOWN MY COVER.

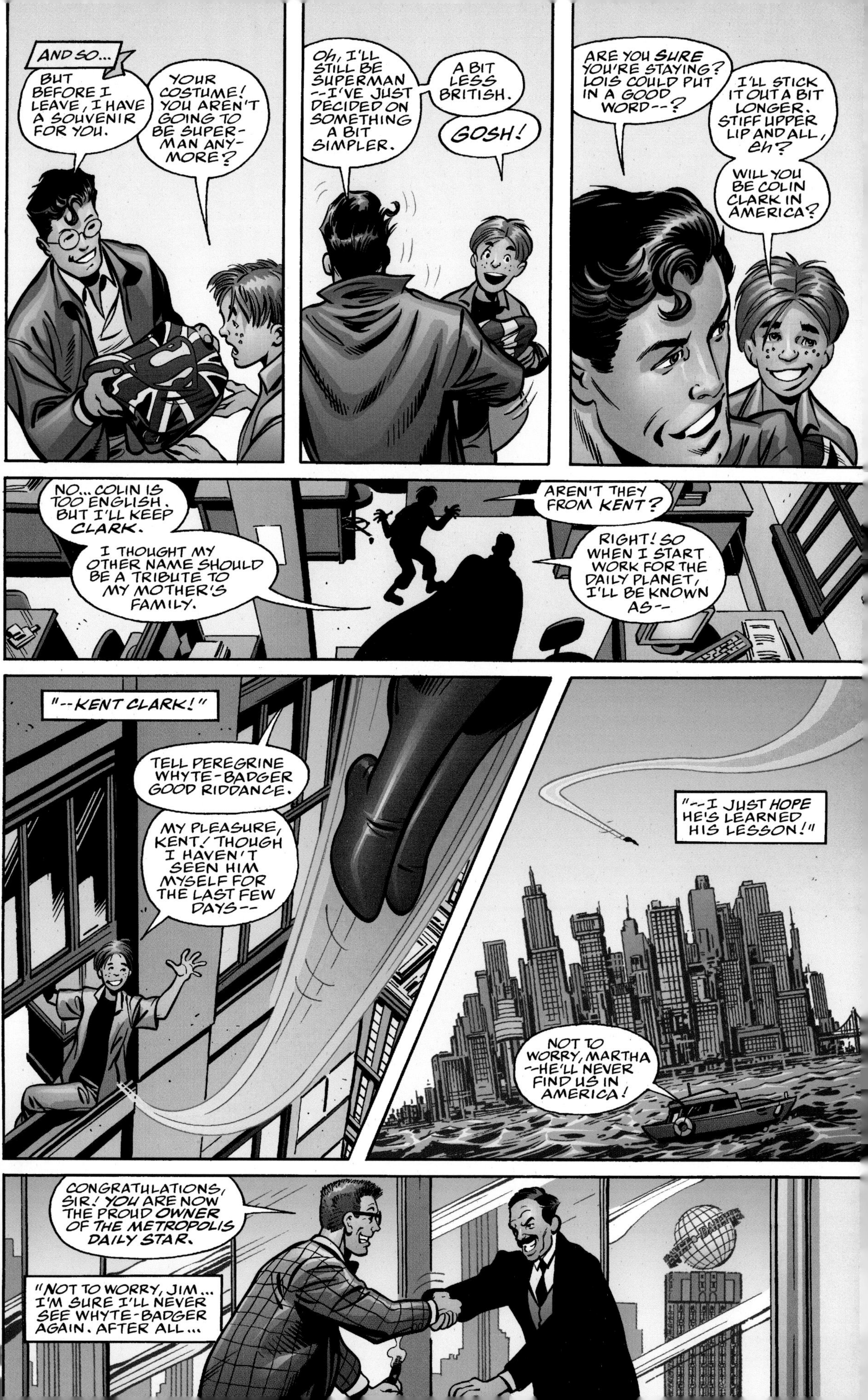
AND SO...
BUT BEFORE I LEAVE, I HAVE A SOUVENIR FOR YOU.
YOUR COSTUME! YOU AREN'T GOING TO BE SUPER-MAN ANY-MORE?
Oh, I'LL STILL BE SUPERMAN --I'VE JUST DECIDED ON SOMETHING A BIT SIMPLER.
A BIT LESS BRITISH.
GOSH!
ARE YOU SURE YOU'RE STAYING? LOIS COULD PUT IN A GOOD WORD--?
I'LL STICK IT OUT A BIT LONGER. STIFF UPPER LIP AND ALL, eh?
WILL YOU BE COLIN CLARK IN AMERICA?
NO... COLIN IS TOO ENGLISH. BUT I'LL KEEP CLARK.
I THOUGHT MY OTHER NAME SHOULD BE A TRIBUTE TO MY MOTHER'S FAMILY.
AREN'T THEY FROM KENT?
RIGHT! SO WHEN I START WORK FOR THE DAILY PLANET, I'LL BE KNOWN AS--
"--KENT CLARK!"
TELL PEREGRINE WHYTE-BADGER GOOD RIDDANCE.
MY PLEASURE, KENT! THOUGH I HAVEN'T SEEN HIM MYSELF FOR THE LAST FEW DAYS--
"--I JUST HOPE HE'S LEARNED HIS LESSON!"
NOT TO WORRY, MARTHA --HE'LL NEVER FIND US IN AMERICA!
CONGRATULATIONS, SIR! YOU ARE NOW THE PROUD OWNER OF THE METROPOLIS DAILY STAR.
"NOT TO WORRY, JIM... I'M SURE I'LL NEVER SEE WHYTE-BADGER AGAIN. AFTER ALL...

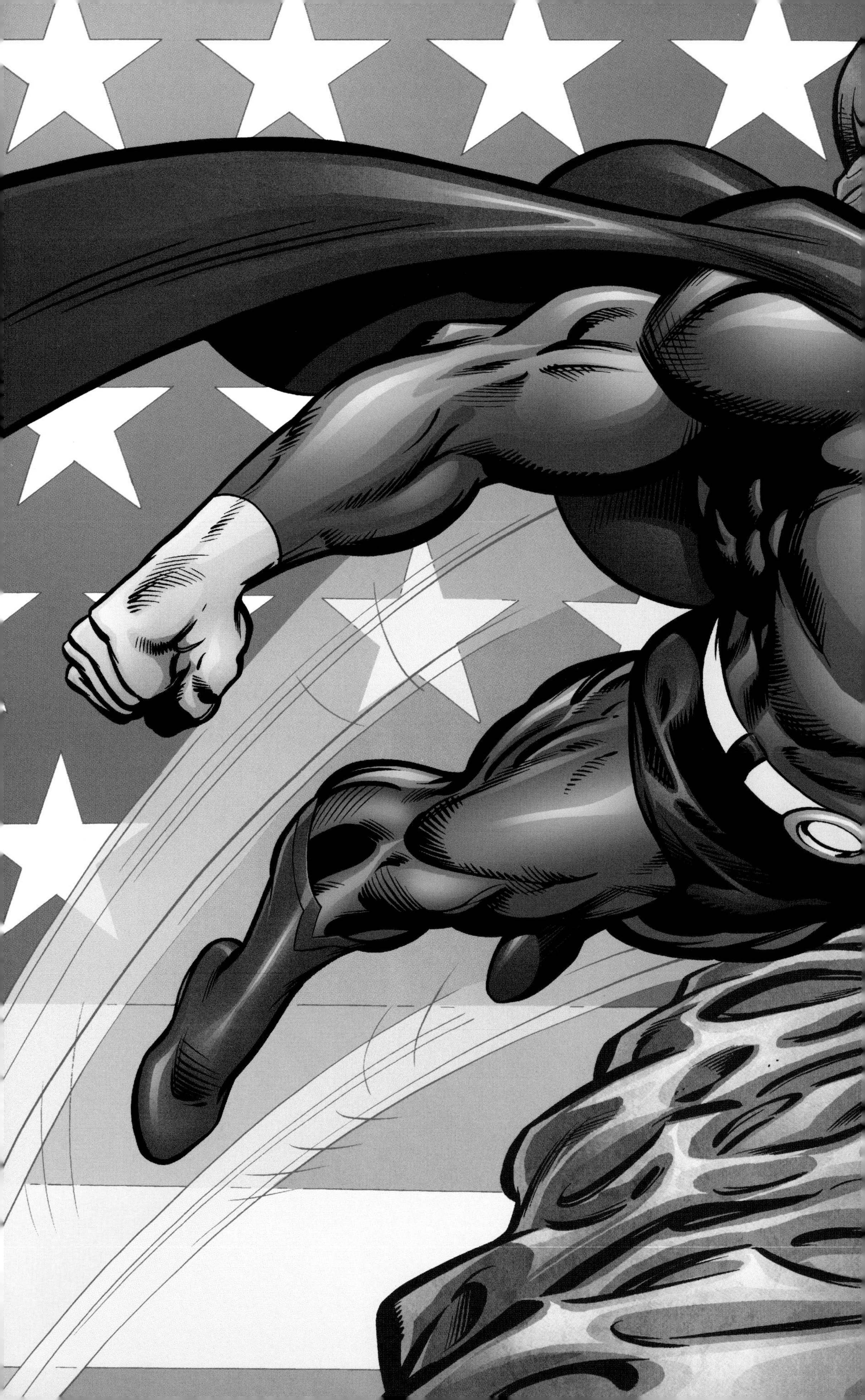

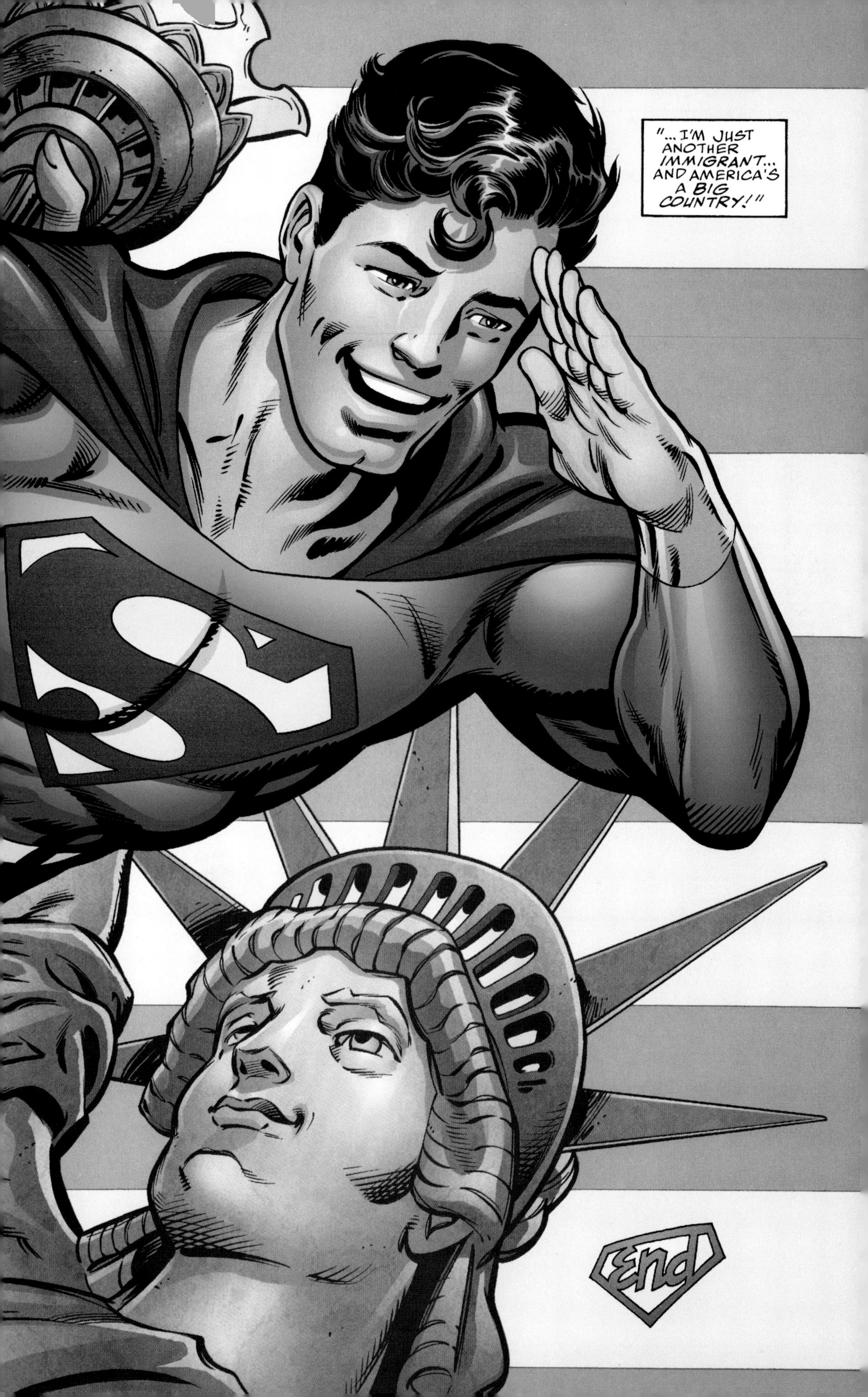
"...I'M JUST ANOTHER IMMIGRANT... AND AMERICA'S A BIG COUNTRY!"
End

S U P E R M A N

THE NEVER-ENDING BATTLE CONTINUES IN THESE BOOKS FROM DC COMICS:

FOR READERS OF ALL AGES

SUPERMAN: ADVENTURES OF THE MAN OF STEEL
P. Dini/S. McCloud/R. Burchett/ B. Blevins

SUPERMAN: PEACE ON EARTH
Paul Dini/Alex Ross

GRAPHIC NOVELS

SON OF SUPERMAN
H. Chaykin/D. Tischman/ J.H. Williams III/M. Gray

SUPERMAN: END OF THE CENTURY
Stuart Immonen/José Marzan Jr.

COLLECTIONS

THE KENTS
J. Ostrander/T. Truman/ T. Mandrake/M. Bair

KINGDOM COME
Mark Waid/Alex Ross

LEGENDS OF THE WORLD'S FINEST
Walter Simonson/Dan Brereton

STEEL: THE FORGING OF A HERO
Various writers and artists

SUPERGIRL
P. David/G. Frank/T. Dodson/ C. Smith/K. Story

SUPERMAN & BATMAN: GENERATIONS
John Byrne

SUPERMAN & BATMAN: WORLD'S FINEST
Gibbons/Rude/Kesel

SUPERMAN: CRITICAL CONDITION
Various writers and artists

SUPERMAN: THE DARK SIDE
J.F. Moore/Kieron Dwyer/ Hilary Barta

SUPERMAN: THE DEATH OF CLARK KENT
Various writers and artists

THE DEATH OF SUPERMAN TRILOGY
THE DEATH OF SUPERMAN
WORLD WITHOUT A SUPERMAN
THE RETURN OF SUPERMAN
Various writers and artists

SUPERMAN/DOOMSDAY: HUNTER/PREY
Dan Jurgens/Brett Breeding

SUPERMAN: THE DOOMSDAY WARS
Dan Jurgens/Norm Rapmund

SUPERMAN: ENDGAME
Various writers and artists

SUPERMAN: EXILE
Various writers and artists

SUPERMAN FOR ALL SEASONS
Jeph Loeb/Tim Sale

SUPERMAN/GEN13
Various writers and artists

SUPERMAN IN THE FIFTIES
Various writers and artists

SUPERMAN IN THE SIXTIES
Various writers and artists

SUPERMAN IN THE SEVENTIES
Various writers and artists

SUPERMAN: NO LIMITS!
Various writers and artists

SUPERMAN: OUR WORLDS AT WAR Vols. 1 & 2
Various writers and artists

SUPERMAN: PANIC IN THE SKY
Various writers and artists

SUPERMAN: PRESIDENT LEX
Various writers and artists

SUPERMAN: TALES OF THE BIZARRO WORLD
Siegel/Forte/Boring/Swan

SUPERMAN: THE TRIAL OF SUPERMAN
Various writers and artists

SUPERMAN: THEY SAVED LUTHOR'S BRAIN
R. Stern/J. Byrne/B. McLeod/ J. Guice/K. Dwyer/various

SUPERMAN: 'TIL DEATH DO US PART
Various writers and artists

SUPERMAN VS. PREDATOR
Michelinie/Maleev

SUPERMAN VS. THE REVENGE SQUAD
Various writers and artists

SUPERMAN: THE WEDDING AND BEYOND
Various writers and artists

SUPERMAN: WHATEVER HAPPENED TO THE MAN OF TOMORROW?
A. Moore/C. Swan/G. Pérez/ K. Schaffenberger

SUPERMAN: THE DAILIES
Jerry Siegel/Joe Shuster

SUPERMAN: THE SUNDAY CLASSICS
Jerry Siegel/Joe Shuster

ARCHIVE EDITIONS

SUPERGIRL ARCHIVES Vol. 1
(ACTION COMICS 252-268, SUPERMAN 123)
Siegel/Binder/Mooney/Plastino

SUPERMAN ARCHIVES Vol. 1
(SUPERMAN 1-4)

SUPERMAN ARCHIVES Vol. 2
(SUPERMAN 5-8)

SUPERMAN ARCHIVES Vol. 3
(SUPERMAN 9-12)

SUPERMAN ARCHIVES Vol. 4
(SUPERMAN 13-16)

SUPERMAN ARCHIVES Vol. 5
(SUPERMAN 17-20)

All by Jerry Siegel/Joe Shuster

SUPERMAN: THE ACTION COMICS ARCHIVES Vol. 1
(ACTION COMICS 1, 7-20)

SUPERMAN: THE ACTION COMICS ARCHIVES Vol. 2
(ACTION COMICS 21-36)

SUPERMAN: THE ACTION COMICS ARCHIVES Vol. 3
(ACTION COMICS 37-52)

All by Jerry Siegel/Joe Shuster

WORLD'S FINEST COMICS ARCHIVES Vol. 1
(SUPERMAN 76, WORLD'S FINEST 71-85)

WORLD'S FINEST COMICS ARCHIVES Vol. 2
(WORLD'S FINEST 86-101)

All by B. Finger/E. Hamilton/ C. Swan/various

TO FIND MORE COLLECTED EDITIONS AND MONTHLY COMIC BOOKS FROM DC COMICS, CALL 1-888-COMIC BOOK FOR THE NEAREST COMICS SHOP OR GO TO YOUR LOCAL BOOK STORE.

Visit us at www.dccomics.com

SM0011